LET IT MAKE SENSE

MY TRUTH, MY JOURNEY

LET IT MAKE SENSE

MY TRUTH, MY JOURNEY

GABRIEL SOLOMON

TRIBE MEDIA BOOK PUBLISHING

OAKLAND, CALIFORNIA

LET IT MAKE SENSE:

MY TRUTH, MY JOURNEY

Published by
Tribe Media Book Publishing.
Oakland, California
tpngmediainfo@gmail.com
www.tpng.biz/solomon-magazine

Gabriel Solomon, Publisher/Editorial Director
Yvonne Rose/Quality Press, Book Packager

Paperback ISBN: 979-8-3305-7856-6

Ebook ISBN: 979-8-3305-7917-4

Library of Congress Control Number: 2024924673

ACKNOWLEDGEMENTS

I would like to give full Acknowledgments to the Creator of both heaven and earth, YHWH. Throughout my journey upon earth, I have been scolded when I needed reprimand and blessings to let me know that Elohim truly exists. Yahuah has been a father, mentor, protector and guide while navigating through turbulent times on rough seas.

My woman of thirty-six years and counting that has been my pillar, best friend and love, though at various times during our companionship we have reached the point of no return.

My mother that has given me life and able to see her son reach this point. My aunt Cynthia that kept my brother and me in check with a firm hand and made education in both secular and theology a must. My sister for being beautiful, intelligent and remarkable. My son, the tinder lover. Remain vigilant and keep rising with or without companionship because only a warrior can survive when his head is not preoccupied with distractions. My grandsons need you to guide them as they accomplish tasks and reach success. My daughters that have been my joy and love. Thank you for giving us a tribe that continues to expand and be fruitful under the halakha of the Torah.

My uncles Ronnie, Vernon, Robert, that taught me game of the streets and what it is to be a solid and standup guy. My Uncle Anthony for being cool and normal away from the killing fields of Oakland,

California. My aunts for being the salt of the earth and remaining steadfast. My niece for being a carbon copy of my sister in every way. My nephew for remaining strong without a dad and carrying on the Turner name. All my cousins that were there for my brother and me when we needed shelter during adolescent years. My second and third generation of cousins that are making the definition of family a priority.

Brother Pietre for visiting me during my rehabilitation and encouragement in keeping the ruach active. All the brothers and sisters at the school that are gaining Chokmah of the Torah. My loved ones (RIP) Lamont and Donnell Jr, gone too soon to realize their greatness. Momma and Papa Johnny for raising us and teaching us to be men. My Aunt May for being stern and loving.

My business partners YNG OG, K Styles, Victor, and Angelique for helping us to grow in the industry. A heartfelt thank you to Yvonne Rose and Quality Press for their exceptional work in professionally bringing my book to life, from cover to cover. Your dedication and expertise are deeply appreciated. To all those I have irked and not included on this journey, please forgive my mistakes.

TABLE OF CONTENTS

Journaling, a tool to help us express, rather than suppress, our thoughts, feelings, and insights. Journaling has strength to lower distress and depression, enhance psychological well-being, and improve physical health. This is especially true when we try to make sense of a situation and deal with it constructively as we write about it.

- Noel Brick, lecturer, and researcher at Ulster University.

INTRODUCTION

Hello, my name is Gabriel Solomon, and what you are about to discover as you examine this book, is my reality. Throughout my journey, I have finally concluded that every aspect of life, as we perceive it, is uncertain. Because of this, my soul has experienced mood fluctuations like the four seasons of nature. Those that truly know me will say my disposition may go from serene to chaotic, like a scorpion aroused by agitation. I have never been a skeptic of religious dogma but recently I began questioning the conundrum of racism, classism, and idolatry from a western philosophy.

The circumstances that have driven me to rethink theories embedded in my psyche from public education, mainstream media, and organized religion are the dissolution of family structure and oblivious recognition of ethnicities other than Europeans in American society. The paradox of the values spoken by politicians and conservative news pundits is a contradiction to the treatment of residents in urban communities.

Kanye West in "All Fall Down" was on point when he said, " We are all self-conscious, I'm just the first to admit it." This is the case for individuals trying to escape poverty by engaging in nefarious activities that have increased the prison population and national murder rate. This literary project is motivating while managing the musical career of YNG OG and producing film and television projects: "She's Not Mine," "Run" currently airing on TUBI and Amazon Prime Video, and the video series "Set Trippn TV" with limited episodes on YouTube.

Within the following 11 chapters, I will discuss my rehabilitation process of 271 days in which I engulfed myself in theocratic research using the eighty-seven books of the CEPHER. (For readers unfamiliar with the CEPHER, a collection of writings pronounced et' sef'-er is a restoration of the books traditionally recognized as set-apart (holy) Scripture and includes Chanoch (Enoch) and Yovheliym (Jubilees) as found in the Dead Sea Scrolls, together with the recaptured writing of Ha'Yashar (Jasher), Apocalypse of Baruch (2 Baruch), recognized in the Septuagint. Writings of the Makkabiym (3 and 4 Maccabees) restores the names of over 3,100 people and places found in the original Ivriyt (Hebrew) language, translated into English.

This writing project has rekindled memories suppressed since my childhood that I am sharing with readers, which has restored my confidence in the restoration of humanity. Since seeing the hypocrisy of mainstream religion and media that causes division among ethnicities, I have included opinions and spiritual quotes as to why humankind has endured since the founding of the world in 'Let It Make Sense.' Once again, Shalom for buying my first published writing endeavor and coming this far in your everlasting journey towards restoring the covenant of Noach and Avraham.

We come under fire daily like the prophet Job, and I was at my snapping point contemplating if the consequences outweighed the offense. I genuinely believe without the Divine intervention while in my unconscious state at night, I would never manifest my dreams into reality during the day in my conscious state without the discipline, sacrifice, determination, and courage needed to evolve.

There is no other factual principle that speaks volumes regarding dreams other than the lyrics sung by the rapper Game, "It's a hard knock life, then you pass away." They say sleep is the cousin of death, so my eyes are wide open, cause a dream is akin to your last breath." Those few short verses have shaped my psychological perception of the behavioral patterns within myself. Throughout my life I was trying to build upon my fantasies only to realize that if it derives not from El Elyon in your visitation, set not your heart upon them. For dreams have deceived many, and they have failed to put their trust in them. SIRACH (ECCLESIASTICUS) 34:6-7 את CEPHER.

I more than often have compromised my core values to network with individuals and organizations to achieve success in the entertainment industry, while putting my spiritual wellbeing in jeopardy, often forgetting that I must acknowledge the RUACH Elohim which has regarded my affliction during my trials and setbacks. He heard my cries and despair when many of my dreams did not grow into reality, and I squandered resources both financially and morally while trying to build alliances and partnerships with individuals to live a secular lifestyle that I often dreamed of. While I was questioning my own self-worth and mental ability, it was RUACH HA'qodesh that remembered for them his covenant and repented according to the multitude of his mercies. TEHILLIYM (PSALMS) 106:44-45 את CEPHER.

The most difficult decision I had to come to grips with in drafting this book is transparency. Like many converts who attended a religious denomination during their adolescence, the fear of sin and ending up in sheol after death inculcated in my spiritual conscience. The actions I chose during my adolescent years had a strong impact on my future development in my adult years. The concept that the mind is the engine that works the whole body and what you see through the eyes and hear through the ears implanted within your reasoning and is strongly associated with your belief of humanity. This has been so true and affected my journey up to this point about my pursuit of achieving sensuous pleasure, regardless of the consequences. While I choose to gain traction in an industry that is doused with greed, sexual gratification, vanity, and idolatry, I tried to walk a fine line in the music and film industry knowing that the mind is like a computer database that will store information that will include sensory and non-sensory experiences.

Everyone has their own cross to bear and their own journeys to either repent or continue unrepentant. I have been fully aware of the choices that humankind offers in entertainment, politics, finance, education, and religion. It is an ongoing battle with the notion that individuals cannot serve Yahweh: during the Sabbath and partake in Hellenized rituals in secret, for he is a holy Elohim; he is a jealous El; he will not forgive your transgressions nor your sins. If ye forsake Yahweh, and serve strange elohai, then he will turn and do you hurt, and consume you, after that he has done you good. YAHUSHA (JOSHUA) 24:19-20 את CEPHER.

I will attempt to "MAKE SENSE OF IT" and be as transparent as possible by including episodes from my youth as a young hyena in urban settings, to numerous mistakes pursuing carnal reasoning while thrusting aside the counsel of the RUACH HA'qodesh who instructed him, and taught him in the path of judgment, and taught him knowledge, and showed to him the way of understanding. YESHA'YAHU (ISAIAH) 40:13-14 את CEPHER.

I will not glamorize but use my past as choices up to this point and the friends and associates met on my path of enlightenment. I must continue to praise Elohim for his love and discipline because when I was a child, I spoke as a child, I understood as a child, I thought as a child: but when I became a man, I put away childish things. For now, we see through a glass, darkly; but then face to face: now I know in part; but then shall I know even as also I am known. And now abides faith, hope, love, these three; but the greatest of these is love. QORINTIYM RI'SHON (1 CORINTHIANS) 13:11-13 את CEPHER.

This is the love that is sustainable and inclines me to be reminiscent of my journey and share with you now! "Let It Make Sense."

NOTES:

CREATION, SHABBAT, FEASTS

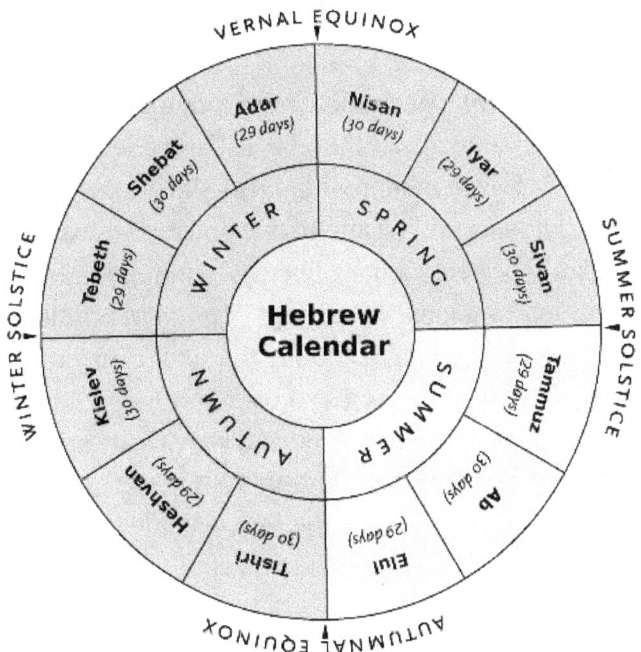

S halom (equivalent in English translation to mean either "hello" or "goodbye"). As an individual who has spent most of his childhood every Sunday in church, I thought it would only be correct to discuss where it all began, in the beginning. Born and raised in Oakland, California, my grandmother migrated from Tennessee and my grandfather hails from Texas. California is where my parents met, so I have chosen to discuss topics that are central to my understanding and have plagued me for many years.

The BIBLE (Basic Instruction Before Leaving Earth) is the manuscript written like a movie from various screenwriters from antiquity who have seen transgression, nation building, divine intervention, idolatry, and bloodshed spilled over religious beliefs, but my question is, how many times does the creator have to push the reset button?

Before we discuss the decimation of the family structure, the rift between genders, ethnicities, and epoch chronicled in the book of BERE'SHIYTH, I must mention the factors that have contributed to millions of individuals finding alternative practices of worship to their detriment. Be it conservative, liberal, or independent political affiliation, the aspirations to disrupt the moral foundations of humanity by enemies bent on disputing the sovereignty of the creator is at an all-time high. We can examine every kingdom and government created since humankind and we will always come to the same conclusion, humanity continues to spiral out of control when morality and halakha (Laws) of the universe are watered down or completely removed.

I take this all-in consideration when individuals discuss racism and classism and the need to separate for the sake of survival, when the only separation needed is humanity dependency upon the antichrists of the world. These are the extremists and scientists debunking the sixth day creation theory when evidence has proven all humankind has two relatable DNA strains that produce deteriorating cells within the body that cause our system to shut down and life to expire. These are facts extremists are not yet to explain or the archeology findings supporting the book of Bere'shiyth not included within the big bang theory. Searching for answers to humanity's beginning, middle, and demise is no mystery if you know where to look.

During my rehabilitation, Google became a useful tool to aid in cross referencing books of antiquity to find if names, locations, and events are akin. I continue to implore readers to fact-check everything someone writes and interpret from a spiritual text for accuracy. Your eyes and ears absorb the information while in your conscious state, but it is the RUACH HA'QODESH that reveals mysteries in your unconscious state of mind. I have more questions than answers needing further interpretation when examining mainstream religion and their part in distribution of fallacy and duplicity in the world. We all know from Sunday school services the story of Moshe and the Mitsvah (commandments), but it was not until I began studying from the Cepher that I enriched and enlightened by halakha of the universe.

Missy Takano holds a BA in Biblical Studies from Multnomah University with an emphasis on New Testament Yavaniym (Greek), and a missionary with TeachBeyond at the Black Forest Academy in Kandern, Germany. Missy says 'As followers of Jesus, God does not expect us to live by Israel's laws. However, we are bound to a promise we enjoy. Sabbath rest is an invitation to practice for eternity in God's presence. It is an act of regular and intentional trust of God's rule on Earth. We *shabbat* to *nuakh*—when we stop working, we can truly rest in God's presence. When we practice this purposeful pause, we make room for God to take up residence in our individual lives and communities. And when we do this, we take part in the new creation story, setting the stage for God to make his dwelling place once again on Earth.' Out of the mouth of babes we read that Missy touched on two prominent issues, Shabbat, and Creation. Thank you, Missy, for your thoughts and offering an opportunity to give parishioners a choice to accept the Lord's Day or Shabbat, or the halakha for spiritual growth is a blessing from the ruach.

The 5 books of the Torah which hold the Mitsvah of adhering to the Shabbat, participation in the Feasts and Pecach (Passover) and clarification of the creation of earth, are the fundamental pillars for faith-based denominations that use the IVIRY (Hebrew) books, and YAVANIYM (Greek) books to achieve spiritual wellness. My perplexity about the Shabbat, Holy Feasts and Pecach derives from me not fully understanding the halakha of the universe. Though I read about creation in the Torah, I still have added questions that go unresolved because of my infancy stages in my journey; but I can report on my growth, and enlightenment is 40 degrees higher this day, than I was five years ago. I was so oblivious to what was truth and what was duplicity from those claiming to be our spiritual leadership that I withdrew from evangelizing for an extended period to refocus on self-teachings.

For two hundred and seventy-one days, I began to Google all rituals associated with religion and I began to uncover the heresy seeped into current beliefs. The added Besorah beyond the sixty-six books of the Bible not included in prescribed publications given to parishioners in my earlier congregations, afforded me the courage to question the stewardship of elders assigned to provide my spiritual nourishment every Sunday. Before we go any further, I want to add a disclaimer that this is not an attack upon Mashiachiy (Christian) denominations or any inherited belief system from your childhood, but information found through research while immobilized during my rehabilitation process that I am sharing with readers of this book.

My research began with Alexander the Great. who conquered empires from Mitsrayim to Afghanistan, and the early Christians of the Roman empire that took part in many pagan rituals. Many of these accounts coincide with locations and names in the chronicles of YAVANIYM TESTAMENT. I also uncovered many rituals and festivals that religious denominations have written in their

Cepheriyms on the expelling of demons and life after death that originated from polytheistic practices. This was very confusing to me initially after putting total faith in the ministers, preachers, priests, and elders ordained to interpret the word of Elohim for my spiritual enlightenment.

I go to church to seek redemption and salvation for my soul bombarded by the sin and corruption of humanity. What the eyes witness, and the ears hear living in urban and metropolitan communities is violence, homelessness, gunfire, profanity, sexual debauchery, overwhelming, numbing my moral compass and taking a toll on my spiritual wellness. In times past, my only source of healing was in the four walls of my congregation on those Saturday and Sunday services, overwhelmed by choir singing, praise dancing and hell-fire preaching over true calls for repentance. My ears were burning from the hand-clapping hymns and musical chorus; but afterward when the music stopped, my ruach was still thirsting for that living water the preacher said Jesus provided.

For ten years, my family experienced the true meaning of spiritual wilderness, feeding my ruach with outdated publications and Watch Tower magazines. Without a Kingdom Hall or weekly fellowship to share insight on the scriptures with, I began each day in heartfelt prayers that I would not return to my former lifestyle among the non-believers. With Cepher safely stored in my backpack while working on the docks, I spent downtimes and lunch breaks for an entire year reading the 87 books thoroughly. This would be my second occasion delving into the scriptures, but I never forgot that I read that the angel of the presence spoke to Moshe according to the Word of Yahweh, saying: "Write the complete history of the creation, how in six days Yahweh Elohim finished all his works and all that he created, and kept Shabbat on the seventh day and sanctified it for all ages, and appointed it as a sign for all his works.

For on the first day he created the heavens which are above and the earth and the waters and all the Ruachoth which serve before him, the angels of the presence, and the angels of sanctification, and the angels of the ruach of fire and the angels of the ruach of the winds, and the angels of the ruach of the clouds, and of darkness, and of snow and of hail and of hoar frost, and the angels of the voices and of the thunder and of the lightning, and the angels of the Ruachoth of cold and of heat, and of winter and of spring and of autumn and of summer and of all the Ruachoth of his creatures, which are in the heavens and on the earth, He created the abysses and the darkness, evening and night, and the light, dawn and day, which he has prepared in the knowledge of his heart.

And thereupon we saw his works, and praised him, and lauded before him on account of all his works; for seven great works did he create on the first day. And on the second day he created the expanse during the waters, and the waters divided. On that day half of them went up above and half of them went down below the expanse that was in the midst over the face of the whole earth. And this was the only work Elohim created on the second day. And on the third day he commanded the waters to pass from off the face of the whole earth into one place, and the dry land to appear. And the waters did so as he commanded them, and they retired from off the face of the earth into one place outside of this expanse, and the dry land appeared. And on that day he created for them all the seas according to their separate gathering places, and all the rivers, and the gatherings of the waters in the mountains and on all the earth, and all the lakes, and all the dew of the earth, and the seed which is sown, and all sprouting things, and fruit bearing trees, and trees of the wood, and the Garden of Eden, in Eden and all.

These four great works Elohim created on the third day. And on the fourth day he created the sun and the moon and the stars, and set them in the expanse of heaven, to give light upon all the earth, and to rule over the day and the night, and divide the light from the darkness. And Elohim appointed the sun to be a great sign on the earth for days and for Sabbaths and for months and for feasts and for years and for Sabbaths of years and for jubilees and for all seasons of the years. And it divides the light from the darkness and for prosperity, that all things may prosper which shoot and grow on the earth. These three kinds he made on the fourth day. And on the fifth day he created great sea monsters in the depths of the waters, for these were the first things of flesh created by his hands, the fish and everything that moves in the waters, and everything that flies, the birds and all their kind. And the sun rose above them to prosper them, and above everything that was on the earth, everything that shoots out of the earth, and all fruit bearing trees, and all flesh.

These three kinds he created on the fifth day. And on the sixth day he created all the animals of the earth, and all cattle, and everything that moves on the earth. And after all this he created man, a man and a woman created he them, and gave him dominion over all that is upon the earth, and in the seas, and over everything that flies, and over beasts and over cattle, and over everything that moves on the earth, and over the whole earth, and over all this he gave him dominion. And these four kinds he created on the sixth day.

And there were altogether two and twenty kinds. And he finished all his work on the sixth day, all that is in the heavens and on the earth, and in the seas and in the abysses, and in the light and in the darkness, and in everything. And he gave us a great sign, the Sabbath, that we should work six days, but guard the Sabbath on the seventh day from all work." YOVHELIYM (JUBILEES) 2:1-18 את CEPHER.

The chronicles of BERE'SHIYTH (Genesis) outlines Elohim ended his work which he had made; and he rested on the seventh day from all his work which he had made. And Elohim blessed the seventh day and sanctified it: because in it he had rested from all his work which Elohim created and made. These are the generations of the heavens and of the earth when created, in the day that Yahweh Elohim made the earth and the heavens, BERE'SHIYTH (GENESIS) 2:2-4 את CEPHER.

This is the story of creation and the Sabbath, so if we equate this to a normal forty hours of labor with eight hours of overtime, I presume any normal business owner, contractor or employee would wish to rest the body, mind and RUACH (spirit). The Sabbath is more of a refreshing and rejuvenation of the soul like what YAHUAH Elohim prescribed for himself after creating all that we have come to understand. I cannot speak for everyone, but dedication to fulfilling the Sabbath has kept me physically and spiritually fit, but this was not the case initially after becoming a rank-and-file member of the International Longshoremen and Warehouse Union (Local 10). Becoming an unidentified casual was an opportunity that I nearly squandered because of my lax work ethics and hood mentality. A mentality I could not shake as former street pharmacist and president of the junior usher board of 7th avenue Baptist Church. I found myself consciously chasing the American dream of material consumption, while not physically and spiritually displaying the same enthusiasm towards my growing family. I was using so many excuses to chase the money while knowing you shall not take the name of Yahweh Elohayka in vain: את, for Yahweh will not hold him guiltless that takes his name in vain.

Guard the day of the Sabbath; to sanctify it as Yahweh Elohayka has commanded you. Six days you shall labor, and do all your work: But the seventh day is the Sabbath of Yahweh Elohayka: in it you shall not do any work, you, nor your son, nor your daughter, nor your manservant, nor your maidservant, nor your ox, nor your ass, nor any of your cattle, nor your stranger that is within your gates; that your manservant and your maidservant may rest as well as you. And remember that you were a servant in the land of Mitsrayim, and that Yahweh Elohayka brought you out thence through a mighty hand and by a stretched-out arm: therefore, Yahweh Elohayka commanded you to see the day of Sabbath. DEVARIYM (DEUTERONOMY) 5:10-15 את CEPHER. Through discovery of BERE'SHIYTH, the concept of the Shabbat was not registering with me while I continued an effort to hustle day and night to receive the benefits of local 10 that conflicted with adhering to Mitsvah of the Shabbat.

I was enjoying the material trappings of ILWU and Co-CEO of No Mercy Entertainment but at what cost? Fooling myself as hearer of the word given to Moshe trying to forget the reasoning of being a doer of the word when I was on the docks or building the entertainment brand. Congregating at Yahuah Assembly only when it was convenient for my work schedule or did not interfere with scheduled trips. Working overtime and not coming home trying to do back-to-back shifts during observation of the Shabbat. A ticking time bomb ready to detonate listening to theories and opinions at parties and industry events that supported alternatives to what I have read in the Holy Bible. Associates who I presumed had our best interests at heart were knowingly or unknowingly sowing seeds of spiritual doubt and we allowed these doubts to manifest for the sake of generating alliances within the entertainment industry.

It was not until I read an article on a trip that I began to question how scientific ideas woven into the fabric of religious dogma could alter your reasoning of the Bible. The discussion in the room centered around the Big Bang Theory and emerging minorities venture capitalists in Silicon Valley. With menial knowledge of the theories, I read an article by The University of Western Australia explaining the early development of the Universe. According to this theory, the

Universe expanded from an extremely small, extremely hot, and extremely dense state. Since then, it has expanded and become less dense and cooler. The Big Bang is the best model used by astronomers to explain the creation of matter, space, and time 13.7 billion years ago.

Early in the 20th century, the Universe thought to be static: always the same size, neither expanding nor contracting. But in 1924 astronomer Edwin Hubble used a technique pioneered by Henrietta Leavitt to measure distances to remote objects in the sky. Hubble used spectroscopic red-shift data to measure the speeds these objects were traveling then graphed their distance from Earth against their speed. He discovered that the speed at which astronomical objects move apart is proportional to their distance from each other. Researchers Professor Snezhana Abarzhi and Ms. Annie Naveh from UWA's Department of Mathematics and Statistics conducted a mathematical analysis of the conditions created from a supernova. Professor Abarzhi said although the supernova explosion was violent but not turbulent and quick as previously thought. "It is traditionally considered that turbulence was the mechanism for energy transfer and accumulation which resulted in chemicals being formed in the supernova," Professor Abarzhi said. "However, our research has revealed it was not turbulent but a slow process where hot spots of energy localized and trapped, resulting in the formation of, for example, iron, gold, and silver from atoms produced by the Big Bang. "The findings are important because they challenge our understanding of the Big Bang Theory and how life formed." Professor Abarzhi said it was fascinating to see the complexity of how the Universe might have formed. "Human beings essentially started as hydrogen atoms and energy, swirling around to create other chemicals and these interactions resulted in life," she said. "The creation of life on Earth will always fascinate and challenge us, leaving more questions than answers, but this latest research brings us one step closer to understanding how we came to exist."

Entrenched in all these alternatives, the theory of creation is factual and taking the creator out of the equation is a recipe for spiritual disaster. Chokmah is greater than material riches that are gained and squandered and faith continues to grow within those that seek that Divine power. And a word came into his heart, and he said: "All the signs of the stars, and the signs of the moon and of the sun are all in the hand of Yahweh. Why do I search for them out? If he wishes, he causes it to rain, morning and evening; And if he wishes, he withholds it, and all things are in his hand." And he prayed that night and said, "My Elohim, El Elyon, you alone are my Elohim, and you and your dominion have I chosen. And you have created all things, and all things that are the work of your hands. Deliver me from the hands of evil ruachoth who have dominion over the thoughts of men's hearts, and let them not lead me astray from you, my Elohim. And prove me and my seed forever that we go not astray from henceforth and forevermore." YOVHELIYM (JUBILEES) 12:17-20 את CEPHER.

Love, reasoning, and repentance, is a recurring theme throughout this book because I want to "LET IT MAKE SENSE" and there is unsurmountable evidence of existence of YHWH though majority of millionaires in Silicon Valley think otherwise. Love is when you genuinely believe in a theory of a Creator that hears your suppressed thoughts that you're too ashamed to share with anyone else. I made the mistake within my proclaimed ideology to emancipate the RUACH HA'QODESH from my conscience to suppress childhood trauma plaguing past, present and future relationships. I did not put distance between astronomers and scientists who devised a theory of a cosmic explosion that has formed the universe and humanity but are clueless to the source of the explosion. Utilizing millions of dollars from grants and donations for exploration among the stars to discover extraterrestrial life that will give credence to their Big Bang Theory. Authoring books and contributing to industry journals to receive praise and become the next acclaimed awardee.

Life is full of twists and obstacles, but it is the choices we make that put us on a course of righteousness or damnation. Faith and penance are the only exigence to discover the veracity that atheists and scientists do not understand. What legacy will I bequeath humankind after my ashes sealed in the urn and placed upon the mantle? Adonai, you have been our dwelling place in all generations. "Before the mountains existed, or ever you had formed the earth and the world, even from everlasting to everlasting, you are El. You turn man to destruction; and say, Return, ye children of men. For a thousand years in your sight are but as yesterday when it is past, and as a watch in the night. You carry them away as with a flood; they are as sleep: in the morning they are like grass which grows up. In the morning it flourishes and grows up; in the evening it is cut down, and withers. Consumed by your anger and by your wrath, we are troubled. You have set our iniquities before you, our secret sins in the light of your countenance. For all our days passed away in your wrath: we spend our years as a tale told. The days of our years are threescore years and ten; and if by reason of strength they are fourscore years, yet is their strength, labor, and sorrow; soon cut off, and we fly away. Who knows the power of your anger? Even according to your fear, so is your wrath. So, teach us to number our days, that we may apply our hearts unto wisdom." TEHILLIYM (PSALMS) 90:1-12 את CEPHER.

These scientific articles made me question the motives of those in higher learning, influencers on social media platforms and alternative news outlets visited by millions of subscribers daily. I stopped attending these events because they created an alternate reality for atheists that I knew eventually would begin to unravel my reasoning of creation and supreme sovereignty from the creator of humankind.

We all have choices to either stand upright or bend to Ciyn (sin), I chose the latter for start-up capital to get www.tpng.biz off the ground floor. Often reminiscing on the last conversation between my brother and I, when he said the industry was increasing the wedge between my family and faith. He said building our recording company conflicted with my spiritual studies and needed to take a breather. Before the motorcycle accident I never contemplated an early demise even though I faced death more than once. Contemplating a lifestyle of protection and placidness that seemed boring while my cousin's lives seemed interesting and unregulated at the time. My grandparents hoped by shielding my brother and me from the harsh realities of urbanization it would extinguish our rebellions; but after cutting school and visiting 23rd Avenue, I knew it was not enough. I had to put my faith through fires, hiding from my grandparents a lifestyle I knew they would never approve of. I needed to explore deeper into the rabbit hole and retrieve answers to mysteries such as my purpose on earth and the assignment given to me. I needed to go beyond the Saturday or Sunday sermons that continue to be smoking mirrors to the untrained disciples of theology.

I have made an earnest effort to extinguish the dogmatic personality that has kept me from fully following the Messiah and his teachings. Stripping the mindset of rebellion is an ongoing process so I cannot be complacent just because I studied more than a few chapters and precepts and uttered to everyone, my salvation! This is a rigorous endeavor requiring restraint and solitude to unshackle the fetters of secular and religious oppression that have tormented humanity for generations. "But they rebelled against me and would not hearken unto me: they did not every man cast away the abominations of their eyes, neither did they forsake the idols of Mitsrayim: then I said, I will pour out my fury upon them, to carry out my anger against them during the land of Mitsrayim. But I wrought for my name's sake, not polluted before the heathen, among whom they were, in whose sight I made myself known unto them, in bringing them forth out of the land of Mitsrayim. Wherefore I caused them to go forth out of the land of Mitsrayim and brought them into the wilderness. And I gave them my statutes, and showed them my judgments, which if a man does, he shall even live in them. Moreover, I also gave them my Sabbaths, to be a sign between me and them, that they might know that I am Yahweh that sanctifies them. But the house of Yashar'el rebelled against me in the wilderness: they walked not in my statutes, and they despised my judgments, which if a man does, he shall even live in them; and my Sabbaths they greatly polluted: then I said, I will pour out my fury upon them in the wilderness, to consume them". YECHEZQ'EL (EZEKIEL) 20:8-13 את CEPHER.

One example that comes to mind is secular celebrations that becomes entrenched within our consciousness because of their world-wide popularity.

Valentines, Easter, 4th of July, Halloween, Thanksgiving, Christmas, New Year's Eve. If you are a Methodist convert, Presbyterian, Catholic, Baptist, 7th day Adventist, Jehovah Witness, Non-denomination, Atheist, Islam or follow Judaism, these secular celebrations are unavoidable because of their commercialization and adherence in many denominations. Those 271 days during rehabilitation was the spark needed to realize family, ministry, Longshore career and TPNG brand could be gone within an instant if the motorcycle accident was a fatality. It was through divine intervention I had the opportunity to redirect my efforts and cease wandering on the road of rebelliousness mentioned within the 87 books of the CEPHER and complete this book to share with humanity. I gained freedom from my confinement and now embrace a new attitude richly enlightened with purpose instead of the carnal lifestyle that irritated the RUACH HA'QODESH within my temple. These changes of moral and spiritual ideologies are still a work in progress and will not manifest in my lifespan, but I must truly be honest with myself instead of trying to augment my own ego and be perceived as a pompous cretin. The first topic that we are going to address are the first courses for children in Sunday school or mandatory education for Divinity and Theological students. Since this is the first chapter of this book, my hypothesis is to expound on the six-day creation between the army of heavenly RUACHOTH and humanity.

Looking back at my youth and trying to find the true religion is not easy. No religious denomination can say they are number one when there is so much evidence from books of antiquity that shows early Christians duplicated beliefs, rituals and texts from ancient empires and rewrote them to fit their own doctrines and rituals. What we have, are books used within many religious denominations cultivating practices from ancient pagan empires that YAHUAH Elohim warned us about in the Cepher. With the creation of life, there is also the creation of death. Losing a loved one is difficult to say the least and when my brother died, I lost it. Making funeral arrangements was stressful and still to this day I reminisce of my brother as though he is still here upon earth. My brother and I were remarkably close and though he included himself in personal affairs that were off limits and crossed boundaries to his own detriment, I still loved him because in the darkest days on my journey, he was there for moral and financial support.

We neither have the power to control our birth and neither know the time of our death, but individuals partake in situations that speed up the process of their demise. I wish not to seem unsympathetic to individuals who have committed suicide, murdered, or died from avoidable or unavoidable incidents but when given an opportunity via divine intervention to avoid end of life, what will you do differently?

After my 2nd surgery, the pain and immobilization induced severe depression which caused me to display acrimony towards nurses and staff. This was completely out of character for me, so I called my woman and told her I had reached the point of no return and was drowning in self-pity and not clinging onto the metaphysical strength that I urged so many to look for in their time of despair. With extreme fatigue in her voice, she asked, what about our children and their children and those who you have mental and spiritual ties with? Did I think how even the mention of ceasing the breath of life the creator gave to me would affect her. I was being inconsiderate, in which she constantly reiterated throughout the night as though I have also become absent-minded from the accident, but her words made me realize that it was not time for me to check out. My awakening was a call to still be courageous like a roaring lion, so this is my testimony and my endeavor to loosen the fetters of religious bondage and pagan celebrations that have become a generational curse upon me and all those seeking redemption since antiquity.

We have discussed the Creation and demise of humanity. The Sabbath and day of rest. The celebrations that have influenced parishioners to take part in pagan rituals; but what is the CEPHER and why is it not recognized among mainstream religion. I want to be as transparent as possible and relate to the readers what influence reading books not included in the Holy Bible, have increased my reasoning and insight on my own behavior patterns. The main factor of my endeavor is inculcating ketuviym (writings) of the CEPHER to interact with family, business associates, members of the union. The slogan "action speaks louder than words" is the correct meaning when trying to infuse your spiritual lifestyle upon individuals with a secular mindset. There are citizens that will follow and obey the laws of the land because they fully put their trust in the government. Men and women study the scriptures because they wish to live a peaceful lifestyle without turmoil. The Bible thumpers and religious converts put faith in the word of Elohim because of the changes they experienced while living a lifestyle of disobedience and sin. Rebellious souls do not believe in divine intervention because it is not right in front of their eyes. These are the individuals that take life as it comes and push it to the limit every day. Moshe experienced individuals with this same mindset throughout his lifespan.

Then there are Individuals like me currently studying the scriptures but struggling to make sense of it. This is especially true when contending with the ideology of the six-day work week and adhering to the preparation of the Sabbath. "And he said unto them, this is that which Yahweh has said, Tomorrow is the rest of the Holy Sabbath unto Yahweh: את bake that which ye will bake today, and את seethe that ye will seethe; and את that which remains over lay up for you to be kept until the morning. And they laid it up till the morning, as Moshe bade and it did not stink, neither was there any worm there. And Moshe said, eat that today; for today is a Sabbath unto Yahweh: today ye shall not find it in the field. Six days ye shall gather it; but on the seventh day, which is the Sabbath, in it there shall be none. And it happened, that some of the people on the seventh day gathered, and they found none. And Yahweh said unto Moshe, how long refuse ye to guard my commandments and my Torah?" SHEMOTH (EXODUS) 16:23-28 את CEPHER.

Like the souls among the lineage of Noach that did not have the complete writings to guide and instruct them to decipher the things shroud in mystery, we too are the unlearned and deceived. Not understanding right and wrong among individuals hellbent on corruption, tyranny, and idolatry. I practiced customs and traditions celebrating feasts with food and songs of a miscreant aligned with the reasoning of the disobedient instead of recognizing holy assemblies fit to restore the obedience of the faithful. Devils have truly infiltrated mainstream religion and have encouraged the religious illiterate to partake in rituals assigned to heathens. I encourage parishioners to explore feats practiced in the Torah. You will not find those activities condemned as Hellenistic, so why do we not speak unto the children of Yashar'el, and say unto them, concerning the feasts of Yahweh, which ye shall proclaim to be holy assemblies, even these are my feasts. VAYIQRA (LEVITICUS) 23:2 את CEPHER.

Our school in Oakland assimilates the Lord's Day and building upon the mitsvah of the Holy Bible instead of spending hours listening to music and songs about the power of Jesus and still shackled to the mental and spiritual chains of our oppression. I have researched the IVIRY calendar, and it is in stark contrast to the Gregorian calendar that western culture uses. The Hebrew calendar can be a bit complicated, but the basics, however, are that it is lunisolar (dictated by the sun and moon), and that the year count will always be ahead of the Gregorian calendar by 3,761 because the years count from 3761 B.C.E. Finally, the months dictated by the moon: if there is a new moon, it is a new month. A full moon will be in mid-month. The names that we use for the IVIRY calendar are from the nation of Babel and the founder Nimrod from the Kush lineage and adopted by the IVIRY nation as of their time of exile from Babel in the sixth century BCE.

The Bible writes down that until then the months called simply by their numerical position in the year (First Month, Second Month, etc.), just as the days of the week — except for Shabbat — still are in Hebrew. In addition, the Bible does record some ancient names for the months that disappeared once the IVIRY nation adopted Kushite names. These include the now-forgotten months of Bul and Aviv, among others. The Gezer Calendar from the 10th century BCE, the oldest Hebrew inscription ever discovered, refers to the months according to the agricultural activities associated with them. The IVIRY months are, in order: Nisan March – April, Iyar, April – May, Sivan, May – June, Tammuz, June – July, Av, July – August, Elul, August – September, Tishri, September – October, Heshvan, October – November, Kislev, November – December, Tevet, December – January, Shevat, January – February, Ada Feb- March. The IVIRY calendar begins on Nisan and not Shevat so if we are praising Jesus who is the descendant of the Semite lineage then should we not also follow the IVIRY calendar that he adhered to?

I will list the fourteenth day of the first month (Nisan) which is Yahweh's Pecach. And on the fifteenth day of the same month is the Feast of Matstsah unto Yahweh: seven days ye must eat Matstsah. This observation follows the seeds of Yashar'el and mix company Exodus from the bondage of Mitsrayim, like Independence Day but without fireworks and cookouts. In the seventh month, on the first day of the month (Tishrei), is a memorial of blowing of shofars, a holy assembly. According to tradition, it was in Tishri that the world came to be. In the Torah, the month termed "the seventh month," written: "In the seventh month, on the first of the month, it shall be a Sabbath for you, a memorial of blowing of horns, a holy occasion. Also on the tenth day of this seventh month is Yom Kippuriym or day of atonement and it shall be a holy assembly unto you; and ye shall afflict your souls and seek repentance and salvation. The month of Tishri is like Thanksgiving because we are grateful for our creation and celebrate on the fifteenth day of this seventh month with the Feast of Sukkoth for seven days unto Yahweh instead of one. Sukkoth are huts that the Yashar'el nation dwelled in when YHWH brought them out of the land of Mitsrayim.

While attending Crozer Theological Seminary c.1950, Martin Luther King Jr. authored an essay titled "The Influence of the Mystery

Religions on Christianity." King noted that the place at Bethlehem selected by early Christians as Jesus's birthplace was an early shrine of a pagan god, Adonis. After the Bar Kokhba revolt (c. 132–136 CE) was crushed, the Roman emperor Hadrian converted the Christian site above the Grotto into a shrine dedicated to the Greek god, Adonis, to honor his favorite, Greek god Antinous.

The search engines on the web are not helpful at all. because images and entire depictions of religious patriarchy are from a European concept with men and women of brown or black hue non-existent. Wikipedia was no better, but at least I downloaded texts of Pagans and Jews decorating their burial chambers with art, later followed by early Christians with visual expressions of the human soul delivered from death to an everlasting life. The Jewish faith puts little emphasis on immortality, and the afterlife was vague, uncertain, and sometimes dismal. So, it would be safe to say that early Christians contrived teachings contrasting the writings within the IVIRY testament.

While new texts discovered in the Christian catacombs under Rome – i.e., the Good Shepherd, Baptism, and the Eucharistic meal – the Orant figures (women praying with raised hands) enriched pagan art. Pagan symbolism in the form of victories, cupids, and shepherd scenes scattered throughout the catacombs. Jewish and pagan use of sheep and goats, birds in a tree or vine, or eating fruit, especially grapes, seven steps leading up to a tomb, a pair of peacocks, the Robe of sanctity, the reading of scrolls, are all found in pagan art and adapted in the Christian art to express the hope of immortality in Christian terms. Pagan sarcophagi had long carried shells, and portraits of the dead often had shells over the heads of the dead, while some put a shell over a grave. Christians and Jews adopted the convention, showing it with another symbol – the halo. For the Christians who made the catacombs, these symbols were necessary to convey their message of death and the afterlife to visitors and away from the scrutinizing eyes of the Pope and bishops.

The early Christian art inside their catacombs depicting death and the afterlife, is like the Mitsrayim nation original conception or taken in part from the hieroglyphics found in burial chambers within pyramids. Many ancient Egyptians believed that there was a place they went to when they died called the *Duat*. We translate this word as 'underworld' or 'afterlife.' To get to the afterlife, a deceased person's spirit had to travel on a long and challenging journey. Each person made of several elements: essence (*ka*) and personality (*ba*), which joined together in the afterlife to form a perfect being called an *akh*. The *ba* shown as a human-headed bird. The deceased traveled through the *Duat* in his own form and in the form of the *ba*. The goal was to reach a special place called the Field of Reeds – Egyptian heaven. Most of the evidence from ancient Egypt comes from funerary monuments and burials of royalty, or the elite class, and for the late period of animals. Little is known of the mortuary practices of the working class or common population. Alongside the fear of the dead, there was a moral community between the living and the dead, so that the dead were an essential part of society, especially in the 3rd and 2nd millennia BCE.

This chapter entails creation and the Sabbath, but death also plays a significant role in humanity history. In the third chapter of BERE'SHIYTH, Yahweh Elohim put a curse on the first man that will become a genetic DNA imprint for all generations after him. No man or woman would be able to cure the plague caused by the first man and woman's disobedience. Death is the eventuality of everyone when Elohim said, "Behold, the man has become as one of us, to know good and evil: and now, lest he put forth his hand, and take also of the tree of life, and eat, and live forever." The offspring of the first man and women were selfish and did not consider the consequences for their offspring. Thank you for going this far on my journey of enlightenment and please remember to follow and fellowship with YAHUAH Assembly www.tpng.biz.

LINKS

The Story of Josiah Henson, the Real Inspiration for 'Uncle Tom's Cabin'/ Journey to The Afterlife/ The world of the dead in ancient Egyptian religion/ Pagan influences on early Christianity/ Sol Invictus/ Funeral/ HEBREW CALENDAR – JEWISH MONTHS/ Hebrew Calendar | History, Months & Holidays

EVOLUTION OF MANKIND

"Defile not ye yourselves in any of these things: for in all these the nations defiled which I cast out before you: And the land defiled: therefore, I do visit the iniquity thereof upon it, and the land itself vomits out her inhabitants. Ye shall therefore guard my statutes and my shall not commit any of these abominations; neither any of your own nation, nor any stranger that sojourns among you: (For all these abominations have the men of the land done, which were before you, and the land is defiled;) That the land spue not you out also, when ye defile it, as it spued out the nations that were before you. For whosoever shall commit any of these abominations, even the souls that commit them cut off from among their people. VAYIQRA (LEVITICUS) 18:24-29 את CEPHER".

History tends to repeat itself when we choose to forget or misalign the truth. I say this with the utmost respect to individuals fighting to hide the scars inflicted on those who only want freedom: you cannot justify brutality by only telling one side of the story. I reiterate that a nation that continues to inflict misery upon citizens will only increase conflict and resentment.

"Go down Moses/Way down in Egypt land/Tell old Pharaoh/To let my people go!/Oh when Israel was in Egypt land/Let my people go!/Oppressed so hard, they could not stand/Let my people go!/So the Lord said, go down (go down) Moses (Moses)/Way (way) down (down) in Egypt land/Tell all Pharaohs/To let my people go (let my people go)" - Louis Armstrong 1956.

This chapter will begin where chapter one left off discussing the elevation of humanity and the migration of nations populating the earth. In the BERE'SHIYTH account of the Tower of Babel, all humankind spoke one language until dispersed from ancient Babylon that is the present-day Iraq. This was the second migration, but it is the first migration theory that is causing an uproar with the destruction of all humanity except 8 people that lived. For atheists and separatists, the Noachian story is a bitter pill to swallow and does not fit into their agenda and core beliefs.

Unlike the struggles of individuals during the periods following the Emancipation Proclamation and during Jim Crow, I have yet to experience the hardships of individuals living in southern and northern America in my lifespan. This statement is not meant to remove the pain caused by organizations and individuals determined to "Make America Great Again" with the abstraction that lineage of Japheth should exist separately from all inferior ethnicities by setting up an all-exclusive nation. Albeit my generation never endured periods of racial unrest experienced by activists during the height of the Jim Crow era, but the ramifications of an agenda to suppress the economical and intellectual structure of American citizens is incessant. My warning to all parishioners that take the CEPHER lightly, which is based on ancient nations, traditions, and archaeological sites proven through research and online search engines, to replenish the faith and build courage in a land not fully embracing diversity.

Religion has both pros and cons that can either divide or coalesce, but continued dogmatism based upon race is the destructive mechanism to our Constitution that guarantees that "all men are created equal" and "equal protection under the laws." The Declaration of Independence which Thomas Jefferson wrote in 1776, set up for European immigrant's rights, which natives and slaves could not call upon. No individual or organization can deny a taxpayer the rights and freedoms afforded to them under the social security system. This is the essential Chokmah of political science that "We hold these truths to be self-evident, that all men are created equal, that they are endowed by their Creator with certain unalienable Rights, that among these are Life, Liberty and the pursuit of Happiness." The Fourteenth Amendment grants citizenship to all people born or naturalized in the United States, including formerly enslaved people. It also guarantees all citizens "equal protection under the laws". The concept of "all men are created equal" influenced by European entitlement philosophy, embedded within education, religion, politics, arts and entertainment, finance, and local government.

John Locke (29 August 1632 – 28 October 1704) was an English philosopher and physician, who believed that all people are born with certain "inalienable" natural rights, such as "life, liberty, and property; so I advise the readers to relinquish membership in any theocratic and political organization not striving for unity among mankind. Unification is the essence of antiquarianism and the process of gathering evidence of the past and using that information to educate interested parties in the hope of reducing illiteracy that has kept many parishioners of western religions in the dark. As a perpetual theology student, the CEPHER has been my road map to understanding humankind history and the analysis of diversion from original genealogy, but it is the 18th-century antiquary, Sir Richard Colt Hoare, who said it eloquently, "We speak from facts, not theory." This path of jealousy and envy is the trait of disobedience that dwells within all humankind and when Individuals recognize treachery and say nothing, then the individual becomes an accomplice to the sin.

Science has aided in the smiting of our neighbors when the research analysis pushes a wider separation of creation and morality. In the 18th century, craniologist Samuel George Morton and German anatomist Friedrich Tiedemann researched human skulls to compare the brain size of five ethnicities. Tiedemann's research emphasized that all humanity was not different and treated as such to prove racial equality and the abolition of slavery. Morton's research analysis took a darker path with the sole intention to further racial division, hierarchy, and slavery within the United States. As president of the Academy of Natural Sciences, he was funded for his research and afforded with the ability to correspond with scientists around the world to secure samples. As one of the leading scientists to prove scientific racism or biological racism which is the pseudoscientific belief that humanity subdivided into biologically distinct ethnic groups and support or justify racial discrimination.

Scientific racism was accepted throughout the scientific community and used by politicians, social and religious groups looking to continue slavery and divide humanity using science instead of the Bible that seeks reasoning and insight. Morton's books helped further the division of humankind into biologically separate groups that set up stereotypes that still exist in our generation on physical and mental characteristics among ethnicities. Scientific racism is the evil contrived by those opposed to the creator's purpose for mankind to live in harmony and a common theory prominent in European and American academic writings from the mid-19th century through the early-20th century without considering physical anthropology that discredits racist worldviews based upon theories that racial categories are necessary along with the hierarchy of superior and inferior races.

Morton claimed the Bible supported polygenism while his books said that each ethnicity was separate with specific, irrevocable characteristics. Morton asserted through his scientific analysis of the examination of individual skulls that the intellectual ability of an ethnicity measured by skull ability. His theory meant a large brain equated to high intellectual abilities, and a small skull showed decreased intellectual abilities. Morton held the largest collection of skulls at the time in America and that each ethnicity had a separate origin and the book of BERE'SHIYTH on Noach and his three sons was incorrect. In all three of his published books, his writings helped push the notion that Caucasians are at the pinnacle of evolution and Ethiopians at the lowest point, with various other ethnicities falling in between these perimeters.

Morton's scientific study of skulls excavated from graves of individuals buried in Mitsrayim (Egypt) was that Morton theory of hierarchy had always existed throughout antiquity and should be the law of the land. When confronted with evidence that many ancient Egyptians had dark skin like other Ethiopians, Morton used skull measurements to solidify the writings of Georges Curvier: that said, "whatever may have been the hue of their skin, they belonged to the same ethnicity of Caucasians." Attempting to justify his theory of a dark-skinned Caucasian ruling class and skull measurements of the five ethnic groups led him to include that "Negroes were numerous in Egypt but must be classified as the same as American and European servants and slaves." Morton contributed to Egyptology and the theory that any evidence of civilization in Africa must have derived from Caucasian presence or influence. Morton's skull collection featured at the Academy of Natural Sciences of Philadelphia until 1966, when transferred to the Penn Museum.

The anthropologist Aleš Hrdlička called Morton "the father of American physical anthropology". Crispin Bates has noted that Morton's "systematic justification" for the separation of ethnicities, has proved him as a benefactor for aiding most materially in giving to the negro his true position as an inferior race. Morton wrote that "I am more than ever confirmed in my old sentiment, that Northern Africa was populated by an indigenous and aboriginal people, who were dispossessed by Asiatic tribes. These aborigines could not have been Negroes, because the latter were never adapted to the climate, and are nowhere now, nor ever have been, inhabitants of these latitudes. Were they Caucasian or some better race, intricately linked to the Arabian race?" Morton, it seems, from his writings were contrary to the theological teachings recognized as the basis for moral and spiritual beliefs for individuals seeking not separation but non partiality.

Then God said, "Let us make mankind in our image, in our likeness, so that they may rule over the fish in the sea and the birds in the sky, over the livestock and all the wild animals, and over all the creatures that move along the ground." So, God created humanity in His own image, in the image of God, He created them; male and female, He created them. BERE'SHIYTH 1:26.27.

On the Origin of Species by Natural Selection, or the Preservation of Favored Races in the Struggle for Life is a work of scientific literature by Charles Darwin considered to be the foundation of evolutionary biology; published on 24 November 1859. Darwin's book introduced the scientific theory that ethnic groups evolve over the course of generations through a process of Natural selection which is the theory that the reproduction of individuals is due to differences in the heritable traits characteristic of ethnicities over generations. Variation of traits, both genotypic and phenotypic, exist within the organisms of all humanity. However, some traits are more likely to help survival on the next generation. If new traits become more favored due to changes in a specific environment, new species can arise especially if these new traits are radically different from the traits owned by their predecessors. These traits are decided by many factors including adaptation to their environments. Others passed down from sexual selection because these traits derived from mating partners.

Natural selection is contrary to Morton's theory and science helps solidify the biblical Chokmah that the entire world had one language and a common speech. As people moved eastward, they found a plain in Shinar and settled there. They said to each other, "Come, let's make bricks and bake them thoroughly." They used brick instead of stone, and tar for mortar. Then they said, "Come, let us build ourselves a city, with a tower that reaches to the heavens, so that we may make a name for ourselves; otherwise, we will be scattered over the face of the whole earth." But the Lord came down to see the city and the tower the people were building. The Lord said, "If as one people speak the same language, they have begun to do this, then nothing they plan to do will be impossible for them. Come, let us go down and confuse their language so they will not understand each other." So, the Lord scattered them from there over all the earth, and they stopped building the city called Babel because there the Lord confused the language of the entire world. From there, the Lord scattered them over the face of the whole earth." BERE'SHIYTH 11:1-9.

The theories published by Darwin and Alfred Russel Wallace in 1858, elaborated in Darwin's influential 1859 book On the Origin of Species of Natural Selection, or the Preservation of Favored Races in the Struggle for Life. To make sense of it, I needed to understand why the majority accepted the theories of Morton and not Darwin's and why Morton's writings passed down like a generational curse that makes one genetic group superior and the others inferior? I also wanted to explore why slaves on many plantations outnumbered their oppressors, but there was little resistance against torture, forcible rape, and wives and children being sold off to other plantations without widespread uprisings or rebellions. Slaves were forbidden from speaking in their native dialect or severely beaten if caught reading books or educating themselves. Both the slave and master faced the threat of violence and murder as a reminder of daily life on the plantation. Negroes who did not speak the English dialect and practiced western religious rituals and traditions were labeled infidels and were not considered the most desirable converts to Christianity.

There was little effort by early colonists of proselytizing negroes because a Christian could not be a slave. Missionaries had a huge moral dilemma on their hands since slavery was fundamental in the South, but the Bible was revered as a guide for high morality and love of neighbor regardless of ethnicity. And the sons of Noach began to war on each other, to take captive and to slay each other, and to shed the blood of men on the earth, and to eat blood, and to build strong cities, and walls, and towers; and individuals began to exalt themselves above the nation, and to found the beginnings of kingdoms, and to go to war, people against people, and nation against nation, and city against city, and all began to do evil, and to acquire arms, and to teach their sons war, and they began to capture cities, and to sell male and female slaves. YOVHELIYM (JUBILEES) 11:2 את CEPHER.

The book of BERE'SHIYTH details all the names of Noach and his woman Emzara, their sons, wives, and children, but gives minimal datum on their complexion. Utilizing the scriptures and comparing the information from textbooks and videos, we will track first the seven sons of Japheth and his women Adataneses, followed by his brothers Cham and Shem. The first-born son to Japheth is Gimer (Gomer), and the book of YOVHELIYM lists his land inheritance towards the East from the North side to the River Tina. The ancient names of the CEPHER have changed over the generations, but Tina River is in South Africa, as supplied by the US military intelligence in electronic format, including the geographic coordinates and location name in various dialects, Latin, Roman and native characters.

According to experts that research the history of the African continent, the original ancient name of Africa was Alkebulan. This name translates to "mother of mankind," or according to other sources, "the Garden of Eden." Alkebulan is an extremely old word, and its origins are Indigenous. Many nations in Africa used this word, including the Ethiopians, Nubians, Moors, and Numidians. YOVHELIYM (JUBILEES) 9:8 את CEPHER.

The second son to receive his land inheritance was Magog, gifted with all the inner portions of the North until it reached the sea of Me'at. It was exceedingly difficult to find the River Re'at, but the Bible says son of A'dam, set your face against Gog, the land of Magog, the chief prince of Meshek and Tubal, and prophesy against him, YECHEZQ'EL (EZEKIEL) 38:2 את CEPHER.

The Jewish historian Josephus of the 1st century CE claimed that Gog and Magog were the Scythians, and in the 5th and 6th centuries understood to be the Huns. Gog and Magog equated with the Magyars in the 10th century and thought of as the primogenitor of Muslim sect led by Muhammad and Saladin, in the Middle Ages. The book of

QOLASIYM says "Where there is neither Yavaniy nor Yahudiy, circumcision nor uncircumcision, Barbarian, Scythian, bond nor free: but Mashiach is all, and in all." QOLASIYM (COLOSSIANS) 3:11 את CEPHER.

Japheth's next son Madai was written about quite extensively and associated with the Ashshur tribe and nation. In the ninth year of Husha the King of Ashshur who conquered Shomeron, and carried Yashar'el away into Ashshurah, and placed them in Chalach and in Chavor by the River of Gozan, and in the cities of the Madai. MELEKIYM SHENIY (2 KINGS) 17:6 את CEPHER. King Husha or Hoshea was the last king of Yashar'el in 732 B.C.E. and during his reign, Israel was conquered by Assyria and taken into exile. Biblical scholars named the Iranian Medes with Madai and the Iranian city of Hamadan. The Kurds and Balochs still support traditions of descent from Madai. According to the *Book of Jubilees* (10:35-36), Madai had married a daughter of Shem and chose not to dwell in his land inheritance beyond the Black Sea (corresponding to the British Isles). The fourth son Javan who inherited land islands towards the border of Ludiy dwells in the land of Macedonia, YASHAR (JASHER) 10:13 את CEPHER.

I had to be very diligent in researching names and locations when I began studying from the Cepher, because the names in the Cepher pronounced differently in the Bible. Javan's name search revealed in the Cepher that Javan was the progenitor of the Greeks. The sixth son of Japheth is Meshech and according to Archibald Sayce, a Professor of Assyriology at the University of Oxford from 1891 to 1919, his articles in the 9th, 10th and 11th editions of the Encyclopedia Britannica, identified Meshech with Muska, a name appearing in Assyrian inscriptions, and generally believed to refer to the Mushki. Most reference books since Flavius Josephus name Meshech in Ezekiel's time as an area in modern Turkey.

Tiras was the final son of Japheth, and his land inheritance was four great islands near the part of Cham land inheritance. (Genesis 10:2, 1 Chronicles 1:5). Gomer's three sons were Ashkenazi who were linked to the Scythian nation in eastern Europe, the Slavic nation in Central Europe, Eastern Europe, Southeastern Europe, the Baltic states, Northern Asia, and Central Asia. Riphath and Togarmah which scholars have claimed Togarmah as the legendary ancestor of various tribes in western Asia and the Caucasus. (Genesis 10:3, 1 Chronicles 1:6). Javan's four sons were Elisha linked to Cyprus, and nation in the eastern Sea, north of the Peninsula, south of the Anatolian Peninsula, and west of the Levant. It is geographically a part of West Asia, but its cultural ties and geopolitics are overwhelmingly European. Cyprus is the third largest and third-most populous island in the Mediterranean. It is east of Greece, north of Egypt, south of Turkey, and west of Lebanon and Syria. Tarshish, Kittim and Dodanim (Genesis 10:4, 1 Chronicles 1:7).

Japheth and his descendants, after the flood, believed to have migrated to areas around the Black and Caspian Seas, Asia Minor, and the Greek islands (Aegean Sea Region). They thought to have settled in the islands of Cyprus, Crete, and Rhodes. According to the first century historian Josephus (Antiquities of the Jews, book 1, Chapter 6), the descendants of Japheth also populated the areas around the Taurus and Amanus mountains, living in Asia as far as the river Tansis and inhabiting Europe to Cadiz. The sons of Cham and his woman Na'eltama'uk did not migrate a long distance unlike his brother Japheth and his clan that propagated nations among islands and seaports in Asia and Europe but chose to dwell in much warmer climates in Alkebulan (THE MOTHER OF HUMANKIND, THE GARDEN OF EDEN) and the Mediterranean basin.

The descendants of Cham were Cush whose land inheritance is Nubia in what is now northern Sudan and southern Mitsrayim, centered along the north-flowing Nile River in northeastern Alkebulan, which flows into the Mediterranean Sea. Cush's brother Mitsrayim land inheritance is northern Mitsrayim named after himself which is a transcontinental country that straddles more than one continent spanning the northeast corner of Alkebulan the Sinai Peninsula, in the southwest corner of Asia. Mitsrayim borders alongside the north Mediterranean Sea, the northeast Gaza Strip of Palestine, and Israel, the eastern Red Sea, the south of Sudan, and western Libya. The Gulf of Aqaba in the northeast separates Mitsrayim from the nations of Jordan and Saudi Arabia.

I had difficulty researching the land inheritance for Cham son Put, but Canaan chronicled extensively throughout the Cepher. Canaan land inheritance was initially the Eastern Mediterranean region of West Asia that consists of Anatolia, a large peninsula in Turkey which is bounded by the southern Mediterranean Sea, the western Aegean Sea, the north-west Turkish Straits, and the northern Black Sea. West Asia is an enormous land mass containing the Arabian Peninsula, Iran, Mesopotamia, the Armenian highlands, the Levant, the island of Cyprus, the Sinai Peninsula, and the southern part of the Caucasus Region. West Asia is separated from Alkebulan by the Isthmus of Suez in Mitsrayim and separated from Europe by the waterways of the Turkish Straits and the watershed of the Greater Caucasus. Central Asia lies to its northeast, while South Asia lies to its east.

Canaan, who many Bibles scholars claim cursed, blessed among his brothers because his land inheritance would encompass Syria, and present-day Israel, Jordan, Lebanon, the Palestinian territories, most of Turkey, southwest of the middle Euphrates, the land bridge between Alkebulan (Africa) and Eurasia. The Eastern Mediterranean shores, extending from Greece in Southern Europe to Cyrenaica, Eastern Libya in Northern Alkebulan. Canaan became the father of Sidon, his firstborn, and of Seth that would later propagate the nations of the Jebusites, the Amorites, the Girgashites, the Hivites, the Arkites, the Sinites, the Arvadites, the Zemarites, and the Hamathites. Afterward, the clans of the Canaanites spread out, so that the Canaanite borders extended from Sidon all the way to Gerar, near Gaza, and all the way to Sodom, Gomorrah, Admah and Zeboiim, near Lasha. The descendants of Kush: Seba, Havilah, Sabtah, Raamah, Sabteca, and Nimrod remembered in the book of BERE'SHIYTH as a mighty hunter and in defiance of the sovereignty of Elohim. Nimrod whose kingdom originated in Babylon, Erech, and Accad, found in the land of Shinar in southern Mesopotamia.

The creation of government and advances in human development traced back to the progeny of Noach's son, Cham. As a child, educated on many characters of the scriptures, one person sparks my interest more than the rest, the story of Nimrod. The book of Genesis skimmed over his life journey and conquest chronicling how he went forth to set up Assyria, where he built Nineveh, Rehoboth-Ir and Calah, as well as Resen, between Nineveh and Calah, the latter being the principal city. It would be much later in life that I would discover the descendants of Raamah, who are Sheba and Dedan. Mizraim became the father of the Ludim, the Anamim, the Lehabim, the Naphtuhim, the Pathrusim, the Casluhim, and the Caphtorim from whom the Philistines derive from. The sons of Shem and his woman Sedeqetelebab include Elam whose land inheritance is named after himself in what is now southern Iran. The principal dialect spoken was an extinct Semitic language called Akkadian that scholars believe was spoken in Mesopotamia, Assyria, and Babylon in the third millennium BC among Assyrians and Babylonians until the 8th century BC.

Ashshur, Shem second son and Nimrod are both debated by historians as to which individual founded the cities Nineveh, Rehoboth, Calah, and Resen. Shem's third son Arpakshad, whose woman was Rasu'aya, land inheritance was in northern Mesopotamia. Eber, the son of Arpakshad, bore two sons: the name of one was Peleg; for in his days the earth divided; and his brother's name was Yoqtan. And Yoqtan begat Almodad, and Sheleph, and Chatsarmaveth, and Yerach, and Hadoram, and Uzal, and Diqlah, and Oval, and Aviyma'el, and Sheva, and Ophiyr, and Chaviylah, and Yovav. Lud land inheritance was along the Halys River and Alis River within Turkey. Aram, the fifth son of Shem is the ancestor of the Aramean people of Syria and West Asia. The children of Aram; Uts or Uz is the eldest of the four brothers and Flavius Josephus states that Uz founded the cities of Trachonitis and Damascus.

Muslim scholar Ibn Kathir is an Arab Islamic exegete, historian, and renowned scholar on tafsir (Qur'an exegesis), the tarikh (history), and fiqh (jurisprudence). Kathir, considered a leading authority on Sunni Islam, quoted as saying in Uts is the father of 'Ad, the progenitor of the nation of Ād. Australian Chinese revolutionary Tse Tsan-Tai names Uts with the Indigenous peoples of the Americas, his descendants are native to a specific region, which inhabited the Americas before the arrival of European settlers in the 15th century. Tse Tsan-Tai also insists that Chul, the second son of Aram, traced to the Austroasiatic peoples in Taiwan in Maritime Southeast Asia, parts of Mainland Southeast Asia, Micronesia, coastal New Guinea, Island Melanesia, Polynesia, and the Madagascar nation that speak Austronesian languages. They also include Indigenous ethnic minorities in Vietnam, Cambodia, Myanmar, Thailand, Hainan, the Comoros, and the Torres Strait Islands.

Aram had two other sons, Gether, and the fourth son Mash or Mesgach, but little mentioned about these two brothers. Arpakshad begat Shelach. Shelach begat Eber, who is a progenitor of the Ishmaelite's, and father of the original Arabs who lived in the Arabian

Peninsula in West Asia, situated northeast of Alkebulan on the Arabian Plate.

Twelve seas surround the Arabian Peninsula making it a huge maritime region. The Aegean Sea, the Sea of Marmara, the Black Sea, the Caspian Sea, the Persian Gulf, the Gulf of Oman, the Arabian Sea, the Gulf of Aden, the Red Sea, the Gulf of Aqaba, the Gulf of Suez, and the Mediterranean Sea. The area populated by many of the descendants of Shem dwelling in the Middle East, excluding most of Mitsrayim and the northwestern part of Turkey and including the southern part of the Caucasus.

When I began this journey of enlightenment, the history to unlock the questions surrounding the origin of Chamites and Semites descendants living in America hidden in books never offered in public education. I included the lineage of the sons of Noach in the beginning of this chapter in the hopes that many will take this information, change the agenda, and call it the "All Souls Movement." Configuration of a narrative set up by a small number of "political and economic elites" who control media conglomerates via media ownership, distribution concentration, and marketing integration, on traditional distribution channels and corporate streaming platforms. This brings us to theological interpretation and my displeasure of epic biblical films from Moses to Jesus Christ with minimal non-European cast members as co-stars or leads.

The Torah lists nations in Africa and Mediterranean regions that major film producers seem to overlook when it comes to capturing the authentication of their films. Even today, leading religious denominations producing biblical productions have gone the way of Hollywood film studios that shy away from productions that portray African slave traders and their tribal partners, capturing and enslaving other Chamite and Semite tribes and nations. The Iviry bible from

BERE'SHIYTH to MACCABEES chronicles enslavement upon nations exiled for unholy practices, and temples sacked and destroyed before the occupation of the YAVANIYM, Alexander the Great in eastern Mediterranean, Mitsrayim, Europe, and parts of Asia.

There are many stories that film producers are yet to bring to light that depicts Chamite and Semite history before American slavery. I have truly believed that the stigma that slavery brings is generational and if we can understand the plight of slaves from antiquity within the Iviry nation, then we can compare the grand strategy, and begin to realize "All things are full of labor; man cannot utter it: the eye is not satisfied with seeing, nor the ear filled with hearing. The thing that has been, it is that which shall be and that which is done is that which shall be done and there is no new thing under the sun. Is there anything whereof it may be said: See, this is new? It was already of old time, which was before us. There is no remembrance of former things; neither shall there be any remembrance of things that are to come with those that shall come after. Qoheleth (Ecclesiastes) 1:8-11."

These are the generations of the sons of Noach, Shem, Cham, and Japheth: and unto them were sons born after the flood. The sons of Japheth; Gimer, and Magog, and Madai, and Javan, and Tubal, and Meshek, and Thiyrac. And the sons of Gimer; Ashkenazi, and Riyphath, and Togarmah. And the sons of Javan; Eliyshah, and Tarshiysh, Kittiym, and Dodaniym. By these were the isles of the other nations divided in their lands; everyone after his tongue, after their families, in their nations. And the sons of Cham; Kush, and Mitsrayim, and Put, and Kenyan. And the sons of Kush; Ceva, and Chaviylah, and Cavta, and Ra`amah, and Cavteka: and the sons of Ra`amah; Sheva, and Dedan. "And Kush begat Nimrod: he began to be a warrior and hunter in the earth. He was a warrior and a hunter before Yahweh wherefore said, Even as Nimrod the warrior hunter before Yahweh. And the beginning of his kingdom was Babel, and Erek, and Akkad, and Kalneh, in the land of Shin'ar.

Out of that land went forth Ashshur, and built Nineveh, and the city Rechovoth, and Kelach, And Recen between Nineveh and Kelach: the same is a great city. And Mitsrayim begat Ludiym, and Anamiym, and Lehaviym, and Naphtuchiym, And Pathruciym, and Kacluchiym, (out of whom came Pelishtiym,) and Kaphtoriym. And Kenyan begat Tsiydon his firstborn, and Cheth, And the Yevuciy, and the Emoriy, and the Girgashiy, And the Chivviy, and the Arqiy, and the Ciyniy, And the Arvadiy, and the Tsemariy, and the Chamathiy: and afterward were the families of the Kena`aniym spread abroad. And the border of the Kena`aniym was from Tsiydon, as you come to Gerar, unto Gaza; as you go, unto Cedom, and Amorah, and Admah, and Tseviym, even unto Lesha.

These are the sons of Cham, after their families, after their tongues, in their countries, and in their nations. Unto Shem also, the father of all the children of Eber, the brother of Japheth the elder, even to him were children born. The children of Shem; Elam, and Ashshur, and Arpakshad, and Lud, and Aram. And the children of Aram; Uts, and Chul, and Gether, and Mash. And Arpakshad begat Shelach; and Shelach begat Eber. And unto Eber were born two sons: the name of one was Peleg; for in his days the earth divided; and his brother's name was Yoqtan. And Yoqtan begat Almodad, and Sheleph, and Chatsarmaveth, and Yerach, And Hadoram, and Uzal, and Diqlah, And Oval, and Aviyma'el, and Sheva, And Ophiyr, and Chaviylah, and Yovav: all these were the sons of Yoqtan. And their dwelling was from Mesha, as you go unto Cephar a mountain of the east. These are the sons of Shem, after their families, after their tongues, in their lands, after their nations. These are the families of the sons of Noach, after their generations, in their nations: and these were the nations divided in the earth after the flood." BERE'SHIYTH (GENESIS) 10:1-32 את CEPHER.

Before we travel further down the rabbit hole in this chapter, the proceeding findings may seem offensive to individuals. I have spent my entire life up to this point in church and mingling in social circles being politically correct, but this is the first time that I am finally getting it. Since I began drafting this book and researching facts, scripture verses, textbooks and academic search engines, my behavior, mindset, and priorities are evolving. This chapter is consuming all my time because there is so much to understand and repent for because of the frivolous B.S that consumed my teenage years up to my adulthood. I want to scream and laugh hysterically at the same time, bamboozled, brainwashed, and indoctrinated into philosophical theories that were a deterrence to my enlightenment.

Please bear with me if I sidestep from time to time while drafting this book, but this is an awakening for me and you, and the journey is just getting underway. When I say unto you, Ask, and given you; look for, and ye shall find; knock, and opened unto you. For everyone that asks receives; and he that looks for finds; and to him that knocks, it shall be opened. If a son or daughter asks for bread from any of you that is a father, will he give them a stone? Or if they ask a fish, will he give them a serpent? Or if they shall ask for an egg, will he offer them a scorpion? If ye then, being evil, know how to give good gifts unto your children: how much more shall your heavenly Father give the Ruach Ha'Qodesh to them that ask him? LUQAS (LUKE) 11:9-13 את CEPHER.

I added "them" instead of "he" in the verse above because many of the writers were men addressing men, and giving spiritual counsel to men, while women at the time, prohibited from speaking or recognized within the congregation. Throughout the scriptures, women played a prominent role in antiquity and are the majority as congregation parishioners in mainstream religious denominations. Since the early 1990s, women have filled the void in empty congregations and became shepherds over men seeking spiritual petitions, repentance, and salvation, while harassed by controversy, discrimination, and biased church bylaws. I will use several quotes and reasonings from men and women of antiquity and past generations that are either spiritually grounded or can contribute with vital information to emphasize a topic within a chapter. We have included Flavius Josephus c. AD 37 – c. 100) an officer in the Roman army and converted Jewish historian. Tubal is the fifth son of Japheth, considered to be the father of the Iberians. Iberia, centered on present-day Eastern Georgia, which bordered on Colchis in the west, Albania in the east and Armenia in the south.

We must always acknowledge the Creator for letting the remnant finally breathe that are suffocating from lack of enlightenment. The difficulty of my journey is distributing time to juggle projects while supporting a robust study habit to continue this book promptly. While proofreading the chapters, I have a clearer reasoning of the role of spiritual wellness and the administration of religious dogma. Culture separation within all societies from as early as Babylon has been consistent and evolves each millennium that consists of the Upper class: the elites, natives, and merchants. Middle class: migrants, foreigners, entrepreneurs. Lower class: serf, defenders, citizens who were former slaves. Slaves: had no rights.

I encourage readers that genuinely want to change the narrative to take neither the blue or red pill but remain sober to examine societal factors, and those capable of inflicting brutality, the inhabitants of each social class, and unvarying proliferation of slavery. Most public-school curriculum highlights slavery and the civil rights movement without addressing nations outside of European lineage that the Bible chronicles. The elevation of humanity thoroughly scrutinized in textbooks and scholastic writings but filmmaking with artistic and commercial significance is yet to address the social and political endeavors of individuals before pre–Atlantic Slave Trade.

Not only do we have to come to sound reasoning with our faith but also with our inner prejudices against each other to shatter the mental chains of enslavement, so if breaking both of my legs on my Harley is undeniably a sign of the Divine intervention of YAHUAH Elohim, then so be it. Like the Roman convert, Paul, on the road to Damascus that experienced divine revelations on his donkey, we must examine the collapse of morality in the world and ask why. It is a travesty and a disservice to continue to stigmatize the name Uncle Tom after reading the true history of Josiah Henson (June 15, 1789 – May 5, 1883). The name downgraded as a demoralizing insult to individuals with aspirations of enlightenment and prosperity. The perpetrators of misinformation have unknowingly aligned themselves with elitists bent on the desecration surrounding the narrative of anti-slavery movement. The truth is Josiah Henson aka Uncle Tom was a former slave that courageously gained his freedom by escaping from his oppressor. His oratory skills were renowned as a religious minister who became an abolitionist, who founded a settlement and laborer's school for other fugitive slaves at Dawn, near Dresden, in Kent County, Upper Canada, of Ontario. This long held inimical characterization of persons being an Uncle Tom based upon adverse belief of their character is false. The motivational exemplary of Henson to change the narrative of individuals oppressed and mentally abject is contradictory to the servile label that has been adapted by agents of bamboozlement. It seems at times; our nation is at war from outside and inside influencers that are detrimental to the creed of Emancipation Proclamation.

The writing is on the wall that the presidency of Donald Trump emboldened organizations that were once archaic in campaigns to suppress the so-called Woke movement, have risen with great boldness to increase division between the ethnicities. State and federal politicians claiming to be the voice of the people have pushed an agenda of inclusion by trying to ban historical facts, while others depict America as not the melting pot it claims to be. If we do not address the past issues, separating all citizens based upon gender and race, there will continue to be dissent among a nation tearing itself apart at the seams. When we begin believing the fabrications of individuals with the resources to misconstrue the truth like those that take the name uncle Tom for something derogatory, it makes me wonder, what else have they lied to us about?

The concentrated effort to enshroud evidence that will enlighten millions of individuals recognized as ancestors of former slaves and native Americans would be hysterical and incredulous from outsiders if the attestation were not factual. The narrative of the annuals told to myself, and others listed within my ethnicity is pure comedy, so I ask all individuals reading this book, "Who raised you?" Having gone through 20 years of the public educational system, it is still difficult to navigate through the continuous stream of various intellectuals seeming ridiculous when trying to embellish proven history, "but these ain't jokes." T.K the comedian, says you get spiritual when you hit 2nd and 3rd gear in your lifespan, and you begin contemplating your accomplishments and reasoning. You start off analyzing your past mistakes and regrets that will haunt you in the hereafter. This is the sole reason I have started a campaign of correcting the verbal offenses hurled at prior acquaintances and family members. Building a Teflon consciousness to understand the rationale of individuals spewing bigotry and hatred but there are only so many waking hours in the day to absorb the propaganda that spews out of the mouth of these instigators of racial disharmony.

If you have read this chapter up to this point then you will come to realize the existence of an illiberal society and benightedness does more harm than good, and further augments stereotypes among the seeds of Noachian nations. There is no better example of the spark that started the Woke Movement than the movie "Roots" that aired on TV One. Alex Haley was bold and innovative in the methods he used to depict the plight of ethnic cultures clashing in Colonial America. During the marathon broadcast, I found myself spiraling down a sea of uncontrollable fervency. Though I was living in the late nineties, the biopic was earnest with reality of injustice unleashed on an ethnic group. How many times have you overheard your parents or grandparents make disparaging remarks about individuals solely based on ethnicity, but under self-examination did not hold any weight? How many times have you disregarded your learned emotional intelligence but choose to venture outside your political, social, or intellectual boundaries?

It takes a courageous person to admit what we all have known but do not accept, we are experimental lab beasts running at full speed only to realize that our efforts were all for not when we expire. This is the reality and destiny of individuals that stay within the confines of the matrix and accept communication primarily used to influence or persuade preconceived notions over reasoning. Propaganda can further an agenda that coincides with smart marketing to encourage a particular synthesis and narrative. I dare to go as far as saying that for generations, elites in power have used spokespersons in media, politics, religion, and entertainment with coded language to birth emotional rather than rational responses designed to influence or control another, usually in a manner which helps the elites' personal aims.

Robert E Park, in 1904, recognized suggestion theory as the "suggestive influence exerted by people on each other. As an

American urban sociologist with expertise in urban sociology that examines the social, historical, political, cultural, economic, and environmental concepts that have shaped urban environments, Parks is one of the most influential figures in early U.S. sociology making significant contributions to the study of urban communities, race relations and the development of empirically grounded research methods, in the field of criminology. Park focused on studies of collective behavior like rallies and crowds. noting that "when two or more people come in contact, a 'circular process' of mutual suggestibility gets triggered. I must speak on these influencers of communication because they continue to implant stereotypes and slighted images negatively characterizing various ethnic cultures for the amusement of others within their circle. As a child and pre-teen, my comprehension of daily life inside of urban communities was from exploitation films, which gave my brother and I a depiction of life outside my family's gated fence. The changes happening around everywhere else under the watchful eye of our grandmother, Mama Johnny, served as a warning that nothing stays stagnant and dormant because change was happening upon the moral and spiritual landscape.

Is it by coincidence that Conservative political leaders are launching attacks on public education by limiting what instructors can teach about slavery and the continuous institutional racism plaguing American and European societies. Conservative news outlets and podcasts are attacking students and teachers by campaigning on the importance of banning books that they consider "inappropriate." Politicians and the clergy have begun to politicize PTA meetings with the "Stop Woke Act" in public education, starting from early elementary tutelage up to college and university academia. In January 2023, Gov. Ron DeSantis of Florida said he would reject a proposed Advanced Placement African American Studies course that included content such as "intersectionality and activism." The College Board later removed many of the criticized contemporary Black authors and content from its required curriculum nationwide, though asserting that the changes were not in response to political pressure from DeSantis and other conservative leaders attacking the concept of social-emotional learning.

It has only been 60 years since the horrors of Jim Crow devastated millions of Americans in both the North and South, leaving survivors unable to grapple with fire-bombings and reported lynchings in communities that once strived as financial Wall Streets and small business enclaves. I have never seen individuals in hooded white sheets or cross burnings living in Oakland, California, except those portrayed cinematically, but I will never downplay their existence or their antagonistic impact on western culture. Racism is not a laughing matter but with critical race comedy, you can speak to an audience on the abominations and iniquities of the past through jokes. While researching excerpts for this chapter, I came across several jokes that may be offensive spoken by comedians during comedy sketches like "I did an ancestry.com family history today and found out that my great grandfather helped Rosa Parks start the Civil Rights Movement. He was the guy who said, "Get up, that's my seat," or continues to spout bigotry with "I am a police officer caught choking the chicken in public. My badge revoked and sentenced to three years jail time. The chicken filed a Civil Rights lawsuit and received 3 million in reparations." Funny or over-the-line, depending on the audience's belief of the joke and the ethnicity of the comic.

Chamite and Semite comics have labeled descendants of Japheth "honkies," "crackers," and "red necks" for years; but once a Japheth comic label a descendant of Chamite or Semite "nigger" it goes viral instantly with career-ending circumstances. "The Woke Movement" terminology derived from African American Vernacular English (AAVE) meaning "alert to racial prejudice and discrimination" encompassing a broader awareness of social inequalities such as racial injustice, sexism, and denial of LGBT rights that affects all ethnicities in this melting pot we call America. Young people of all ethnic backgrounds began mobilizing against public policies like the war in Gaza to Reparation payments, while protests erupted on college campuses around the country. Before the "Black Lives Matter" movement captured the news cycle nationally and internationally, mainstream media began reporting an upsurge in police shootings of unarmed citizens. The comedian, Richard Pryor, was quoted as saying "The truth is gonna be funny, but it is gonna scare the shit outta folks."

These scare tactics are what enriches network news outlets and media giants to highlight drug abuse, police brutality, and unlawful behavior in urban communities. I cringe every time I see news stories of young adults looting retail outlets knowing this will only push stereotypes of criminality directed towards minorities. Instead of embracing the contributions of immigrants, politicians have lambasted migrants from countries outside of European countries. This is why it is so important that we eradicate stereotypes that corrupt the unification of ethnicities in America. Music and films that contribute to perpetuating racial divides in both cultural representations and institutional racism are more popular in our generation than the sixties and seventies. I liken these culture influencers to agents of an unholy alliance that is prevalent in the entertainment industry. Men and women ordained with power, nobility, and influence with no other occupation than to increase the darkness and confusion among the nations like Elymas the sorcerer (for so is his name by interpretation) withstood them, looking to turn away the deputy from the faith. Then Saul, (as one Pa'al,) filled with the Ruach Ha'Qodesh, set his eyes on him, and said, O full of all subtilty and all mischief, you child of the devil, you enemy of all righteousness, will you not cease to pervert the right ways of Yahweh? MA'ASIYM (ACTS) 13:8-10 את CEPHER.

It takes courage from religious leaders and Hollywood elites to combat racial tensions and prejudices by producing stories of the CEPHER that bring about unity to a wider international audience. We cannot erase historical evidence or try to whitewash human physical bondage set up to sustain the infrastructure needs within the Netherlands, Spain, Britain, and France. These growing nations needed cheap labor for agriculture and construction, but they fear that reparations would further highlight European and Spanish oppression among the elite class, from fully acknowledging the contributions of those enslaved sweat and labor. Conservatives and liberals can no longer hide the vileness of European agents of capitalism without discussing their Chamite and Semite counterparts that became wealthy in present-day Benin, Ghana, Senegal, Gambia, Congo, Nigeria, and Angola. I have yet to fully understand the cruel behavior with routine violence and bloodshed inflicted indiscriminately upon the lower class by the upper class. The strategy of every nation is to convert the middle and lower class by religious dogma to abandon ancestral values and worship idols of higher-class culture. The traditions practiced by individuals migrating after the Noachian flood were either abandoned or banned that which did not coincide with the law of the land.

Security was a priority to support structural mechanisms-imposed millennia ago when humanity found innovative ways to secure territory and harvest resources to satisfy a need for growth and power. Many cultures relied upon idolatry and their military prowess using tactics built to sustain empires and their reputation as fearsome warrior cultures. Mesopotamia was the cradle of civilization, and the ancient Sumerians pioneered war and conquest, and their method of controlling the classifications used by nations of western societies.

Using militia under the guise of agents of the state, Akkadians developed the first professional army, the first military dictatorship, and secret societies to disrupt and rein in the lower classes if necessary. Akkadian warriors were fierce defenders of their nation duplicated in part by loyalists that believed they were acting in the best interests of the people.

From liberation movements during the Jim Crow era and late seventies to a group of former Confederate soldiers in Tennessee which founded an organization in bitter opposition to postwar Reconstruction and its promise of civil and political unrest for men and women recently released from slavery in Southern states. The organization developed as the Ku Klux Klan with elements of a secret fraternal society carried out an agenda of intimidation and violence against those promised equality under the Emancipation Proclamation. During the years of 1866 through 1871, these terrorists hiding behind white and red robes killed thousands of innocent Black Southerners and their white supporters that stood up to them. Documented with the justice department that widespread rape cases on Black women and men occurred by men of the organization during and after that period. A campaign of terror and oppression of Black families in the South, the Klu Klux Klan continued with burning down their homes and killing livestock on a massive scale, Their membership in 1915 was nearly 8 million, mostly Protestant, citizens including women that wore skirted robes and called themselves the WKK (Women of the Ku Klux Klan) a sort of booster club which organized activities that were often separate from the men's.

The KKK believes they are doing the work of their deities to preserve a pure nation under God. Many melanated men and women were seeing how preachers were quoting from the Bible asking parishioners to love thy neighbors and obey the golden rule, but they were active members with the Klu Klux Klan and white supremacy groups. The book of BERE'SHIYTH first nine chapters discussion on lineage of first man, Adam, and woman, Chuah, detailed their sons and daughters which said unto them, "Be fruitful, and multiply, and replenish the earth," have been discarded by atheists and antagonist religious organizations as myths or unbelievable to justify abuse of civil liberties, unwarranted harassment, serfdom, and racial assassinations. *How many times have you felt threatened or afraid of harm when approached by an individual that was not of your ethnicity? How many times have you watched conservative news channels and complained America is worse off now because of the illegal migrants and Blacks? How many times have you sided with law enforcement after the unarmed shooting of innocent Americans?* We must look beyond the hue of our brothers and sisters' skin tone and realize that evil and violence comes from the moral breakdown of humanity no matter what ethnicity they are.

In the first year of the third jubilee, Qayin slew Havel because Elohim accepted the sacrifice of Havel and did not accept the offering of Qayin. And he slew him in the field: and his blood cried from the ground to heaven, complaining because he had slain him. On this account, written on the heavenly tablets, cursed is he who smites his neighbor treacherously, and let all who have seen and heard say, so be it; and the man who has seen and not declared it, let him be accursed as the other. And for this reason, we announce when we come before Yahweh Elohaynu all the sin which is committed in heaven and on earth, and in light and in darkness, and everywhere. YOVHELIYM (JUBILEES) 4:1-6 את CEPHER.

Qayin killed his brother Havel because his heart was full of envy and hate. After being reprimanded by Elohim for his continued thoughts of unrighteousness, Qayin decided to embark on the path of evil and destroyed his brother's body but could not destroy his RUACH that belonged to the creator.

I spoke of repentance and redemption when I began writing after my near fatal motorcycle accident but now, I am asking all parishioners to be the man or woman in the mirror and make a change to increase love among your brothers and sisters, regardless of their ethnicity. My people were destroyed for lack of knowledge because you have rejected the knowledge, I will also reject you, that you shall be no priest to me: seeing you have forgotten the Torah of your Elohim, I will also forget your children. As increased, so they sinned against me: therefore, will I change their glory into shame. They eat up the sin of my people, and they set their heart on their iniquity. HUSHA (HOSEA) 4:6-8 את CEPHER.

Knowledge is power and can change those opposed to racial equality into staunch defenders of racial justice. One central figure that comes to mind is Malcolm X and his conversion from Detroit Red to el-Hajj Malik el-Shabazz May 19, 1925 – February 21, 1965. Part time petty criminal that converted to Nation of Islam becoming a vocal advocate for Black empowerment after incarceration at Charlestown State Prison for larceny and later Norfolk_Prison Colony, both in Massachusetts. At an early age, Malcolm saw many acts of violence, racial injustice, discrimination from unsympathetic European adults as a child that would turn any person in his situation into a high voltage live wire. A majority of newly freed slaves after the Emancipation Proclamation were living in poverty and substandard housing conditions while employment was either denied or limited to sharecropping.

Families were desperate for government aid and relief but only received Jim Crow laws that condoned the brutality of any non-European citizen for the smallest infractions, especially accusations of looking at a European woman or acting self-important. Most often, the local Sheriff, the judge and the preacher who were members of the Klu Klux Klan were the prominent instigators of the lynchings of the accused. This was a factor that led to Malcolm's criticism of Christianity and the hypocrisy that many understood as being a religion that oppressed melanated people while uttering commandments to love thy brother. And A'dam called his woman's name Chuah because she was the mother of all living. BERE'SHIYTH (GENESIS) 3:20 את CEPHER.

Brothers and sisters of all ethnicities needed to combat racism and terrorism with nonviolence, but Malcolm leaned towards the Nation of Islam teachings, including the notion that the lineage of Japheth considered devils. Malcolm initially struggled to accept this belief; however, over time, Malcolm reflected on his past relationships with European immigrants marked by dishonesty, injustice, greed, and hatred. Summoned by the local draft board for military service in World War II, he feigned mental disturbance by rambling and declaring: "Please send me down South so I can organize some nigger soldiers and steal us some guns and kill us those racist crackers." Declared mentally disqualified for military service. I guess the members of the Draft board did not want Detroit Red around their active-duty soldiers and live ammunition.

Zealots have continued to misinterpret the Bible or Koran to corrupt the faith of believers to implement their unlawful and wicked agenda. The religious conflicts between Christians and Muslims started primarily to secure control of holy sites considered sacred by both groups between 1096 and 1291. These conflicts between individuals and nations were either pledging allegiance to Jesus, YAHWEH or Allah waged in the Middle East and on American soil. Malcolm X, like so many religious converts, has fully compromised moral and theological principles for social causes contrary to the spiritual beliefs of Avraham. Malcolm's interpretation of Islam was filled with hate and anger until his pilgrimage to Mecca and came face to face with European Muslims who were his brothers of different skin pigment.

The same moral and spiritual enlightenment has occurred within Skinheads and conservative Christians that genuinely believe in patriotism and ethnic pride duped by ministers of Satan's army. For such are false apostles, deceitful workers, transforming themselves into the apostles of Mashiach. And no marvel; for Satan himself transformed into an angel of light. Therefore, it is no powerful thing if his ministers also transformed as the ministers of righteousness; whose end shall be according to their works. QORINTIYM SHENIY (2 CORINTHIANS) 11:13-15 את CEPHER.

I encourage all denominations to reject works of the devil and follow the commands of the Torah, and not like their ancestors who were not interested in religion, because too much enlightenment of the Torah might inspire slaves to fight for their freedom. In 1743, a missionary school was set up to train freedmen and slaves in Charleston, South Carolina in the field of theology. The appeasement to corrupt fellow slaves came via indoctrination of Nigger Harry and Nigger Andrew taught the rudiments of education and basic doctrines of the Catholic Church. Serving as the training school for missionary workers in various parts of the colony of South Carolina, the school shuttered in 1763 because one of the instructors died and the other proved inefficient. After researching various documents on slavery and the church, I often wondered if the Catholic Church appeased slave owners by making slaves passive with religious doctrines that never prescribed salvation through freedom of bondage.

Not until Methodism and the Quakers took a stand for racial equality did slaves ever expect to be free of the chains and whips under the institution of thralldom. Subjected daily to cruelty and forced labor under the threat of violence, forced converts of Christianity never afforded the same privileges and protections enjoyed by European Christians because missionaries taught slaves to obey their earthly masters as they would Jesus. Stripped of ancestral values and traditions by missionaries that moderated their passions and behavior requiring passive and submissive reasoning through the interpretation of selected Scriptural verses of the Negro Bible. Selected slave Negroes converted to Evangelicals prevented fellow slaves from sinning against God by offending against the laws of the 1800s. The few bible verses that slaves who converted to missionaries used to help quiesce chatter of insurrections at any time proved effective against incendiarism or rebellion in slaveholding communities. *What made millions of oppressed people continue day after day terrified to the point of allowing themselves classified as nothing more than chattel and nescient in nature?*

For centuries, individuals with resources and influence have peddled theories as to why a majority of Chamite and Semite citizens continue to allow European oppression in the 20th century. The role of illiteracy of antiquity and hidden artifacts that will unlock mysteries of life in 2348 BC, after the antediluvian period that began with Creation at 4004 BC, is a major factor in the division of ethnicities. The hatred and ignorance towards individuals because of the diversity of their skin tone was never a factor in antiquity, but learned prejudice beginning in 1661 with The Barbados Slave Codes. Until we erase the theories of one ethnicity being superior to another or the rights of the United States constitution meant for a chosen few, daily life for all citizens will not be "The One Nation Under God" that continues to be controversial when we recite the Pledge of Allegiance. The migrants of antiquity were the pillars of civilization and ignorance of antiquity is the chief advocate for dissension that stands in opposition to unification and justice.

British naturalist, Charles Darwin (February 12, 1809- April 19, 1882), was quoted as saying "that all species of life that have descended from a common ancestor is now generally accepted and considered a fundamental concept in science." This is the scientific evidence that supports the BERE'SHIYTH account of all humanity derived from the first man, Adam. All known forms of life are based on the same fundamental biochemical organization: genetic information encoded dices in DNA, (Deoxyribonucleic acid that is a polymer composed of two polynucleotide chains that coil around each other to form a double helix). The polymer carries genetic instructions for the development, functioning, growth and reproduction of all known organisms and many viruses.

Now please bear with me as I give readers a brief description of genetic information for all humankind. DNA and ribonucleic acid (RNA) are nucleic acids. Alongside proteins, lipids, and complex carbohydrates (polysaccharides), nucleic acids are one of the four major types of macromolecules that are essential for all known forms of life transcribed into RNA. It has become widely accepted in science that early in the history of life on Earth, prior to the evolution of DNA and possibly of protein-based enzymes as well, an "RNA world" existed in which RNA served as both living organisms, the storage method for genetic information, a role fulfilled today by DNA, except in the case of RNA viruses and potentially performed catalytic functions in cells, a function performed today by protein enzymes, with the notable and important exception of the ribosome, which is a ribozyme. Through the effect of protein (Once formed, proteins only exist for a certain period degraded and recycled by the cell's machinery through the process of protein turnover. A protein's lifespan measured in terms of its half-life and covers a wide range. They can exist for minutes or years with an average lifespan of 1–2 days in mammalian cells. Abnormal or misfiled proteins degraded more rapidly either targeted for destruction or due to being unstable) and RNA-enzymes (proteins that act as biological catalysts by accelerating chemical reactions. The molecules upon which enzymes may act called substrates, and the enzyme converts the substrates into different molecules known as products.

All metabolic processes in the cell need enzyme catalysis to occur at rates fast enough to sustain life.) then translated into proteins by (highly similar) ribosomes, (bind to messenger RNAs and use their sequences to decide the correct sequence of amino acids to generate a given protein. Amino acids selected and carried to the ribosome by transferring RNA molecules, which enter the ribosome and bind to the messenger RNA chain via an anti-codon stem loop. For each coding triplet (codon) in the messenger RNA, there is a unique transfer RNA that must have the exact anticodon match and carries the correct amino acid for incorporating into a growing polypeptide chain. Once the protein produced, it can then fold to produce a functional three-dimensional structure) with ATP, NADPH, and others as energy sources. There are some 23 proteins found in all organisms, serving as enzymes carrying out core functions like DNA replication. The fact that only one such set of enzymes exists is convincing evidence of a single ancestry. Natural selection is the process that drives evolution or change within a species. His classic theory published in "On the Origin of Species" in 1859, more than 150 years ago.

I have just listed all the nations and ethnicities among humanity found in the first book of the Bible, and two organizations, separate but equal in ideology. This is not a push to turn you against your beliefs but facts you can easily research and draw your own conclusions to, because racism is created by individuals that do the bidding of the ruler of the earth, Satan. You have the first book that details humanity evolution from the seed of A'dam and his woman, Chuah, that debunks the big bang theory and theories of scientists that have successfully created division among humankind with race terms black, white, brown, and yellow. If we are to believe what the scriptures tell us that individuals lived for hundreds of years, but now have only 70 plus years tested for obedience and understanding, what have you done with your time and resources to unite all humanity?

What mistakes have you made through assumptions and close-minded thinking that keeps you awake at night? As you read this paragraph, I have used "we" and "you" because I am also guilty of bigotry and applying stereotypes to predetermine brothers and sisters from the lineage of Japheth, Shem, and Cham before befriending them and fully knowing their behavioral trait.

Ignorance is a vital tool of oath keepers of devils that have pledged to keep humanity divided via entertainment, politics, education, and finance with noble lies propagated by elites to keep social disharmony. Plato aka Aristotle's: 427 – 348 BC examined in my psychology course and considered foremost in ancient Yavaniy philosophies and one of the most quoted writers in Western philosophy. My dear friend and colleague, Teasley, shared with me the "noble lie" known as the myth or parable of the metals in Book III. Socrates provides the origin of the three social classes of ancient Yavaniy society, but these social classes as you read below, are not classified or even discussed as ethnicities but rather as precious metals and their worth among humanity. The earth, as being their mother, delivered them, and now, as if their land were their mother and their nurse, they ought to take thought for her and defend her against any attack and regard the other citizens as their brothers and children of the self-same earth.

While all of you, in the city, are brothers, we will say in our tale, yet God, in fashioning those of you who are fitted to hold rule, mingled gold in their generation, for which reason they are the most precious; but, in the helpers, silver, and iron and brass in the farmers and other craftsmen. And, as you are all akin, though, for the most part, you will breed after your kinds, it may sometimes happen that a golden father would beget a silver son, and that a golden offspring would come from a silver sire, and that the rest would, in like manner, be born of one another. So that the first and chief injunction that the god lays upon the rulers is that of nothing else are they to be such careful guardians, and so intently observant as of the intermixture of these metals in the souls of their offspring, and if sons are born to them with an infusion of brass or iron they shall by no means give way to pity in their treatment of them, but shall assign to each the status due to his nature and thrust them out among the artisans or the farmers. And again, if from these there is born a son with unexpected gold or silver in his composition, they shall honor such and bid them go up higher, some to the office of guardian, some to the assistantship, alleging that there is an oracle that the city shall then be overthrown when the man of iron or brass is its guardian. I look at this parable as a battle to keep hierarchy among the elites and to limit the influence and power of the working class and poor. Racism plays a leading role since the pigment of a citizen's skin tone does not stand for his worth and nobility among the elites. The prohibited mixing of metals to keep pureness and value so their offspring will not become infected by lesser metals.

This so much resembles the male European immigrants fear of the male Negro slave engaging in coitus with the female European immigrants and the lynchings and terrorism inflicted on innocent men because of rape accusations or procreation between Negro males and European women. Plato's noble lie written to show classism within Greek antiquity, but this tale is for any individual that thirsts for reasoning to interject within their own lives the parable to awaken 9 Other moral and spiritual consciousness of the disobedient mind battle against the unification of all humanity based on status, ethnicity, and ranking. Guardians or gate keepers commanded to keep the metals separated and avoid by any means necessary the cohabitation of the metals with boundaries and restrictions to deaden passions within the mind to accelerate dehydration of fellowship. Without the fellowship and communication of various metals to combine and flourish them, stagnation occurs and the luster and illumination of precious metals no longer become precious, but ordinary and obsolete. "For the temperate mind has power to conquer the pressure of the passions, and to quench the fires of excitement, and to wrestle down the pains of the body, however excessive; and, through the excellency of reasoning, to abominate all the assaults of the passions. But the occasion now invites us to give an illustration of temperate reasoning from history." MAKKABIYM REVIY'IY (4 MACCABEES) 3:17-19 את CEPHER.

It is the only truly just civil society founded on a lie. Socrates prefers to face up to the issue with clarity. A good regime cannot be based on enlightenment; if there is no lie, several compromises—among them private property—made and hence merely conventional inequalities accepted. "This phrase given 'noble lie', a self-contradictory expression no more applicable to Plato's harmless allegory than to a New Testament parable or the Pilgrim's Progress, and liable to suggest that he would countenance the lies, ignoble, now called propaganda.   This is a radical statement about the relationship between truth and justice, one which leads to the paradox that wisdom can rule only in an element dominated by falsehood. It is hardly worth obscuring this issue for the sake of avoiding the crudest of misunderstandings. And modern phenomenon of propaganda might become clearer to the man who sees that it is somehow related to a certain myth of enlightenment which is itself brought into question by the Platonic analysis. The great dragon cast out, that old serpent, called the Devil, and Satan, which deceives the entire world: cast out into the earth, and his angels cast out with him. CHIZAYON (REVELATION) 12:9 את CEPHER

LINKS HUMANKIND

What Darwin Got Right (and Wrong) About Evolution/ Common descent/ Malcolm X/ Klu Klux Klan and Christian churches/ A new take on the 19th-century skull collection of Samuel Morton/ On the Origin of Species/ Why?/

The Plantation Preacher/ The History of the Negro Church/ Geographical Names/ What Was The Original Name Of Africa?/ Gog and Magog-religion and mythology/ Hoshea/ Right-Wing Attacks on Education and Student Expression/ Ancient Warfare: 8 of the Greatest Warrior Cultures of Ancient Times

ONE FLESH

And the man said, this is now bone of my bones, and flesh of my flesh: she called Woman, because she was taken out of Man. Therefore, shall a man leave his father and his mother, and shall cleave unto his woman: and they shall be one flesh. BERE'SHIYTH (GENESIS) 2:23-24 את CEPHER.

Are we making some headway yet on our belief of humanity and how we interact with each other? So far, we have discussed the creation of heaven and earth while exploring the evolution of humankind. The last chapter was on the discovery of DNA that ties all humankind together and the behavior patterns within social classifications. By understanding the reasoning from both temporal and spiritual perspectives, our hope is to change the dynamics of western culture for the mindset that all ethnicities share so many distinct characteristics from a genetic standpoint that racism and bigotry abolished. It does not matter if you live in Oakland, California or on Easter Island, we are all creatures of a single species refuted by the big bang theory or renowned scientists publishing evolution theories to classify ethnicities.

I genuinely believe that incognizant of history and narrow-minded skeptics that continue to attack the DNA evidence that all nations upon the earth derived from one source is our worst enemy. Those who believe that the Torah (Instructions) is the story of mankind's existence, migration, and conclusion guided by reasoning with an unbreakable faith in a Creator of the universe. These same individuals accredit celestial beings having the ability to interact with mortals on earth and provide enlightenment to mysteries of past, present and future. I can lean upon the ruach for peace when my soul is in turmoil; but when it comes to understanding my woman and controlling her mood swings, I am clueless. I hear the same argument from men and women that complain their mate does not understand them, or things have changed since they got married. Before I learned to bridle my anger and refused to be an accomplice to my woman's mood swings, I was all in with the tit for tat and loud outbursts throughout the home. This is not only for men, but women too have given second thoughts to the reasoning of getting married. If you have, you are not alone, because I too have come to discover that I will never fully achieve completeness with my mate before I expire upon the earth.

As you read further within this chapter, we will provide you with other information beside scriptural excerpts for you to research that I hope will give credence to the phrase "Let It Make Sense." The Webster dictionary defines sense as; conscious awareness or rationality—usually used in plural and for technical assumptions this definition seems to sum up what we are trying to express but I would also like to add the sense when it comes to attraction of opposite gender, the sense that better suits this discussion is a particular sensation or quality of sensation, usually down in the genital area. We cannot discuss the mental without the physical since most marriages start off physically from the honeymoon and after 20 plus years of monogamous matrimony is strictly mental.

The A'dam and Chuach story of the woman created from his rib would make many skeptical of the validity of the Bible and the contributing writers of the holy scriptures, but I ponder not on the physical but the mental reasoning of the story as the two become one. Even though they are completely different genetically, they should have allowed the power of the ruach that dwells within all, to decrease their inclinations to act independently as a couple. There was no dating stage for the first couple to examine the pros and cons necessary to weigh the likelihood of marriage but instantly thrust together, and we saw the nature of self-determination that distracted the two from seeking insight and reasoning to go the distance. Their failure to fully grasp the instructions to rely upon each other and keep the Chokmah of the Creator as a roadmap to alleviate the problems and pitfalls of life is our testimony. If you have been with your man or woman for quite some time and never made it a three-cord bond between you, him/she and the creator, what is stopping you? The phrase "why buy the cow when you can get the milk for free" hits dead center when couples are playing house.

I have heard divorcees say they have been married before and do not want to get married again, or couples that are dating but categorized their relationship as friends with benefits. How many sermons have the minister warned us, "Be not unequally yoked together with unbelievers: for what fellowship has righteousness with unrighteousness? And what communion has light with darkness? Qorintiym Sheniy (2 Corinthians) 6:14". This verse is profound and kept me from engaging with many sexual partners during college years. After watching a horror film, I began contemplating my sexual activity after seeing the girl's memory transferred during coitus to the boyfriend that starts dreaming about every guy she has slept with. The moral dilemma laid upon those choosing pleasure over principles and the mental issues or sexual ailments passed along during coitus. The film may have been the imagination of a screenwriter. but the implications of demon possession made me look at girls in college differently. When the scriptures warn you that the two shall be one, and do not become unevenly yoked with unbelievers, you begin measuring the consequences of unprotected sex, teenage pregnancy, vanquished by the enemy using coitus as their weapon.

There are many tales too unbelievable to be factual like evil spirits that attack you while sleeping or awake called Incubus. Myth or reality, this evil spirit attaches to women in their sleep through sexual intercourse disguised as a dream. The power that sexual intercourse has upon both humans and beasts is phenomenal. How many times after engaging in coitus have you felt exhausted and powerless? Our strength diminished, and completely drained and weak. Samson's strength was his locks, but he was deceived by his woman after coitus and his power taken away, so do not be like Samson or Delilah. "And it happened afterward, that he loved a woman in the valley of Soreq, whose name was Delilah. And the cereniym of the Pelishtiym came up unto her, and said unto her: Entice him, and see wherein his great strength lies, and by what means we may prevail against him, that we may bind him to afflict him: and we will give you every one of us eleven hundred pieces of silver. And Delilah said to Shimshon: Tell me, I pray to you, wherein your great strength lies, and wherewith you might be bound to afflict you. Shofetiym (Judges) 16:4-6".

The Bible (Basic Instructions Before Leaving Earth) has spiritual messages and parables chronicled for every temptation, dilemma, and issue that comes upon us while trying to navigate upon the earth. We gain insight on our interaction with each other physically and mentally, which taken lightly since every man regardless of social classification tempted when the mind is battling seduction. The same statement is true for women when they meet a man that sparks their hidden fantasies. The human physique is remarkable and appealing to the senses but also a weapon when used to manipulate and control the lighthearted and faint of spirit. Reminiscing upon my own shortcomings, enticed by the flesh while trying to stay upright with the ruach. I have never considered myself a ladies' man by any stretch of the imagination, but I was promiscuous often allowing lust to overpower me when I should have known better. I will not justify my indiscretions or make excuses like cheating mates that blame their infidelity on intoxication, abandonment issues, lack of parental guidance, or one-night stands. I have chosen to take responsibility for my actions and own it and face whatever consequences derived from my transgressions and learn from it. This has not always been easy, and I had to deal with many serious repercussions for not heeding red flags and warnings from the ruach or self-control of the genitals that are more worthy than pleasurable sensations. "For when we were in the flesh, the motions of sins, which were by that mitzvah, did work in our members to bring forth fruit unto death. But now delivered from that mitzvah, that being dead wherein held; that we should serve in the newness of the ruach, and not in the oldness of the letter" Romaiym (Romans) 7:5-6".

We are in a much better position to fully vet our prospective significant others with all the investigative tools at our disposal. A'dam could not woo Chuach and get a better perspective as to her true character in the presence of adversity. The same opinion can also apply to Chuah regarding A'dam as a suitable husband and protector.

Led astray by temptations of the soul before they disobeyed the commandments of YHWH, and A'dam being the firstborn of human creation did not stand up for Chuah when she needed him the most. The bond of marriage is not only for companionship but protection and defense against any enemy that tries to create a wedge between the man, woman, and Father. "Now the serpent was more subtle than any beast of the field which Yahweh Elohim had made. And he said unto the woman: Yes, has Elohim said, Ye shall not eat of every tree of the garden? And the woman said unto the serpent: We may eat of the fruit of the trees of the garden: But of the fruit of the tree, which is during the garden, Elohim has said: Ye shall not eat of it, neither shall ye touch it, lest ye die. And the serpent said unto the woman: Ye shall not surely die: For Elohim knows that in the day ye eat thereof, then your eyes opened, and ye shall be as Elohim, knowing good and evil. Bere'shiyth (Genesis) 3:1-5".

My reasoning tells me that this was not the first time the serpent beguiled Chuach because of the serpent's courage to call the Alpha and Omega a liar, and Chuach manifesting the lie existing in her heart. How many times have you heard a marriage breaking up because a third party stepped in with a lie? Was one or each spouse beguiled by a friend they trusted that turned out to be an enemy to the marriage bond? When two becomes one, a decision that affects both individuals should be discussed before any action is taken or the consequences can be devastating. Case in point, A'dam and Chuach bringing death upon themselves and offspring. This is an excellent time to introduce self-control to the marriage equation, because most couples lack willpower that is valuable and necessary to put the best interests as a unit in front of their independent reasoning. Each mate brings qualities they have gotten during their lifespan to the relationship that the other may not own but is essential to equip them for any quandary arising within the marriage.

From my own experiences dealing with women in many relationships before marriage, we began to see the changes happening and the quandary of us both raised in single-parent homes as negative examples when we began dating. All the counsel from family and friends could not prepare us with the mental strength necessary to initially defeat the obstacles we faced after matrimony. We both continued to associate with unmarried acquaintances that only added turmoil to their single lifestyle that did more harm than good. Several occasions arose within the marriage that almost pushed us to divorce because of our stubbornness and unwillingness to separate our former lifestyle for the sake of the marriage. This was especially true when associating with friends of the opposite gender and confessing to them issues that we were facing and seeking their advice on the matters. This was a wow factor to be discussing coitus with them because their opinions were always negative while their friendship was bringing us closer to crossing the line of adulterous behavior.

I honestly believe when I became conflicted with the book of BERE'SHIYTH which chronicles the pairing of beasts of the field and the reasoning for finding a mate that is compatible with your spiritual, emotional, mental, and financial well-being. I hope that individuals can heed the warnings of bringing an outside influence into marital disputes that are not certified marriage counselors or stealthy attempts to undermine the bond between you and your mate. There was never a time while dating that my grandparents did not meet the girls that I became interested in. In fact, there is only one girl that my grandmother and aunt scrutinized as being unfitting because of her questionable background and demeanor that continues to be a roller coaster ride three decades later. From faith to housekeeping, my women and I were raised differently but over the years we learned to compromise, and this strengthened our love for each other. When the Creator emphasizes "evenly yoked," this announcement has been true from day one because the divorce rate is exceptionally high for individuals that think with fleshly mindset without recognizing the spiritual bonding needed to go the distance. I have seen many individuals raised under the banner of theocracy, succumb to the pressures of the flesh, and admit they were unprepared with an unbelieving mate.

I can tell anyone who is contemplating matrimony, to look beyond the outward appearance since Chokmah lifts the head of them that is of low degree and makes them to sit among great status. Commend not a person for their beauty; neither abhor a person for their outward appearance. The bee is little among flies; but her fruit is the chief of sweet things. Beauty is only skin deep but an ugly cut to the bone. "And now I announce unto you that the children of Yashar'el will not guard true to this ordinance, and they will not circumcise their sons according to all this Torah; for in the flesh of their circumcision they will omit this circumcision of their sons, and all of them, sons of Beliya'al, will leave their sons uncircumcised as they were born. And there will be great wrath from Yahweh against the children of Yashar'el. Because they have forsaken his covenant and turned aside from his word, and provoked and blasphemed, since they do not see the ordinance of this Torah; for they have treated their members like the other nations, so that they removed and rooted out of the land. And there will be no more be pardon or forgiveness unto them so that there should be forgiveness and pardon for all the sin of this eternal error. Yovheliym (Jubilees) 15:33-34".

In my estimation, we are under attack with every method known by humanity to disrupt the order of the universe. Even the definition of marriage changed and altered by the mechanisms of the elites. Organizations and political parties have interpreted the foundation of marriage incorrectly and have instituted behavior that is grossly contrary to what the Torah says is the basis of marriage. Love is the overall theme of the Bible as well as obedience and discipline, but when we begin injecting our own opinions on what morality should look like, we are heading down a dead-end street with no lights on and brakes malfunctioning.

I have studied several books and verses of the Bible repeatedly because metaphors and parables have different interpretations that are often confusing. The book of Mishlei (Proverbs) says "Every wise woman builds her house: but the foolish plucks it down with her hands." Is this talking about the physical aspect of structural engineering or family parenting? Or "Let the woman learn in silence with all subjection. But I suffer not a woman to teach, nor to usurp authority over the man, but to be in silence. A'dam formed, then Chuah. And A'dam was not deceived, but the woman being deceived was in the transgression."

The book of TIMOTHEUS RI'SHON (1 TIMOTHY) has a strong command for women to be silent in religious ceremonies but, it also poses two questions. How can women continue to grow from a theological education if the men are teaching false doctrines? Or are these verses calling for women to be in a lower-class status than men within the religious circle because of Chuah disobedience? The word YAH should not be taken lightly but approached with a vigorous examination for accuracy and applied to your own lifestyle to achieve insight to grasp the difficulties of living as one. When I visit congregations from the east to west coast, women parishioners outnumber the men in many denominations. This is why the commandment of listening with both ears and seeking discernment is critical to understanding parables that can change the dynamics of your spiritual consciousness. If we approach the books of the scriptures as a study in human psychology, we shall decipher the reasoning of human behavior taught. Who does not need intelligence of the inner workings for sustainability in marriage, family, economics in turbulent times, and sustaining our Faith while transforming your mind from carnal to spiritual? If only I had taken what I learned in my youth to heart, I would not have repeatedly made so many blunders in my romantic relationships. Why do young people raised within a religious environment succumb to temptation often?

Christianity emphasizes the need to rely upon Jesus with all your basic needs but for those battling with sexual impulses and infidelity, the concept of faith and morality is hard to swallow. "If you love to hear, you shall receive understanding, and if you bow your ear, you shall be wise. Stand in the multitude of the elders and cleave unto him that is wise. Be willing to hear every holy discourse and not let the parables of understanding escape you" SIRACH (ECCLESIASTICUS) 6:32-35 את CEPHER.

The above reasoning is simple to understand and align your inner Ruach with the creator of creation to prosper under the remarkable wonders within the six-day period. Our physical attributes that make male and female compatible studied and theorized throughout the ages and though we differ in ideologies and traditions, our genetic similarities in physical appearance, such as facial features, skin color, and body proportions prove we derive from the same DNA. We also inherited the emotions that make us love and "there is no fear in love; but perfect love casts out fear: because fear has torment. He said that fear not made perfect in love" YOCHANON RI'SHON (1 JOHN) 4:18 את CEPHER.

Since my adolescent years, the only emotions I experienced were positive from my grandparents disciplined for immoral behavior. As a child I could shift most of the blame on adolescence, then I felt a leather strap on my backside. I had no excuses for not acting accordingly when I became a teenager, but it was the love I felt at my grandparents' home that brought me back to safety whenever I would choose to steer off course. There was never a time I could remember that profanity and violence displayed in my grandparents' household. The interaction between my grandparents was a complete opposite of the relationship between my biological mother and father that divorced when my brother and I were still toddlers. The separation played a derogatory role in both our lives, and it would not be until our teenage years that we would come to would come to grips with our mother fleeing because of physical and mental abuse and non-participation of our dad". As I look back on those years with pops when he would severely punish my brother and me for not addressing him by his first name, while parading multiple women as overnight guests in the home, we would eventually take on his womanizing personality in our own adult lives. Our dad became the primary caregiver, but it was our grandparents and our aunt Irene and Cynthia that raised us, that became the mediators between us and the mean streets of Oakland, California.

I would later contemplate the impact my parents continuing in matrimony would have had on our own relationships and marriage. The countless hours sitting in church every Sunday, listening to the rants and theatrical discourses of the Reverend did not address the issues that teenagers face entering puberty. As I approached my teenage years and began to realize the shift in my character related to testosterone growth, compelled to keep these emotions suppressed from grandparents and church elders. My attraction to female anatomy accelerated with the discovery of my dad's hidden pornography magazines and polaroids. This was a huge burden upon my psyche knowing that pre martial coitus was a sin and the desires from temptation fought with righteousness and reasoning. As a child I had the desires of a child, but upon puberty, my eyes opened, and I began to realize that our bodies were different, like A'dam and Chuah when they sewed fig leaves together and made themselves aprons. "And they heard the voice of Yahweh Elohim walking in the garden in the cool of the day: and the man and his woman hid themselves from the presence of Yahweh Elohim amongst the trees of the garden. And Yahweh Elohim called unto A'dam, and said unto him, where are you? And he said, "I heard your voice in the garden, and I was afraid, because I was naked; and I hid myself. And he said, who told you that you were naked? Have you eaten of the tree, whereof I commanded you that you should not eat? And the man said, the woman whom you gave to be with me, she gave me of the tree, and I did eat." BERE'SHIYTH (GENESIS) 3:7-12 את CEPHER.

During my adolescent years, eating from the tree of temptation with pornography and moments of self-gratification would further blur my theological reasoning and beliefs. In the earlier chapter we explored the generation of Noachian tribes in 2448 BC expanding upon the earth and the expansion of ethnicities and nations populating the earth in 2024 CE. The scriptures chronicle the interactions between the sexes, but King Shalomah (Solomon) whose reign as a monarch of ancient Yashar'el and Yahudah from 970 to 931 BCE fascinated me the most with his vast chokmah (wisdom) and many wives. Solomon was portrayed as a man ordained with divine chokmah in Judaism and Christianity, excelling in divinity and considered to be a major Islamic prophet. In the Quran, Shalomah also came to be known as a magician and an exorcist, but it was the biblical account of his 700 wives and 300 concubines described as foreign princesses and women of Moab, Ammon, Edom, Sidon, and the Hittites that filled his harem that drew my attention. In a twisted scenario from an urban perspective, King Solomon, considered the ultimate player and philanderer, gave insight into his interaction with his various women and concubines.

With the onslaught of men coming under fire from the #MeTooMovement, the exploits of Shalomah were frowned upon with utter disgust in our modern era due to women speaking out against womanizers and predators influenced by Western culture.

Once again, Hollywood tried to glamorize the image of harems within the dynasties of royalty; however, the seclusion of women did not originate with Judaism or Islam, but instead where polygamy allowed in pre-Islamic Assyria and Persia where the ruler's wives and concubines lived with female attendants and eunuchs. You would have to live with your head in the sand to disbelieve that intercourse does not play a significant role in humanity. Even the book of BERE'SHIYTH sixth chapter details when men and women were engaged in sexual relationships and began to procreate and daughters were born unto them, the sons of Elohim who are either deemed angels in heaven or carnal man recognized as religious zealots, saw the daughters of men that they were fair; and they mated with women through force or mental persuasion.

The creator's superior workmanship in creating the female anatomy and facial beauty developed an insidious behavior within celestial creatures that would make them forsake righteousness for lecherous intentions. Many religious scholars have deep skepticism about the account, but the CEPHER reveals that Yahusha appeared first to Miriam of Migdal, from whom he had cast out seven demons and was casting out a devil, and it was dumb. When the devil was gone out, the dumb spoke; and the people wondered and said, he casts out devils through Baal Zebub the chief of the devils. The powers of celestial beings over humankind wholeheartedly indulging in disobedience and corrupt reasoning, become easy prey to devils and eventually owned or influenced by demons. The influence of demonic possession is not as far-fetched as some would imagine with many books and writings detailing physical and psychological ailments which cause the individual to do evil.

Though the CEPHER details demon possession, mainstream religion has yet to include in their discourse to parishioners the battle of sexual promiscuity enhanced by supernatural ability beyond their own learning. *How many nights have you experienced hallucinations of a sexual nature with the clear effect of phenomena ejaculation?* I genuinely believe that Naphaliym were born in the earth in those days who also gathered afterward, when the sons of Elohim came in unto the daughters of men, and they bore children unto them, the same became warriors and tyrants which were from everlasting, mortal men of the name. The thirst for sexual gratification shared among all ethnicities and genders, and it was common for men to have several wives and elites were famous for creating harems. Hugh Heifer, founder of Playboy magazine ran a harem from his mansion that is like ancient monarchs that kept a group of women, consisting of wives, concubines, and servants for the purpose to satisfy the desires of the king.

Many Hollywood films in the early sixties influenced by European Renaissance paintings dating to the 16th century often depicted the harem as a hidden world of sexual subjugation where many women lounged in the nude or sheer robes. Shalomah was not the only royal elite to have many wives, but it was his parables like "Whoso finds a woman finds a good thing and obtains favor of Yahuah" that many critics have ordained a hypocrite for interacting with hundreds of women and being a staunch supporter of polygamy. The Torah (Instructions) says Elohim told Abraham, "And I will make your seed as the dust of the earth: so that if a man can number the dust of the earth, then shall your seed also be numbered." In the earlier chapter the sons of Noach migrated and began to populate the earth with their seeds and from their offspring we now have diversity and many cultures enriching humankind. Little is known and written about the women that the sons of Elohim had sexual relations with before the deluge, or the women and offspring of the ruler of Babel, Nimrod, after the deluge. It was not until people began to spread out into distant lands, that we discovered through ancient writings the treatment of the women of antiquity.

Fast forward to my generation the rumors spoken by elders about mix-race children born on southern plantations, but it was movies like "Roots" that exposed a tale of sexual assault among slave and slave owners. The continuous rapes and assaults of European men against Chamite and Semite women before and after Jim Crow, and the lynchings of Chamite and Semite men for suspension of gazing upon European women. I've yet to discover that research conducted within urban communities of the harmful effects of institutional rape and what part it plays in destroying the Black family. The devastating impact of debauchery inflicted on Chamite and Semite women has always angered men that sought justice but never found any. One has only to examine the behavior of angels that forced themselves on women before the deluge and European men on slave plantations that forced themselves on slaves. The one central theme among those I consider men of strength against those powerless to fend off their assaults, is their propensity to engage in sexual misconduct against those effete in nature. I often wonder about the mindset of wives married to these perpetrators and their minimal objections to the crimes inflicted upon rape victims. *What were their conversations with their children after they discovered the heinous crimes of their husbands?*

The spiritual and moral reasoning from my grandmother that tried to instill values of virtue into boys not ready for manhood speaks volumes into her character. As children, geared towards merriment while navigating through our adolescent years, my brother and I were protected from harm and criminality that many youths face today. From a lifestyle of privileges or the unspeakable horrors of poverty, the foundation of marriage and family life is a struggle, no matter what ethnicity you derive from. I want you to take a moment and reflect on your adolescent years and release any horrible feelings you have stored deeply within your subconscious. For this mental exercise we are going to examine your interaction with the opposite gender and how you approached the situation. *Did you know the right words to say to make them smile? Or did they approach you and lay down the ground rules before you could even utter a sentence?* My high school years clouded with self-inflicted mishaps and blunders, attracted me to the girls displaying low self-esteem with single-parent issues that allowed me to go the distance with little effort. I can never recall my father giving my brother and me the sex talk and what to look for in a suitable mate. My grandfather never discussed it, and my grandmother taught us to be self-sufficient in our adult years. I had to learn about supporting a companionable relationship through trial and error, because in my estimation, my dad was too embarrassed to speak truthfully with an adolescent boy.

All the Sunday sermons would have been worthwhile if only the preacher would have instructed his teenage parishioners to speak the things which become sound doctrine. "That the aged men be sober, grave, temperate, sound in faith, in love, in patience. The aged women, likewise, that they be in behavior as is becoming holiness, not false accusers, not given to much wine, teachers of good things; That they may teach the young women to be sober, to love their men, to love their children, to be discreet, chaste, keepers at home, good, obedient to their own men, that the Word of Elohim be not blasphemed. Young men likewise exhort them to be sober minded." TITUS (TITUS) 2:1-6 את CEPHER.

This sound advice from antiquity would have deterred me from being sexually promiscuous and sowing oats like a sailor on weekend leave. The need for companionship began at an early age and developed into full-blown lust with our introduction into the music industry. The more my brother's and my popularity grew, girls and women became more accessible with little effort. Raised in a Baptist denomination, abstinence and sexuality were never discussed from a clinical perspective. As adolescent students of theology, we were taught to suppress our sexual desires because they are sinful in nature. I had to fight daily during elementary and middle school with the flesh. I always wondered if the sons of Elohim experience the same sexual feelings after seeing from the heavens the daughters of men bathing or engaging in sexual relations with the sons of men. Also, Greek mythology speaks on many female goddesses known as Succubi, which are demons or supernatural entities from folklore who often seduce unsuspecting men and then feed on their life forces. Like the male incubus, the Succubi (singular: succubus) have nefarious intentions with names that lean on their seductive purposes, which can lead to a wide variety of succubus names for characters in fantasy, literature, and even gaming. *Was there intense anger created without the fleshly attributes of humankind and restricted from pleasures afforded to carnal men and women? Were angels truly pure in heart and what was the compromising factor that made them forsake their duty of aiding humans expand upon the earth?*

The apocrypha chronicle their guilt and sadness when detected of wrongdoings and punished for sexual fornication and manipulation. The Creation of men and women is remarkably like the beasts of the field with erogenous zones within the body that allows and welcomes sensuous feelings that naturally release, and the body returns to equanimity. Religions tend to draw a distinction between passion and lust by condemning lust as a sinful desire that goes against the spiritual commandment to control lust, but the passion that heighten sexual relations is morally acceptable. Lust is defined as an immoral premeditated act because the thoughts and desires of a person are to engage in coitus to dissolve the sexual appetite from the object of affection.   According to the *Catholic Encyclopedia*, "A Christian's heart is lustful when venereal satisfaction is sought for either outside of marriage or, before marriage in a manner which is contrary to the laws that govern marital intercourse." Pope John Paul.

Whereas passion, regardless of its strength, to be something God-given and moral, because the purpose, actions, and intentions behind it are benevolent and ordered toward procreation, while also governed by the person's intellect and will. A primary school of thought on this is Thomism, which speaks on the intellect, will and appetite, and draws from principles defined by Aristotle. However, the exact definitions assigned to what is morally definite and multiplicity of roots toward procreation depend on the religion. For example, religions based in pantheism and theism will differ on what is moral according to the nature of the "God" acknowledged or worshiped. Some denominations allow sodomites and fornication within their congregation or let unrepentant parishioners continue in evangelical and missionary work. This lackluster approach to harvesting seeds for salvation is not what the Cepher instructs for parishioners, "but the commandment is a lamp; and the Torah is light; and reproofs of instruction are the way of life: To guard you from the evil woman, from the flattery of the tongue of a strange woman. Lust not after her beauty in your heart; neither let her take you with her eyelids. By a whorish woman, a man brought to a piece of bread: and the adulterer will hunt for the precious life. Can a man take fire in his bosom, and his clothes not burned? Can one go on hot coals, and his feet not be burned?" MISHLEI (PROVERBS) 6:23-28 את CEPHER.

I have known lust firsthand before marriage when the strange women were backstage after every performance or the VIP mansion parties. The motorcycle annual runs or late-night rendezvous. It got complicated quickly for me when I began substituting truth and transparency for lies and B.S. It gets equally toxic when your women begin doing the same things for as long as you. The old saying "It isn't no fun when the rabbit got the gun" stings like a horde of hornets because my ego bruised, and humiliation took over where laughter once was. What started off as companionship to fill the void of emptiness and boredom on rainy days and football season, turned into self-analysis and the realization that the grass is never greener on the other side of town. I spent valuable time trying to upgrade women that had already reached their limit in life. I was starting to wonder what was wrong with me and why I am continuing to attract the exact profile of women that did not fit my criteria two friends ago.

As a teenager you really do not contemplate the luggage you discard while hustling because it is always new luggage that you pick up with little effort. Then hit with the thunderbolt and find a girl that is your match without even knowing that this was Yah plan all along. For a moment you do not care that she comes with her own drama and back story because she completes you in every sense of the word. YHWH creation of A'dam used the Iviry word *yi'ser*, which stands for taking some existing substance and molding it into shape. In the case of women, however, the Iviry root word is *banah*, meaning "to build." YAH "built up" the woman from the foundation of A'dam's rib. That word is similar in meaning but carries some sense of "adding" what was not there before. But I give this warning to all men rushing into a long-term relationship with short-term memory if you cannot escape the consequences of one's actions, do not expect your women to be one hundred if you are not at least sixty percent committed to making a marriage successful. Ladies, my advice from past experiences is do not expect your man to be completely transparent if you still have male friends that you occasionally visit and communicate with when you need to discuss your marriage because this is a recipe for disaster.

Married couples experience the honeymoon phase but then comes the "seven-year itch" that happens in a large majority of marriages, referring to a perceived decline in happiness in relationships around the seventh year. Most people tend to get divorced in their late 20s to early 30s, because it takes maturity on both spouses to be transparent and communication is the key in resolving any issues in the marriage before they become major. I had to learn this by countless tribulations within my marriage because both my wife and I were raised in single parent households and were too immature while raising two kids to seek marital counseling in our early twenties. We were behaving like teenagers and not taking the spiritual counsel of the JWs (Jehovah Witness) to heart that could have deterred us from a future separation. "When I was a child, I spoke as a child, I understood as a child, I thought as a child: but when I became a man, I put away childish things." QORINTIYM RI'SHON (1 CORINTHIANS) 13:11 את CEPHER.

The phrase "If I would have known what I know now" correctly fits my state of mind today. I separated and dated other people while being still cordial but that only complicated the situation. If I can give a morsel of advice to the readers so it can make sense and preserve the family unit, please keep outside influences out of your marriage and rely upon the words of Chokmah (wisdom) from couples who have weathered the storm and are still celebrating anniversaries. Divorce is never good for children and can wreak havoc on finances but if there is violence and abuse within the household, seek safety at once. My wife and I were teenagers and through our adulthood we both made blunders and mistakes, but we were committed after our second separation to repair the damage caused by infidelity and lack of communication.

The American Psychological Association (APA) estimates that the probability of a first marriage ending in divorce within the first 10 years is approximately 33% in 2023. According to the National Fatherhood Initiative's "National Survey of Marital Strengths," a lack of commitment is the most often mentioned reason for divorce. In many cases, one or both partners feel unprepared for the commitment needed for a long-term relationship, which leads to their separation. The main cause of us splitting up was immaturity and not taking on the role of parenting seriously. According to the AAMFT, about 15%

of married women and 25% of married men have had extramarital affairs. The National Coalition Against Domestic Violence (NCADV) states that many victims of domestic abuse cite it as a primary reason for seeking a divorce.

We would argue in front of friends and our children over menial issues that could have resolved as easily as they started. I would say a remark that would trigger her pressure point and sparks would fly throughout the night. I saw many couples grow apart over time and people would say that this is what happened to us, but it was a lack of transparency and communication. We both ride or die with each other, like so many couples that find that they want different things from life or have disparate values. We enjoyed the same activities and learned to take part in each other's hobbies if only for one time, then discussed the likes and dislikes because 'incompatibility' often leads to divorce.

The National Survey of Marital Strengths highlights incompatibility as one of the leading reasons for divorce. Substance abuse can strain a marriage, leading to financial problems, emotional distress, and loss of trust. The National Institute on Drug Abuse (NIDA) reports that substance abuse is a significant contributor to marital dissolution. The above statistics and data apply to any ethnicity that wants to repair the bonds of marriage and continue to build on the purpose of the family unit. Humanity has evolved over four thousand, four hundred and forty-two years and though there are genetic and environmental variations among humans, we share many similarities when it comes to etiquette, alliances, and conjugality. The creator of the heavens and earth created all things for a purpose from our birth to our end so we can inculcate reasoning via trials and tribulations that either teaches us to walk upright or suffer the consequences of disobedience.

Even if raised among the elites or dwell in an improvised community, those that love trueness abide in the light, and there is no occasion of stumbling in them. I have always marveled at the creative process of forming man and animals out of the earth, the dust of the ground. He could have formed a woman in the same way but chose not to. This was to emphasize the nature of the relationship between men and women. At the same time, this creative process says something important about the differences between men and women. Man "formed" from the dust and Elohim blew the breath of life in him, but woman formed from man.

The CEPHER says in the book of BERE'SHIYTH that woman was formed to become a mate to man and aid in the procreation process. While man and woman intimately linked, and made for each other, also created as unique and separate genders. Male and female are not interchangeable or replaceable: they are exceptional. The creator who provides all things for his purpose has now given man the greatest of all possible earthly gifts: a helper, a companion, a wife. YHWH is the giver of all good things and to achieve reasoning to fight against temptation after a man and woman bonded in marriage is the greatest gift. Blessed is the man that endures temptation: for when tried, he shall receive the crown of life, which Yahweh has promised to them that love him. Let no man say when tempted, tempted of Elohim: for Elohim cannot tempt with evil, neither tempts he any man: But every man tempted, when drawn away of his own lust, and enticed. Then when lust has conceived, it brings forth sin: and sin, when finished, brings forth death. Do not err, my beloved brethren. Every good gift and every perfect gift are from above, and come down from the father of lights, with whom there is no variableness, neither shadow of turning. YA`AQOV (JAMES) 1:12-17 את CEPHER.

When we fight temptation and lust from the strange woman or man, we increase the love that encompasses a range of strong and positive emotional and mental attributes that increase virtue and affection to enjoy happiness and pleasure: most commonly, love refers to a feeling of strong attraction and emotional attachment.

"Behind every successful man, there is a woman and behind every unsuccessful man, there are two. - Mark Twain

LINKS FOR FLESH

Women_in_ancient_Egypt/ /divorce-statistics/ Code-of-Hammurabi/ Caranus of Macedon/ Franklin United Church-East Franklin Union Church/ Everything you need to know about erogenous zones/ Let's Talk About Sexual Energy

NOTES:

WHO IS ELOHIM?

"I think very deeply" is a quote from the rapper KRS-One, expressing consciousness instead of the subliminal messages that corrupt the minds of youth and adults. Music and images are tools used to influence the minds and souls of humanity, but what happens to individuals when their audio and video content becomes a portal that allows evil forces to blanket their thought pattern? Supernatural film script writers and producers knowingly have aligned themselves to witchcraft for wealth upon earth. The psychological impact that most cast members experience during production of a supernatural horror film are never researched. What makes a person want to play demons in movies and not leave them unscathed? Most entertainers have signed on the dotted line to follow unrighteousness instead of morality for a paycheck. The heavy metal music genre in the 70s and 80s introduced teens to lyrics praising demons upon earth, and their worship of fallen angels was placed subliminally so that many listeners did not know idolatry attached to the song. Now hip hop and pop artists have displayed satanic imagery during stage performances at award shows and public appearances, that have many people screaming illuminati.

I am not a conspiracy theorist but take for example the lyrics of singers who receive heavy rotation on national radio stations. "Been tryna hide it, Baby what is it gonna hurt if they do not know? Makin' everybody think that we solo, if you know you got me (You got me) And boy I got ya' Cause tonight I am making deals with the devil, And I know it is gonna get me in trouble, just as long as you know you got me." Disguised as songs about romance, do these songs hold a deeper meaning?

YouTube saturated with interviews and videos from entertainers, politicians, and athletes, engaged in religious ceremonies leaked to news outlets to acknowledge their complete participation. "For I was envious of the foolish when I saw the prosperity of the wicked. For there are no bands in their death: but their strength is firm. They are not in trouble as other men; neither are they plagued like other men. Therefore, pride compasses them about as a chain; violence covers them as a garment. Their eyes stand out with fatness: they have more than the heart could wish for. They are corrupt and speak wickedly concerning oppression: they speak loftily. They set their mouth against the heavens, and their tongue walks through the earth. Therefore, his people return hither: and waters of a full cup wrung out to them. And they say: How does El know? And is there knowledge in El Elyon? Behold, these are the wicked, who prosper in the world; they increase in riches" Tehilliym (Psalms) 73:3-12 YOCHANON (John) aka the Baptist, spoke on the carnal mind and untrained heart that is a character trait all ethnicities inherited via A'dam and Chuah.

Like a cancerous ailment that spreads throughout the body if not fought vigorously, it does not hide itself but is shown in behavioral patterns of individuals that express self-will and are self-seeking. After the migration of Shem, Cham, Japheth into lands outside of Ararat "And in the seventh week in the first year thereof, in this jubilee, Noach planted vines on the mountain on which the ark had rested, named Lubar, one of the Ararat mountains, and they produced fruit in the fourth year, and he did guard their fruit, and gathered it in this year in the seventh month." Yovheliym (Jubilees) 7:1.

Those that chose not to maunder, began building nations and conquering smaller less protected brethren, which created a superiority temperament among the gentility that is not able to fully surrender to YHWH. These pillars of the elite class began to focus on the things of the flesh, which allowed them to sin without retribution and repentance. Simulating conduct like "the Naphaliym famous from the beginning, that were of such great stature, and so expert in war. "Those did not Yahweh choose, neither gave them the way of knowledge unto them: But destroyed, because they had no Chokmah, and perished through their own foolishness." Baruk Ri'shon (1 Baruk) 3:26-28."

The worship of deities carved into lifeless idols passed on from generation after generation, and reasoning of the Creator substituted by the carnal person according to the senses that aligned with the things of the flesh. PA'AL (Paul) during the rule of the Roman Empire in lands within Mediterranean and Kemet, also had the mindset of the carnal man; but because of divine intervention engulfed with spiritual reasoning "For we know that the Torah is of the Ruach: but I am carnal, trafficked by sin. For that which I do I allow not: for what I would, that do I not; את but what I hate, that do I. If then את I do that which I would not, I consent unto the Torah that it is good. Now then it is no more I that do it, but sin that dwells in me. For I know that in me (that is, in my flesh,) dwells no good thing: for to will is present with me; but how to perform that which is good I find not. For the good that I would I do not: but the evil which I would not, that I do. Now if I do that I would not, it is no more I that do it, but sin that dwells in me. I find then a rule, that, when I would do good, evil is present with me. For I delight in the Torah of Elohim after the inward man: But I see another Law in my members, warring against the Torah of my mind, and bringing me into captivity to the Law of sin which is in my members" Romaiym (Romans) 7:14-23.

In the last chapter, we discussed parables and metaphors used to pronounce a message of salvation to believers and atheists of antiquity. During the dark ages when spiritual corruption was rampant among the priests of the Catholic church and the Holy bible given to priests and Jesuits that interpreted the gospel to parishioners through their own reasoning, polytheism interwoven into biblical doctrines and disguised as Christian beliefs and traditions. Greek mythology was introduced to students of theology by priests naming their gods and goddesses after planets found in scholastic textbooks today. The above scripture depicts a person of antiquity seeing immorality and sinfulness to a degree that is 10 times more detrimental to a person because of the riches and prestige of the world. This parable is an excellent pre-warning for individuals contemplating the pros and cons engulfed in industries with questionable archfiend overtones.

I have experienced subliminal temptation and moral decadence inside of the entertainment industry and heard of individuals so thirsty for fame, they have allowed the ruachoth of darkness to take control of the person completely. There is a message in the madness of both men and women that experienced the perils of their youth and miraculously through spiritual and moral counseling can tell war stories of their past. You can ask any person that lived for years with a target on their back, and they will tell you that living in the Devil's playground was pure hell. They were battling demons for their sanity, and they never expected that they would lose everything chasing a dream. The drug epidemic and high unemployment were devastating to rural and urban communities across America, but it was the abandoned children and fatherless homes that turned entire cities into war zones and murder capitals. Even though I was on the other side of the equation, the tremendous peer pressure to fit in would forever alter my life in my pursuit to become popular in sports and street credibility. Sidetracked by the influence of my cousins that were in the family apprenticeship program run by my uncles, I would have continued my training in radio broadcasting and aspirations for a football career. Instead, I chose the life of a street pharmacist without an exit plan before the alphabet team put us on their radar.

At sixteen I did not have expectations for the future and my life was spiraling out of control. Looking back on the earlier years, I was lucky to stay above ground and live to fight another day. Stay on point and keep your head on a swivel and "whatsoever your hand finds to do, do it with your might; for there is no work, nor device, nor knowledge, nor wisdom, in Sheol, whither you go. I returned, and saw under the sun, that the race is not to the swift, nor the battle to the strong, neither yet bread to the wise, nor yet riches to men of understanding, nor yet favor to men of skill; but time and chance happens to them all. For man also knows not his time: as the fish taken in an evil net, and as the birds caught in the snare; so are the sons of men snared in an evil time, when it falls suddenly upon them." QOHELETH (ECCLESIASTES) 9:10-12 את CEPHER.

This parable I go to over and over when I find myself depressed and reminiscing about the many blunders and traps for the carnal mind. I chose to include a chapter that addressed the dilemma many youths and adults like me face daily, I cannot seem innocent when I am also guilty of acting on impulses without considering the ramifications of my actions. Hindsight would have led me to make wiser decisions, but speaking on my trials hopefully will not be the next generation tribulations. I had much more to gain but chose to risk it all on a paper chase that rewards those who live life on the edge of their seat. I honestly believe that anyone can turn dreams into reality if not disillusioned by smoking mirrors. I wish individuals to manifest goals that will carry out their desires and there's nothing wrong with aiming to be among the stars and transform your presence among the universe, but more than often, individuals become pawns on the chessboard and easily discarded, not knowing the rules of the game.

Poverty that coalesces with illiteracy brings forth mayhem filled to the brim with wasted dreams and unaccomplished goals. From my observation, you must be on guard of influences that may seem harmless but can create irreversible damage that overwhelms the heart and mind. During my heyday, I must acknowledge individuals who have pushed their talents to the forefront without compromising their ancestral moral beliefs. This is also a warning to students of theology and parishioners of all religious sects because parables also appear in the Quran used to instill values that convey profound moral and spiritual truths. This is the quandary presented to me quite often after my motorcycle accident when networking with business partners and vendors within the entertainment industry. I have come to realize that everyone upon earth is dealing with their own trials and tribulations, and your assignment may not align with their purpose and journey. I have traveled from darkness to enlightenment in an industry of unhealthy habits and the wild carefree lifestyle of individuals with pompous attitudes, inflated egos, like my earlier lifestyle on the streets of Oakland. An industry where young minds manipulated with strategic planning and excelled by gatekeepers with their own agendas.

The light was upon me, but I jeopardized all that in the hopes of becoming wealthy but found myself traveling on a road full of unscrupulous sinners, sitting in the seat of the scornful. A majority within my new circle was only looking out for themselves and ready to do whatever and whenever for the fame. I was losing traction with my growing family by trying to gain traction in Hollyweird. Compounding sinful desires upon my conscience with lies, deception and adulterous intentions. At one point, I could not get a handle of my life and needed to walk away or lose my sanity. "But their delight is in the Torah of Yahweh; and in his Torah they meditate day and night. And they shall be like a tree planted by the rivers of water, that brings forth their fruit in their season; their leaf also shall not wither; and whatsoever they do shall prosper. The wicked are not so: but are like the chaff which the wind drives away. Therefore, the wicked shall not stand in the judgment, nor sinners in the assembly of the righteous. For Yahweh knows the way of the righteous: but the way of the wicked shall perish." TEHILLIYM (PSALMS) 1:1-6 את CEPHER.

This parable explains my continuous transformation in choosing to understand the purpose of my existence. To self-check my own demeanor when individuals try to blow smoke up my buttocks and accept the mystery of the light while confronting the darkness in the world. I equate this to a sea of exposed high voltage wires that do not care who gets shocked or injured. I shed no tears for those who open doors by deception, and oaths that must stay intact, unless you are strong enough mentally and spiritually to accept the consequences. Grateful that I never became one of the individuals that chase fame and fortune under the paparazzi lights, and years later, on TMZ, crying that their life is like a supernatural horror film. They played in the devil workshop but soon found out that demons discard broken pieces. "Smite a scorner, and the simple will beware and reprove one that has understanding, and he will understand knowledge." Mishlei (Proverbs) 19:25 "

While searching for a distribution firm for my licensed Releases, I noticed most of the films distributed each year involve soft pornography, violence, profanity with a PG-13 and R rating. A co-writer on my latest project wanted to include sex and nudity to attract a younger audience but I had to either face the situation or forego the spiritual beliefs of my youth and adulthood or alter the final script with subliminal moral undertones. There was the dilemma of allowing myself to understand false reasoning and reach a consensus that would circumvent Torah commandments and morality for a huge payout. I had already compromised my integrity with hip hop music produced during the first era of gangsta rap. Widening the gateway for unclean ruachs to penetrate heart and mind. "And there exists in pleasure a malicious disposition, which is the most multiform of all the affections. In the soul it is arrogance, and love of money, and vaingloriousness, and contention, and faithlessness, and the evil eye. In the body it is greediness and gormandizing, and solitary gluttony. As pleasure and pain are, therefore, two growths of the body and the soul, so there are many offshoots of these passions. And reasoning, the universal husbandman, purging, and pruning these severally, and binding round, and watering, and transplanting, in every way improves the materials of the morals and affections. For reasoning is the leader of the virtues, but it is the sole ruler of the passions. Observe first, through the very things which stand in the way of temperance, that reasoning is the absolute ruler of passions." MAKKABIYM REVIY`IY (4 MACCABEES) 1:25-30 את CEPHER.

A warning to all aspiring musicians and actors invited to explore the unknown of spiritualism, be careful you do not become a cast member in the sequel of "Devil's Advocate." Mesmerized with illusions that appear and disappear like a puff of smoke, choking the life out of those starring in "Vampire in Brooklyn." The names are too many, and their private life is no longer secret once they have outlived their useful skills and face "Def by Templeton." Examining what shallow women have done to themselves to stay relevant and now "Death Becomes Her." This also becomes a Segway into the topic of Spirit possession which is an extremely popular theme for Hollywood film producers. Supernatural horror movies with a demonic plot are stable revenue source for production studios and script writers depicting humans and sometimes beasts with unusual behaviors in an altered state of consciousness under the control of ruachoth, demons, angels, or elohiyms.

The first horror movie I saw as an adolescent was "The Omen" which was a concept of spirit possession and the antichrist which exists in many cultures and religions, including Buddhism, Christianity, Haitian Vodou, Hinduism, Islam, Wicca, African and Native American traditions. The movie was so popular with an anti mashiach plot ripped from the book of YOCHANON RI'SHON (1 JOHN) 4:3 את CEPHER that the producers followed up with three added sequels. Americans have an unquenchable thirst for the evil supernatural with voluntary or involuntary spirit possession that have beneficial or detrimental effects upon their behavior. When I see a new horror movie trailer on network television or at the cinema, it baffles me, and I have tried on many occasions to make sense of the fascination with spirits, deities, or demons. Since I was a pre-teen and still to this day, movies dealing with the supernatural have always been off limits to me.

My grandparents owned a spacious Victorian home and my brother, and I would stay up late on the weekends watching the series Creature Features. It was hysterical for my younger brother to see my fear every Halloween when movies like Nightmare on Elm St, Carrie, or Friday the 13th would air. What made matters worse is the fact that my aunt and grandmother kept a 4ft doll in the darkened living room on display. The doll was so life-like that guests were startled by her presence and jumped whenever they came into the living room. All I can say is fear is a monster and telling stories about the supernatural is a billion dollar a year Industry. People like Stephen King, John Carpenter, Tobl Hooper and Steve Miner have created a genre that is both lucrative and cult classics. With so many films produced that delves into the supernatural, one must wonder, where do these writers get their inspiration from? Movies like "Rosemary Baby" "The Conjuring" "Hellraiser" have aspects of the occult and include paganism in the storyline. *If life is a movie and everyone has a part to play, what character role have you auditioned for all your life?* Be truthful with yourself while there is breath within your body to make amends for every wrong spawned by hatred, vanity, greed, lust, selfish reasoning, and pompous behavior.

C.T Johnson would quote a verse or two every Sunday from the scriptures, and later break out in his holy ghost dance, to excite the parishioners with theatrics that are common with Baptist preachers. I did not know it then, but the energy it takes for him to skillfully belt out one discourse to keep his parishioners captivated, would prove to be inspirational for me later in life when addressing large audiences or reiterating an elevator pitch to potential investors on new projects. We unknowingly assimilate the character traits of individuals we most admire, be it positive or negative, altering our own demeanor to simulate someone else. You do not have to be a believer or student of theology to realize that we all have succumbed to temptation before in our lives like characters in horror films. In the feature films, we see the plot before carried out and we say to ourselves, "if that was me." But to be honest, how many times have you veered left or right instead of going forward? How many occasions has your consciousness told you to flee from the scene, but you stayed, and the results were devastating?

All the above has happened to me and I regret every poor decision I have made. These are the subtle quandaries that give most of the human beings buyer's remorse. Wishing we could have been stronger in our ability to stay focused when we noticed a beautiful woman in a tight-fitting dress or man well-endowed in underwear advertising and lust suddenly parked in your mind. Your co-worker or neighbor bought a new car or item making you become envious or slightly jealous. For me, lasciviousness and covetousness are a sinful nature that gets the best of me at times, but I got to keep my eyes on the prize. Living life and pushing it to the limit, I must admit, forces me to take it to the extreme at times and go beyond my moderation limit. Although the concept of the seven deadly sins written about extensively, began to attach the character traits listed above to my own nature that I began to take notice. I knew that self-improvement started with my commitment to altering issues that kept me stagnant if I wanted to be a better me. I did not need to align myself to any secret organization or pledge an oath for membership that you see in religious cult films, and if I was not growing spiritually and financially then I had to question myself, why? What were the distractions that kept me from reaching my goals? And I had to ask myself whether I was really distributing 2-4 hours daily for meditation and education. Nope! I continue to reiterate that it was divine intervention that put me on this journey of discovery and enlightenment, not a pledge or oath of secrecy or accepting foreign deities as my guiding light.

It is the nature of humanity to be curious about the unknown and unlock the mystery of antiquity, but at what cost? "And it shall come to pass in those days that all the inhabitants of the earth shall be moved one against another because they know not that my judgment has drawn nigh. For there shall not be found many wise at that time, and the intelligent shall be but a few. Moreover, even those who know shall most of all be silent. And there shall be many rumors and tidings, not a few, and the doings of phantasmatic shall be manifest and promises not a few to be recounted. Some of them shall prove idle, and some of them shall be confirmed. And honor shall be turned into shame and strength humiliated into contempt and probity destroyed and beauty shall become ugliness. And many shall say to many at that time: Where has the multitude of intelligence hidden itself and where has the multitude of wisdom removed itself? And while they are meditating on these things, then envy shall arise in those who had not thought ought of themselves and passion shall seize him that is peaceful, and many shall be stirred up in anger to injure many, and they shall rouse up armies to shed blood and, in the end, they shall perish together with them. And it shall happen at the same time that a change of times shall manifestly appear to every man because in all those times they polluted themselves and they practiced oppression and walked every man in his own works and remembered not the Torah of El Elohim. Therefore, a fire shall consume their thoughts and in flame shall the meditations of their mind be tried. For the Judge shall come and will not try. Because each of the inhabitants of the earth knew when he was transgressing, but my Torah they knew not by reason of their pride. But many shall then assuredly weep, yea over the living more than over the dead. BARUK SHENIY (2 BARUK) 48:32-41 את CEPHER"

For those trying to dabble in spiritism to conjure up mysteries of antiquity may feel their endeavors harmless but for me there are always consequences from wanting to travel further down the rabbit hole. Both the bible and overall theme of the movies listed above discuss the ransoming and pawning of souls for material gain, but both John and Paul wrote similar verses of the parable "For what shall it profit a man, if he shall gain the entire world, and lose his own soul?

Or what shall a man give in exchange for his soul"? MARQUS (MARK) 8:36-37 את CEPHER".

After reviewing the parable, I thought *how much is your soul worth?* YAHUSHA was bribed with kingdoms and wealth if he would follow the enemy of righteousness, and I had to deeply ponder my overall worth outside the boundaries of righteousness. To accept reasoning that was less moderate, upright, and sanctified. Religious sects introduced the devil as an evil entity avoided at all costs, but as I began to materialize in a world of Hip Hop and Christian music, many times the devil comes in human form. The devil was not a myth, but a deity worshiped and glorified with the same aspirations of YAHUSHA but in secret ceremonies and behind closed doors. Now gatekeepers have kicked the doors open beginning in 1996 with the founding of The Church of Satan in San Francisco, Ca. This may seem wild or float above the head of individuals venturing outside the safe boundaries of Christianity, but should it really amaze any individual that confesses to follow Yahusha.

Religious denominations since the creation of the Negro Bible have warned parishioners about Satan as a Mashiach, but few would wrap their heads around a religious organization dedicated to the religion of Satanism? The gauntlet thrown down since the 6th day creation and between two powerful spiritual beings chronicled in Cephers that either manipulate or warn humanity about life on earth. If you have prescribed to the Cephers of Christianity, Islam or Judaism for direction and insight, then is it far-fetched that the Satanic Bible with only 4 chronicles, would be in circulation? The Book of Satan, The Book of Lucifer, The Book of Belial, and The Book of Leviathan. Now, I must confess that while writing this chapter, I had to seek strength and courage beyond my own measure. At the top of this page, I delivered a parable that expressed my current spiritual and mental state and why the supernatural are not taken lightly.

The mind is a database that collects thoughts, information, and visuals from both righteous and unrighteous sources, so I must be very restrictive to what is stored in the corridors of my psyche. Now let us get to it! The Satanic Bible was written by a confessed follower of darkness named Anton Szandor LaVey, whose occupation was author, musician, and full time Satanist. After founding the Church of Satan, he would later become a staunch supporter and marketing guru of the religion of Satanism. LaVey authored The Satanic Bible, The Satanic Rituals, The Satanic Witch, The Devil's Notebook, and Satan Speaks! that I presume had a profound effect on the reader since estimated that the Satanic Bible sold a million copies. In the publishing industry, like the entertainment business, it is all about numbers, and one hundred thousand copies would get you invited to dinner parties, college campuses and talk shows. From this boost of popularity, LaVey released three albums, including The Satanic Mass, Satan Takes a Holiday, and Strange Music.

Are you beginning to realize the significance of the power vacuum the entire world has been in since Cain and Abel? Every religious sect has Cephers for parishioners to examine and music to enjoy, so why wouldn't Satanism be any different? The door is beginning to open wider and reveal that Hollywood and the entertainment industry are no longer hiding in the shadows or concealing their alliance to Beelzebub with the publication of the Satanic Bible. Satanic influence entwined with Christianity, Islam and Judaism since writers began to interpret ancient Cephers, scrolls and hieroglyphics of Mitsrayim. In forensics, every crime is investigated to examine the cause and perpetrator mindset, so the Satanic bible extols the virtues of exploring one's own carnal behavior and influence. I no longer appear amazed that parishioners believe that the Creator and Satan are not external entities, but rather projections of an individual's own personality, passions, and reasoning.

The Book of Satan challenges the Ten Commandments and the sovereignty of YHWH when Elohim spoke את to Moshe all these words, saying, "I am Yahweh Elohayka, which have brought you out of the land of Mitsrayim, out of the house of bondage. You shall have no other Elohim before me. You shall not make unto you any graven image, or any likeness of anything that is in the heavens above, or that is in the earth beneath, or that is in the water under the earth: You shall not bow down yourself to them, nor serve them: for I Yahweh Elohayka am a jealous El, visiting the iniquity of the fathers upon the children unto the third and fourth generation of them that hate me; And showing mercy unto thousands of them that love me, and guard my commandments. You shall not take the name of Yahweh Elohayka in vain; for Yahweh will not hold him guiltless את that takes his name in vain. Remember the day of the Sabbath, to keep it holy. Six days shall you labor, and do all your work: But the seventh day is the Sabbath of Yahweh Elohayka: in it you shall not do any work, you, nor your son, nor your daughter, your manservant, nor your maidservant, nor your cattle, nor your stranger that is within your gates: For in six days Yahweh made the heavens and the earth, the sea, and all that in them is, and rested the seventh day: wherefore Yahweh blessed the day of Sabbath, and hallowed it. Honor your father and your mother: that your days may be long upon the land which Yahweh Elohayka gives you. You shall not kill. You shall not break a wedlock. You shall not steal. You shall not bear false witness against your neighbor. You shall not lust after your neighbor's house, you shall not lust after your neighbor's woman, nor his manservant, nor his maidservant, nor his ox, nor his ass, nor anything that is your neighbor's. SHEMOTH (EXODUS) 20:1-17 את CEPHER".

This is contrary to the mindset of aristocrats that recommend individuals become their own Elohim by taking an oath of Epicureanism, a system of philosophy founded around 307 BCE. Most ivy league schools' philosophy courses founded upon the teachings of Epicurus, an ancient Greek philosopher. Epicurus was an atomist and believed in the existence of atoms and the void, and his writings reflected his interest in applying Democritus' theories to aid humanity in taking responsibility for themselves and for their own happiness since the role of elohiyms are moral ideals and there are no elohiyms around that can help them. This is why I never prescribed the notion that the Black man is God, or considering that Caucasian men are white Devils, since there is always a hidden agenda in every religious sect. After the clergy and ministers serve you, the tainted spiritual food disguised as palatable to the soul, is digestive with materialistic reasoning seasoned in the web of deceitfulness.

Epicurus pushed the Materialism agenda that is prevalent in religion today and preached by mega church pastors on network television and internet. Interpretation can vary but is a concept of philosophical monism which holds that matter is the fundamental substance in nature, and that all things, including mental states and consciousness, are results of material interactions of material things. According to philosophical materialism, mind and consciousness caused by physical processes, such as the neurochemistry of the human brain and nervous system. Materialism directly contrasts with idealism, according to which consciousness is the fundamental substance of nature. Though Epicurus was a deist that held a philosophical position and rationalistic theology that rejects spiritual consciousness as a source of divine knowledge, he based his rational thought without any reliance on revealed religions or religious authority. More simply said, Deism is the belief in the existence of Elohim who Epicurus believes does not intervene in the universe after creating it. Deism emphasizes the concept of natural theology and YHWH existence revealed through nature.

The floodgates breached when many European and Western theologians formulated a critical rejection of religious texts held sacred by theocratic organizations, which led to a domino effect chipping away at truths proven by reason as the exclusive source of divine knowledge. This should not come as a surprise to anyone that has seen the decline of morality and increased adulteration of the Torah and mosaic laws since the early sixties. The quotes "money is power" and "For the love of money" are the most used phrases and, have infiltrated the consciousness of every religious body worldwide. I have seen the weakening of rules meant to keep religious denominations holy for the sake of increased tithes and offerings, does not hold parishioners accountable "who erred from the faith, and pierced themselves through with many sorrows. But you, O man of Elohim, flee these things; and follow righteousness, virtue, faith, love, patience, meekness. Fight the good fight of faith, lay hold on eternal life, whereunto called, and have professed a good profession before many witnesses. TIMOTHEUS RI'SHON (1 TIMOTHY) 6:10-12 את CEPHER"

This is the core principle of Basic Instructions Before Leaving Earth via divine inspiration and reasoning but contrasts with the beliefs of individuals thirst for materialism like Epicurus that led him to religious skepticism and a general attack on superstition and divine intervention. The Book of Lucifer holds most of the Epicurus philosophy in The Satanic Bible, with twelve chapters discussing topics such as indulgence, love, hate, and sex. LaVey also uses the book to dispel rumors surrounding religion. In The Book of Belial, LaVey details rituals and magic, discussing the required mindset and focus for performing a ritual and provides instructions for three rituals: those for sex, compassion, or destruction. The Book of Leviathan provides four invocations for Satan, lust, compassion, and destruction. It also lists the nineteen Enochian Keys (adapted from John Dee's Enochian keys), provided both in Enochian and in English translation.

Many religious denominations use fear and separatism to attract new converts, but fear is not righteous but derives from the carnal mind. I may have envied during my youth, sinners flourishing and prospering in their ways but now I have reached the mindset that their journey is not my journey. I know of too many people that have moved out of the neighborhood and come back to visit associates still engaged in criminality and murdered. They were at the wrong place at the wrong time, so keep yourselves at a distance from their oppression. Changing your location also equates to changing your lifestyle, so do not be impious in your thoughts of surrendering your former behavior. I finally realized that growth comes with uprightness and the difficulty experienced while shedding the carnal mindset takes great strength and courage. Still today, I grapple with former character traits that will make me transgress against the word of uprightness including the sin of pride. With every task carried out and every set goal achieved, I congratulate not myself but the Creator.

Humility is contrary to vanity often warned against throughout the Bible along with wrath, lust, envy, gluttony, and sloth. The successes and failures over the years I have not attributed to good or bad luck but to things that we often take for granted, or completely ignore. Horror movies remind us, much like religion, that we are not in control of our lives and there are things beyond our understanding. But through this undertaking of moral and spiritual reasoning, comes a beautiful array of possibilities that make the exploration worth it. We prize our moral agency so highly that any attempt to undermine, circumvent, manipulate, control, or end it often leads to conflict. These battles have spanned heaven and earth and have included both individuals and great assemblies.

Leonard Berkowitz, professor of psychology at the University of Wisconsin, asserts that horror-movie violence has a threefold effect on audiences. First, he says, "it makes audiences in general less horrified by, and more indifferent to, violence." Secondly, "audiences may learn the lesson that violence is approved behavior" Third, he goes on, "some can become stimulated by it." Really, does not sympathize and empathize with the sufferings of others or separate humans from brute beasts. The wanton violence of horror movies can only erode that sympathy and remind us of how the apostle Paul condemned those who "because of the insensibility of their hearts" came to be "past all moral sense." He encouraged Christians, however, to "become kind to one another, tenderly compassionate." (, *Kingdom Interlinear*)

Can exposure to large doses of senseless bloodshed help one cultivate these qualities? A 1969 study funded by the National Institute of Mental Health, found spirit possession beliefs exist in 74% of 488 societies in all parts of the world, with the highest numbers of believing societies in Pacific cultures and the lowest incidence among Native Americans of both North and South America. As Pentecostal and charismatic Christian churches move into both African and Oceanic areas, a profound belief can take place with demons becoming representative of the "old" indigenous religions, which the Christian ministers try to exercise. "The strong among the mighty shall speak to him out of the midst of Sheol with them that help him: they are gone down, they lie uncircumcised, slain by the sword. Ashshur is there and all her company: his graves are about him: all of them slain, fallen by the sword: Who are appointed to graves in the bottom of the pit, and her company is round about her grave: all the Naphaliym are pierced by the sword, which gave terror in the land of the living. There is Elam and all her multitude round about her grave, all of them slain, fallen by the sword, which are gone down uncircumcised into the nether parts of the earth, which caused their terror in the land of the living; yet have they borne their shame with them that go down to the pit. They have set her a bed during the slain with all her multitude: her graves are round about him: all of them uncircumcised, slain by the sword: though their terror was caused in the land of the living, yet have they borne their shame with them that go down to the pit: he is put during them that be slain. There is Meshek, Tubal, and all her multitude: her graves are round about him: all of them uncircumcised, slain by the sword, though they caused their terror in the land of the living." YECHEZQ'EL (Ezekiel) 32:21-26 את CEPHER.

In attempting to make sense of my journey upon earth to stay on the path that I have veered from up to this point, I began distributing at least four hours daily studying and researching many publications for enlightenment. This is an arduous task trying to support theocratic education and morality while surrounded by self-absorbed individuals fixated on carnal pleasure and wealth building. Since pushing Tribe Media, and www.tpng.biz to the masses, I have seen other brands with unlimited resources and influence out rank my brand on search engines and on social media. I understand that every individual on earth has a role to play and success comes to those who turn dreams into reality. Various religions condemn entertainment and music as idolatry but the concept of the four idols drawn from St. Thomas Aquinas, who spoke of the four false idols that found in all industries and even religion. Revenue that generated from purchases of products or public donations. Power that increased with noticeable influence and status. Pleasure from the ability to get material possessions and engage in activities afforded to individuals with unlimited resources and finances. Fame achieved via skillful talent or marketing campaigns. Aquinas was a Catholic theologian that wrote Summa Theologica, during the 13th century but would take two hundred years before it published in the late 15th century.

In the mind of Aquinas, the pursuit of these idols was distancing people from Elohim. The theory states that we make most of our daily decisions based on our worship of our leading idol and drawn into idolatry by the things we see on the earth. The material possessions of our neighbors, relatives or coworkers drive us to become envious and spiteful. The pursuit to reach a level of success and status will demand us to build a persona that will take on an attitude of winning even at the cost of our neighbor's demise. Using deception and manipulation to reach levels of grandeur if necessary. Applying force of strength and violence against competitors and rivals that stay on our path after warnings about the consequences. Allocating extended hours on projects at work while bypassing religious services and the sabbath because it does not fit into our schedule, we are all found guilty of putting our pursuit of material possessions, recreational activities, and cravings before our worship to Elohim. Wherefore Elohim also gave them up to uncleanness through the lusts of their own hearts, who changed the Truth of Elohim into a lie, and worshiped and served the creature or idol more than the Creator. For this reason, Elohim gave them up unto vile affections: for even their women did change the natural use into that which is against nature.

The downside of our pursuit to put our cravings before moral reasoning is our endeavor to strive for what is not necessarily the best thing for us to get "closer" to our idol. Be honest and truthful and admit that you have wished more than what you have now. You have estimated a thorough strategy for wealth building, social status, or career advancement assuming this plan will lead you to the promised land of happiness. After your plan and strategy has met all the criteria for success and you have tasted the fruits of your labor, are you happy? Humankind has always steered off course and tried to become self-sufficient without acknowledging the true power of their existence. Mortal men and women have pushed aside spiritual enlightenment and taken oaths to recognize no other divinity but themselves. They are their own Elohim and have forged their own alliances that are separate from the one Elohim theory and beliefs.

Since the creation of Babylonian and Egyptian deities, the sons of Noach began to war on each other, to take captive and to slay each other, and to shed the blood of men on the earth, and to eat blood, and to build strong cities, and walls, and towers, and individuals began to exalt themselves above the nation, and to found the beginnings of kingdoms, and to go to war people against people, and nation against nation, and city against city, and all began to do evil, and to acquire arms, and to teach their sons war, and they began to capture cities, and to sell male and female slaves. YOVHELIYM (JUBILEES) 11:2 את CEPHER.

This is my reasoning to disassociate my family from mainstream entertainment that depicts idolatry and satanic culture in the media. We all have choices, but living a lifestyle that separates us from uprightness is not one of them. What profit is it to sell my soul and live a self-willed lifestyle, and eventually become enlightened and be repentant but my lifecycle upon earth has ended. Examine everyone once wealthy and famous who the world put on a pedestal, but currently in prison for sex trafficking or dead. What is your soul worth?

WHO IS ELOHIM LINKS

wiki/Spirit_possession/_____from-fear-to-fascination-why-we-find-pleasure-in-experiencing-horror/ What's So Horrible About Horror Movies?

POWER OF SIN AND RIGHTEOUSNESS

Honor a physician with the honor due unto him for the uses which ye may have of him: for Yahweh has created him. For El Elyon comes healing, and he shall receive honor of the king. The skill of the physician shall lift his head: and in the sight of great men, he shall be in admiration. Yahweh has created medicines out of the earth; and he that is wise will not abhor them. Was not the water made sweet with wood, that the virtue thereof might be known? And he has given men skill, that he might be honored in his marvelous works. With such he heals men and takes away their pains. Of such the apothecary makes a confection; and of his works there is no end; and of him is peace over all the earth. My son, in your sickness be not negligent: but pray unto Yahweh, and he will make you whole. Leave off from sin, and order your hands all right, and cleanse your heart from all wickedness.

Give a sweet savor, and a memorial of fine flour; and make a fat offering, as not being. Then give place to the physician, for Yahweh has created him: let him not go from you, for you have need of him. There is a time when in their hands there is good success. For they shall also pray unto Yahweh, that he would prosper that, which they give for ease and remedy to prolong life. He those sins before his Maker, let him fall into the hand of the physician. Sirach (Ecclesiasticus) 38:1-15 את CEPHER.

In 2022 and 2023, I broke both of my legs on my Harley Davidson Road King, and I want to thank the physicians, nurses, and staff at Highland Hospital and Kaiser Permanente in Oakland, Ca for their ability to care for me and professionalism. To all those that have experienced major surgery or are currently in rehabilitation for their injury, my prayers are for a speedy recovery while you reconstruct your life back to normalcy. For me, the strength to mentally adjust to the inability of movement upon my own competency was arduous. The phrase "what doesn't kill you makes you stronger" from the 19th century German philosopher Friedrich Nietzsche in his 1888 book Twilight of the Idols, comes to mind each time I was able to scoot up and down our three-story condominium for in-home care. From early within my recovery, I quit cold turkey the pharmaceutical medicines prescribed by my physician to mitigate the pain during rehabilitation and physical therapy. This was a decision based upon my final medical procedure after the prescribed medication made me temporarily unconscious so I could have a more invasive surgery.

Opioids often prescribed for out of hospital patients hold chemicals that relax the body and can relieve pain but are highly addictive. This quandary faced with after my motorcycle accident knowing fully the devastating effect the opioid and fentanyl epidemic was having on American citizens. Since the late eighties, pharmaceutical companies have been running commercials promoting pills for everything from child behavior adjustment to sleep support. The side effects can cause paralysis and blindness but have not slowed down consumers from buying billions of pills annually. Entire households have been devastated by legal and illegal drugs in urban, suburban, and gated communities with religious denominations being on the frontlines with parishioners either addicted or aware of someone battling addiction. At the end of the day, substance abuse is a 500 lbs. gorilla on the back of an addict, but King Shalomah warns humanity in the book of Proverbs about foolishness and not adhering to common sense when confronted by everyday realities.

The evolution of humankind also brings about the evolution of intelligence. We now have the power to change our course in life and alter the path that has enslaved millions of lives before us. The Webster dictionary defines idolatry as extreme admiration, love, or reverence for something or someone and since an addict later makes narcotics or alcohol their Elohim, they will forsake food, hygiene and morality while suppressing a sound nutritional agenda, moral reasoning, intervention, and counseling to defeat intoxication. As is a house vacated, so is wisdom to a fool: and the knowledge of the unwise is as talk without sense.

Many people fall into the pit of addiction and unknowingly travel on the road of substance abuse putting narcotics before the instructions of YHWH. Considered idolatry because the definition of idol worship is bowing down or worshiping any person, image, or thing in reverence as you would the creator of both heaven and earth. Narcotics has evolved after 5000 BCE with ancient Greece manufacturing the opium poppy for suppositories, medicines, and in combination with hemlock for suicide. The Bible does not chronicle individuals under the influence of narcotics, but witness accounts written in other publications hidden in the Vatican mentions opioids in medical journals of antiquity, including the Ebers Papyrus and unprocessed opium for medical use during the American Civil War to treat injury.

In the 18th century, workers of iniquity began peddling dope to new immigrants who inhaled the drug and decades later, cocaine turned urban neighborhoods into war zones. In high school, smoking reefer at the dance or house parties considered cool and a means to meet girls, but the moral decline, health problems, and monetary loss buying that Afghan boogie and base rock plagues all ethnicities to this day. Dr. Burke, president of the American Historical Reference Society and consultant for the Smithsonian Institute, included the following U. S. presidents as marijuana users: George Washington, Thomas Jefferson, James Madison, James Monroe, Andrew Jackson, Zachary Taylor, and Franklin Pierce. Tobacco was not only the plants growing in the fields of the south, but also cannabis was an immensely popular and lucrative product for sale.

Two United States presidents admitted to smoking cannabis while in college and before going into politics. On Mar. 29, 1992, Bill Clinton then-Arkansas Governor had to admit that he had tried pot as a 20-something Rhodes Scholar at the University of Oxford. "I've never broken a state law," he said at a candidates' forum. "But when I was in England, I experimented with marijuana a time or two, and I did not like it. I did not inhale it, and never tried it again." Recalling his autobiography "Dreams From My Father," President Obama said, "Because I had been pretty honest about the struggles I went through as a young man, uh, when I ran for office and there was some big reveal about, 'Oh, the guy smoked pot,' it's like, 'Yeah, no, it's in my book,'" he said to laughter and applause. "I, I, I, and I, I learned from that, I, I, I did not sugarcoat it. I did not suggest that somehow it had been, uh, you know, something that I recommend for everybody. "But that is what teenage kids did at that age when I was growing up. Not everybody. Some were wiser than me. I was not that wise."

My introduction to marijuana came when family members introduced me to Hawaiian gold that gave me the munchies because of the high quantity of the chemical tetrahydrocannabinol (THC). At the time of my first smoke sessions, I never knew while I was indulging in the pleasure of inhaling herbs which held a psychoactive ingredient in the cannabis plant that would induce continuous coughs and tears, that I would get an extreme buzz and an appetite comparable to the jolly green giant. As a teenager I did not think about the side effects, only the puff puff pass and the hip hop music playing in the background. The euphoria was mind-blowing causing calm emotions to sweep throughout my body; but when the rhapsody had abated, the paranoia altered the calmness and jubilation that I once felt. The long walk or bus ride home was excruciating expecting my grandmother to detect my inebriated condition. To make matters worse, I was currently the president of the junior usher board, and I had to give the welcome to visitors and parishioners this Sunday morning at church. *How did I get myself into this?* I would question myself while trying to compose myself from the marijuana high and ask the lord to forgive me because my grandmother that we fondly addressed as Mama Johnny, did not allow any foolishness from us.

This was one of the major reasons I made a serious attempt to deter the usage of cannabis because of my grandparents' disapproval and knowing that YHWH sees everything that we try to hide. My grandparents would discuss my dad's behavior and lack of parenting skills because of his substance problems and the shame of me disappointing them was too much to bear. Raised in a home where church services were mandatory and secular education was necessary, my countless act of rebellion is the character trait I wish I could reverse time on. It would be well into my adulthood after engaging in many heated conversations with my wife about the holier than thou attitude I had on her continuous usage of weed and edibles that I would discover information about cannabis and the medicinal attributes after attending a 420 event. Not misconstrued as a formal endorsement of the cannabis industry since every individual must work through their own salvation and moral agenda and the usage of cannabis has a negative stigma throughout mainstream religious denominations. I just want it to make sense and include the pros and cons of THC and CBD from the cannabis plant and attach many scriptures that I have discovered that may or may not be related to cannabis.

When trying to interpret the Cepher as students of theology, I had to first understand thoroughly what I was reading and understand the message the spiritual passage was trying to evoke. I wanted to use the word medicine as my reference since my main goal is to seek healing for the body without corrupting the Temple that houses your assigned ruach. There are several biblical passages we can reference but the verses listed below should suffice. "And we explained to Noach all the medicines for their diseases, together with their seductions, how he might heal them with herbs of the earth" YOVHELIYM (JUBILEES) 10:12 את CEPHER A merry heart does good like a medicine: but a broken ruach dries the bones. MISHLEI (PROVERBS) 17:22 את CEPHER Yahweh has created medicines out of the earth; and he that is wise will not abhor them. "Was not the water made sweet with wood, that the virtue thereof might be known? And he has given men skill, that he might be honored in his marvelous works. With such, he heals men and takes away their pains. Of such the apothecary makes a confection; and of his works there is no end; and from him is peace over all the earth, my son, in your sickness be not negligent: but pray unto Yahweh, and he will make you whole." SIRACH (ECCLESIASTICUS) 38:4-9 את CEPHER "And by the river upon the bank thereof, on this side and on that side, shall grow all trees for meat, whose leaf shall not fade, neither shall the fruit thereof be consumed: it shall bring forth new fruit according to his months, because their waters they issued out of the sanctuary: and the fruit thereof shall be for meat, and the leaf thereof for medicine". YECHEZQ'EL (EZEKIEL) 47:12 את CEPHER

Before my first motorcycle accident I was deeply against taking any pharmaceutical or organic medicines even for high blood pressure and heart condition because of the addictive components and adverse side effects. I read news reports about counterfeit prescription drugs and learned friends and relatives had died from the opium and fentanyl epidemic. Drug addiction has always plagued the urban communities with little fanfare but the crisis in suburban and rural America brought attention to legal and illegal narcotics on network news outlets to the forefront. In the same breath, congress and mainstream media were debating the pros and cons of legalized marijuana and the revenue share to local and state governments.

Since childhood, I have understood idolatry as interpreted by most religious denominations as the worship of something or someone other than El Elohim. From the three most recognized religious sects, Judaism, Christianity and Islam, idolatry is the worship of manufactured images and carvings as though it were a deity. It is a huge concern for me to live upright and avoid the pitfalls of my youth and abide by the oath of repentance to not bring reproach upon YAHUAH Assembly or my moral and spiritual reasoning. This meant avoiding any business opportunities and social events hailed as immoral or polytheism. In the last five years I also began to grow more health conscious and recognized the harmful effects of tobacco and began making an earnest effort to quit buying cigarettes while also consuming spirits in moderation. This has been an ongoing battle for survival since addiction comes in many aspects that are not related to substance abuse but still harmful to the mind and body.

Many will not realize that they have latched onto many unhealthy habits while hanging with family members and friends until an issue has spiraled into many misdeeds and judicial consequences. I was the literal prodigal son who squandered upright moral instructions and decency to take on a gritty street persona to my detriment. My juvenile delinquency began at 15 and it would be well into my marriage before I could turn it around. During my youth and early twenties, I altered from the path of uprightness, and it was my wife who will always be my best friend and soulmate whose ultimatum aligned me back on the road of enlightenment. I saw others venture on that same path of gloom and destruction that has consumed humankind since El Elohim created both heaven and earth and allowed Satan to draw each person away with lustful desires and idolatry. Nobody can continue to live their life in continuous debauchery or abiding by the temptations of the flesh and remain positive and spiritually conscious. Nobody can outsmart their sinful nature and continue to play the game when the rules are designed for each player to lose miserably.

After my last medical procedure, prescribed opioid painkillers and I experienced an out-of-body experience that shook my soul to the core during the night and vowed in the morning that I would never use prescribed opioids again. "Wherefore is there a price in the hand of a fool to get wisdom, seeing he has no heart to it? A friend always loves, and a brother is born for adversity. A man voids understanding, strikes hands and becomes surety in the presence of his friend. He loves transgression that loves strife: and he that exalts his gate seeks destruction. He that has a forward heart finds no good: and he that has a perverse tongue falls into mischief. He that begets a fool does it to his sorrow: and the father of a fool has no joy. A merry heart does good like a medicine: but a broken ruach dries the bones. A wicked man takes a gift out of the bosom to pervert the ways of judgment. Wisdom is before him that has understanding; but the eyes of a fool are at the ends of the earth." MISHLEI (PROVERBS) 17:16-24 את

CEPHER. King Shalom (Solomon) says a friend loves all time and the father of a fool has no joy.

Have you ever confronted a friend or relative on substance abuse or addiction? Have you ever withheld money from a son or daughter because of your suspension that they will buy drugs? What sort of friend would I be if I did not rebuke a mother of three who spends her entire EBT cash and food voucher on drugs instead of providing for her family? I have seen three mainstays in urban communities that continue to enslave and will never help individuals reach freedom and moral maturity. The neighborhood liquor outlet centralized in impoverished communities but is scarce in middle class suburbs. The 24-hour trap house that provides narcotics to kids and pregnant women. The church pastor who continues to fleece the flock to support a lifestyle of debauchery and lewdness. I must reiterate that the idolatry of antiquity described in the Torah is like many deadly sins of the 19th and 20th century. Crime, unemployment, and addiction is root to the continued issues plaguing urban communities in America because individuals will forgo spiritual counseling and prayer to buy drugs and alcohol to feed their craving.

Having the opportunity to manage several radio stations, occasionally songs came across my desk that made sense of the times we were living in. These songs speak to the heart and soul of anybody regardless of ethnicity, gender, or social status going through uncertainty and affliction that this world has thrust upon them. The first song I will list for your review is a man that played both sides of the aisle when it comes to sexually provocative lyrics, but delivered some of the most gut wrenching true to life tales for us to embrace. "Love comes quick, Love comes in a hurry, there are thieves in the temple tonight. Feel like I'm looking for my soul, like a poor man looking for gold, there are thieves in the temple tonight, Voices from the sky say, rely on your best friend to pull you through, Even if I wanted to, I couldn't really truly, Because my only friend is you."

Three of the most destructive forms of idolatry are the addiction to sex, money, and drugs. Religion runs neck to neck with all three because most parishioners have adapted polytheist traditions created in kingdoms founded by sons of Yapheth and have wholeheartedly over the centuries celebrated these rituals and ceremonies while forsaking memorials chronicled in the Torah.

In the mid-80s, when hip hop music tells the world about the crack cocaine epidemic, before the infiltration of the rap industry by advertising and corporate entities, hip hop lyrics warned people to stay away from danger. This was before rap artist(s) accumulated millions of dollars in endorsement deals and praised gun violence and addiction to drugs. Instead of glorified lyrics of stripper poles, molly, and murderous vendettas, but there still existed positive rappers singing consciousness like this: "Lust for money kept me on the street corner and inside of trap houses as a teenager. The power to control another individual because of the money created an inflated ego. He talks to you like he's alive, And when he talks like bees to a hive, The people come running, the older and the young'n, The place he lives in is the house they hung in, He wants your money, only your money, He'll make you feel good for a real fast twenty, The bill is passed and the dollars go fast, The feeling is high but the high don't last, Long enough for you to even read a paper, But you still thirst and hunger for the vapor, Although he is an animate, he'll make you feel, That he can breathe, think, talk and bleed for real, You should stay away cause all he's about, Is just making you broke and string-in you out, It only takes one kiss and a deep, deep breath, Then you're hooked for life cause it's the kiss of death.

During the crack epidemic, many people lost their lives from either slanging, banging or smoking crack. I was on the front lines watching the drama go down while going back and forth from the church to the streets. The aftermath of the crack era is still felt today in countless urban neighborhoods. The last musical genius needs no introduction but to say the moniker of soul brother number one fits him well. For over five decades he made all ethnicities shuffle their feet and dance to his beat. As a teenager I did not know much about this man, but his music was sampled in most hip-hop songs in the 90s and 2000s. This PSA he recorded aired constantly on the radio stations I managed. "I'm a world of power and all know it's true, Use me once and you'll know it, too, I can make a mere schoolboy forget his books, I can make a world-famous beauty neglect her looks, I can make a good man forsake his wife, Send a greedy man to prison for the rest of his life, I can make a man forsake his country and flag, Make a girl sell her body for a five-dollar bag, Some think my adventure's a joy and a thrill, But I'll put a gun in your hand and make you kill, In cellophane bags, I've found my way, To heads of state and children at play".

The conclusion to idolatry is that some people entwined inside the Devil's playground that their ruach turns evil enough to kill others to stay in power or remain fettered in disobedience. For neither did the mischievous invention of men deceive us, but the mischievous chemistry that turned herbs and plants into addictive narcotics and vegetables into alcohol while humankind continues to create plagues and inflict mayhem upon urban communities beginning with lynchings and terrorism, to Tuskegee experiment and heroin addiction of Vietnam veterans. Communities reached their breaking point during the late 80s when the pandemic of crack cocaine linked with national and foreign governments. For many, the smoking of crack cocaine first became a recreational activity but quickly became their obsession, which dominated their lives and enslaved them.

Anyone that has been addicted to alcohol, prescription drugs, narcotics, or nicotine, knows the courage and willpower it takes to overcome an addiction. How many friends or relatives do you know that have beaten or are currently battling addiction? I know several individuals that are walking zombies because the circuits in the brain get overwhelmed, in a way that can become chronic and sometimes even permanent. One of the most primitive parts of the brain, when activated, releases a chemical called dopamine, which, in turn, develops an addiction to a substance. This happens when addictive substances trigger an outsized response when they reach the brain. Instead of a simple, pleasurable surge of dopamine, many chemicals combined in opioids, cocaine, alcohol, methamphetamine, and nicotine cause dopamine to increase more than usual in the brain. The brain adjusts and associates it with the addictive substance.

I have seen firsthand how individuals who were once recreational users quickly become chronic users of the substance, because the brain's circuits adapt and become less sensitive to dopamine. Their anatomy begins to decrease in size since food is no longer a priority while they pursue that pleasurable sensation that becomes increasingly more important than eating. You can ask anyone that knows a former addict who has or is experiencing problems with their mental focus about short term memory loss. For others, particularly with drug addiction, idolatry begins when they rely on a high or intoxicating substance to release the daily burdens of puberty or adulthood. This is a warning to young people reading this chapter that addiction to cocaine and opioids have allowed themselves to become passions, turning their dreams into terrors for the choices they made. Who will seek justice or retribution on their behalf when the angel of death has them in the crosshairs? The breath of life distinguished, and your entire soul put on display to reminisce or endure ridicule. The power of reasoning over addictions never harnessed when moderation is a roadblock for individuals not leaping out on faith. Replacing courage and strength within their spirit for temporary stimulus to forget their current situation.

History has a funny way of repeating itself and the truth of hallucinating drugs is no longer hidden but revealed in movies, on television and in urban and suburban communities. While researching articles for this chapter, the justice department has analyzed evidence that is contrary to proper understanding and reasoning. It is appalling that discrimination plays a huge role in court sentences for a person smoking crack cocaine and individuals snorting or injecting powder cocaine. As an eyewitness in the late-80s, during the crack wars between rival kingpins, political parties and law enforcement, scared citizens outside of urban communities with daily news reports that crack was one thousand times more potent than powdered cocaine. Nightly news showed addicts smoking crack in abandoned buildings and said crack is more likely to lead to violence than powder cocaine or other drugs.

The United States of America justice system in 1986 created a five-year mandatory sentence for possession of five grams of crack cocaine. (21 U.S.C. § 841 (2006).) Now contrast this to the same Anti-Drug Abuse Act, for powder cocaine which a person had to own 500 grams, or over a pound to face a five-year mandatory sentence. This 100-to-1 ratio was not based on evidence: During the debate on the Act, Congress simply considered various arbitrary ratios (including 20-to-1) and settled on the 100-to-1 ratio, with no evidence to support that figure. I have visited friends and relatives in prison caught up in the crack epidemic either distributing or becoming addicts, and they all wished they could change the hands of time. Men and women that went to prison were tried as adults and released with grayish hairs and arthritis. I am grateful that I experienced the discriminatory sentencing and was able to return home before my daughter was born and my son is still a toddler.

It is a fabrication told to those seeking riches and vanity that you must hustle drugs to feed your family. Do not be deceived when invited to feast at the table and dine among the underworld because this is the beginning of tribulations. Only fools rush in without contemplating the cost of services given. How can you accept the destruction of humankind offered to you without fully knowing your power with the creator?   Humanity is on a crash course to destroy each other with corruption and enslave their brothers and sisters with cruelty since Chuah beguiled by the wicked one and A'dam listened to the counsel of his woman instead of the sound reasoning of EL Elohim.

Our faith is more productive when we stop hoping for miracles to change our lives from individuals who have compromised by political correctness, tax incentives and their denomination governing body. Whether or not the righteous sleep securely, wise men shall then truly perceive. And the sons of the earth shall understand every word of that Cepher, knowing that their riches cannot save them in the ruin of their crimes. "Woe to you, sinners, when afflicted on account of the righteous on the day of the great trouble; shall be burnt in the fire; and recompensed according to your deeds. Woe to you, perverted in heart, who are watchful to obtain a correct knowledge of evil, and to discover terrors. No one shall aid you. Woe to you, sinners; for with the words of your mouths, and with the work of your hands, have you acted impiously; in the flame of a blazing fire, you shall burn" CHANOK (ENOCH) 100:3-7 את CEPHER.

Look throughout history and there has never been a time that humanity has been without bloodshed. From Alexander the great to Hitler, nations have followed men as supreme beings and worshiped them as mystical deities. This is the power of idolatry and can be as simple as veneration of Greek mythology and explode into something far more sinister. Making excuses like A'dam and Chuah beguiled by Satan and not taking responsibility for their actions which led to their offspring engulfed in idolatrous practices is no excuse for disobedience. King Shalomah knew firsthand the power of foreign deities and traditions that did not align with Iviry reasonings. Warned that his many wives would turn him away from righteous practices and give an opportunity for the chief adversary, the devil, to question YAHUAH sovereignty. For if we sin, but I say, not if but when, because all have strayed away from morality at least once during their lifetime. We are yours, and this is the faith that so many cling to during various trials and tribulations when they cannot depend on mortal men and women for aid or salvation.

Every country and nation have an extensive list of issues within their sovereignty they are tackling daily but the risk of living among individuals who assume the characteristics of beasts and savages has been in existence since the sons and daughters of A'dam began migration upon the earth. Sinful individuals will remain upon the earth well after your body is laid in a coffin or turned to ashes and put upon a shelf. Men and women who adhere to the concept of spiritual enlightenment from the neighborhood religious denominations or the television evangelist who is selling you salvation placed in a bottle will continue to exalt themselves over reasoning. They will call their deities by names used to commune with the animate powers of the universe, embodying the honor and the source of the power who owned them. Hoodwinked into thinking I was waging war with Satan only to be an accomplice of building up his kingdom via prayer offerings, ceremonial commitments, participation in songs and hymns that are rooted in Hellenistic practices. The power of disobedience has evolved and is no longer hidden in dark corridors or veiled in secrecy. Nations are committing atrocities while oligarchs and elites are blowing smoke out the pipe with gatekeepers of delusions. Quoting a Sioux Medicine Man: "The Pipe is us! The stem is our soul, the bowl is our belief and faith system, the stone our blood, the opening in the bowl is our mouth, and the smoke rising from it is our breath, the visible breath of humankind." As the smoke from the pipe rises to the sky, we presume our works and prayers heard by the Creator. Peace, obedience, and righteousness restored among the people."

The smoke in the peace pipe means the essence and soul of all those seeking a messiah and calling upon his name. It may be the smoke given off by the fires of passion or the intoxicating scent of reasoning. Most importantly it is the breath of words, spoken from the heart, seeking true understanding. This understanding escapes fathers and mothers born from iniquity and raised among ignorance bred from delusions. Putting their hopes of salvation and misery of this world into lifeless objects that will never save but destroy. Woe to the land shadowing with wings, which is beyond the rivers of Kush: That sends ambassadors by the sea, even in vessels of bulrushes upon the waters, saying, Go, ye swift messengers, to a nation scattered and peeled, to a people terrible from their beginning hitherto; a nation meted out and trodden down, whose land the rivers have spoiled! All ye inhabitants of the world, and dwellers on the earth, see ye, when he lifts an ensign on the mountains; and when he blows a shofar, hear ye. Also, I set watchmen over you, saying, Hearken to the sound of the shofar. But they said, we will not hearken. Therefore hear, ye nations, and know, O assembly, what is among them. Hear, O earth: behold, I will bring evil upon this people, even the fruit of their thoughts, because they have not hearkened unto my words, nor to my Torah, but rejected it.

This is the message delivered to a nation swept up in the rivers flowing with confusion and clinging onto the adulation of Hellenistic traditions and rituals that continue to enslave them. From trees planted with vices and disease, the people eat until their bellies are full, then vomit the stomach content so their children can gormandize what they have spewed out. Interpretation of Holy bible given to parishioners through the mouths of Hellenistic and roman priests, idolatry has flourished in lands that are needing a savior but finding none. The guardianship and the divinity of the messiah along with the message of repentance and endurance corrupted by lawless individuals conspiring with gatekeepers of industry to pollute the sovereignty of YHWH. Who really has the unblemished truth needed to fight idolatry and keep a nation from warring with each other? There is no authority in the land that is fighting for the people, only rag tag groups bombarded by ruthless peddlers that are profiting from the confusion and intoxication of humanity. "All ye beasts of the field, come to devour, yes, all ye beasts in the forest. His watchmen are blind: they are all ignorant, they are all dumb dogs, they cannot bark; sleeping, lying down, loving to slumber. Yes, they are greedy dogs which can never have enough, and they are shepherds that cannot understand they all look to their own way, everyone for his gain, from his quarter. Come ye, say they, I will fetch wine, and we will fill ourselves with strong drink; and tomorrow shall be as this day, and much more abundant." YESHA'YAHU (ISAIAH) 56:9-12 את CEPHER. This passage is a vision that is vivid and is a prolonging of the inevitable.

The past is easy to forget but shown reminders of a nation under fire every time I step out my door. It would be so easy to just pack up and move to a gated community and not see the devastating effects of legal and illegal drugs on a community. I ask every reader to examine the saturation of liquor stores and smoke shops in urban areas compared to those in affluent communities. For the Torah conquers the subtle mind and revitalizes the ruach that was once dormant. The message of sobriety comes alive and prevails over everything while you were in an immature spiritual relationship with El Elohim. I attempted to close my ears when I hear individuals call on the name of a savior at award shows, when majority of their songs glorify alcoholism and drug addiction. I cannot help but cringe when I hear reports of youths and adults succumbing to a fentanyl overdose or died of alcohol poisoning. Even musicians within the gospel industry are behaving badly outside the walls of the church and party like rock stars. The mainstream religious denominations filled with hypocrisy and young people are fleeing in droves from priests and preachers caught on camera with male prostitutes and illegal drugs.

I have always wondered how a minister or gospel singer praises Elohim but allows themselves to succumb to the power of carnal man. I know firsthand how difficult it is to walk a path of glory and redemption but indulge in questionable activities that can tarnish your reputation. Everyone is tempted daily and swept up with temptations, but we petition daily to the creator and his messiah to not remember our former iniquities: "let your tender mercies speedily prevent us: for brought extremely low. Help us, O Elohai of our yeshivah, for the glory of your name: and deliver us, and purge away our sins, for your name's sake." TEHILLIYM (PSALMS) 79:8-9 את CEPHER.

I can still remember my grandfather telling me to always look a person in their eyes when talking to them and a firm handshake displays confidence and strength. Have regard to your name, for that shall continue with you above a thousand great treasures of gold. A good life has but a few days: but a good name endures forever. This has always kept me from doing too much and acting like a wild hyena outside the home and swept up with acts of wickedness. This is the testimony from a rebellious child and wayward teenager who did not cling to the Torah but succumbed to delinquency as an adolescent. Research and analyze before accepting the worthless ideologies that have corrupted all ethnicities in our generation and the generations before us. The first statement in GENESIS tells us who made all things; and who owns power over all things; and all things are open and manifest before you. You behold all things, and nothing concealed from you. In the later chapters of GENESIS, you have seen what Aza'zel has done, how he has taught every species of iniquity upon earth and shown to the world all the secret things done in the heavens. Taught to me in Sunday school lessons when I was a child and revealed without pledges or oath requirements.

The names of the Watchers revealed, but GENESIS also chronicled Shemiy'aza who has taught sorcery, to whom you have given authority over those who are associated with him. These are the chemists that have created concoctions that hypnotized the world with hallucinogenic drugs from the herbs meant to heal, not enslave. Some religious denominations will attempt to confuse you by saying the interpretation in GENESIS that chronicled the Watchers interaction with mankind really means sons of A'dam instead of sons of Elohim, but the Torah says they have gone together to the daughters of men; have lain with them; have become polluted; And have revealed their sins to them. This revealed in books of antiquity when humanity began to populate the earth, and rulers set up polytheism among the people. Truth never hidden within the Bible or CEPHER, but workers of iniquities will tell you Monotheism is not exact and is a creative idea of Judaism, Christianity, and Islam. I am not trying to change your beliefs but make sense of it when he said, "Behold, here am I, my son. And he said, what help, and profit have we from those idols which you do worship, and before which you bow yourself? For there is no ruach in them, for they are dumb forms, and a misleading of the heart. Worship them not" YOVHELIYM (JUBILEES) 12:2-3 את CEPHER.

Blessed with the continued warnings throughout the Bible, Quran and Cephar that inform us not to worship things made from the hands of mortals. You must ask yourself why do individuals continue to indulge in drugs when they are harmful to their body and psyche? No heavy consumption of pharmaceuticals or illegal narcotics will get me to travel down a road once again that I know within my soul is corrupt. Too many politicians, entertainers and corporate headhunters make an oath to live by their own rules and rewarded for their allegiance, but what is the penalty for breaking your oath? For the last 10 years I saw celebrities with huge names in their prospective industries face public humiliation. Once admired for their supernova careers that increased their vanity, now imprisoned for drug charges. Let not him that is deceived trust in vanity: for vanity shall be his recompense Carried out before his time, and his branch shall not be green. He shall shake off his unripe grape as the vine and shall cast off his flower as the olive. For the assembly of hypocrites shall be desolate, and fire shall consume the tabernacles of bribery. They conceive mischief, and bring forth vanity, and their belly prepares deceit. They offer their sacrifices to the dead and they worship evil ruachoth, and they eat over the graves, and all their works are vanity and nothingness. They have no heart to understand, and their eyes do not see what their works are, and how they err in saying to a piece of wood: You are my Elohim, and to a stone: You are my Adonai, and you are my deliverer. And they have no heart. YOVHELIYM (JUBILEES) 22:17-18 את CEPHER.

POWER OF SIN LINKS

cannabis/why-does-weed-make-you-hungry/ potential-health-benefits-of-cannabis/ Opium/ The Severely-Distressed African American Family in the Crack Era: Empowerment is not Enough// how-an-addicted-brain-works

SONS OF ELOHIM VS SONS OF MEN

" AND it happened, when men began to multiply on the face of the earth, and daughters were born unto them, That the sons of Elohim saw the daughters of men that they were fair; and they took them women of all which they chose. And Yahweh said, My Ruach shall not always strive with man, for that he also is flesh: yet his days shall be a hundred and twenty years. There were Naphaliym in the earth in those days, who also gathered afterward, when the sons of Elohim came in unto the daughters of men, and they bore children unto them, the same became warriors and tyrants which were from everlasting, mortal men of the name. And Yahweh saw that the wickedness of man was great in the earth, and that every imagination of the thoughts of his heart was only evil continually." BERE'SHIYTH (GENESIS) 6:1-5 את CEPHER.

Before enthralling myself in research for this chapter, I must admit that I was nescience of religious beliefs outside of Judaism and Christianity. The Nation of Islam (NOI) was an organization that I knew of with the murder of Malcolm X and publishing the Final Call newspaper that featured articles of Louis Farrakhan. Surrounded in controversy and labeled supremacists, my eyes opened, and my consciousness enlightened after discovering for myself the truth of their beliefs. I must always refer to my rudimentary theories of religion in my pre-teens and several years as an adult studying many denominations. Within these religious organizations, the discussion of Islam was either contemptuous or non-existent. Most parishioners fall into several categories but are unaware of their piety because of the theocracy of their congregation.

Since this is a journey, we are both exploring to unlock the spiritual unknown and mysteries of earth and heaven to harness our intellectual capabilities, I will try to be as transparent as possible. I will list the belief systems among ethnicities that many denominational members adhere to, which includes the monotheistic belief system, that one God is the only deity that humankind should worship. *Monotheism* distinguished from henotheism, a religious system in which the believer worships one god without denying that others may worship different gods with equal validity, and monolatrist, the recognition of the existence of many gods but with the consistent worship of only one deity. In polytheistic belief systems, followers worship more than one god, usually assembled into a pantheon of gods and goddesses, along with their own religious sects and rituals.

Many religious converts believe a god is "a spirit or being believed to have created, or for controlling some part of the universe or life, for which such a deity is often worshiped." A few years back I hosted a weekly podcast on KGM1 Radio titled "Spiritual Warrior." I invited men and women of all denominations to become guests of the podcast to discuss their ministries, Christian and gospel music careers, current news, and breakfast table topics that coincide with holy scriptures. On a segment titled "Demons Upon Earth " we invited recurring guests from the 7th day Adventist denomination to discuss the myth or reality of the deluge in the Noach generation. Before we discuss the heated discussion, I want to give readers the backstory of The Seventh-day Adventist Church and their theocratic ideologies. (SDA) is a Protestant denomination that founded in the United States around 1860. The denomination's observance of the "biblical Sabbath" starting at sunset on Friday to sunset on Saturday, differs from mainstream Christian denominations and the Jehovah Witness sect. "Advent" means *coming* and refers to their belief that Jesus Christ will soon return to this earth and bring judgment upon the unrighteous. The doctrine of the heavenly sanctuary, is founded on the works of Jesus who is acting as both priest and human sacrifice while doing investigative judgment to reveal which of the passed away souls of mankind are righteous and the detection of pretenders of the Faith whose lives were not righteous and should not be resurrected at the second coming, Adventists believe that co-founder Ellen G White has been richly blessed by the Lord through the gift of prophecy manifested in her ministry and writings.

The Church teaches that these writings were instrumental in taking the Church from a small group to a worldwide movement. Adventists believe Christ's return will be literal, visible, and worldwide. As the book of Revelations says, "And I saw thrones, and they sat upon them, and judgment was given unto them: and I saw the souls of them that were beheaded for the witness of Yahusha, and for the Word of Elohim, and which had not worshiped the beast, neither his image, neither had received his mark upon their foreheads, or in their hands;

and they lived and reigned with Mashiach a thousand years. But the rest of the dead did not live again until the thousand years finished. This is the first resurrection. Blessed and holy is he that has part in the first resurrection: on such the second death has no power, but they shall be priests of Elohim and of Mashiach and shall reign with him a thousand years. And when the thousand years have expired, Satan loosed out of his prison" CHIZAYON (REVELATION) 20:4-7 את CEPHER. The Adventists have written extensively how Jesus Christ will resurrect the dead that are righteous, take the faithful with him to heaven while executing judgment on the unrighteous.

The Second Coming followed by a period of a thousand years (the Millennium) during which the earth deserted except for Satan and the demons that are here on earth. Adventists strongly believe the Second Coming of Christ will happen soon. Many of the religious denominations founded during American slavery and after the Emancipation Proclamation are remarkably similar if not exactly akin in doctrines and beliefs. Now that you have familiarized yourself with the 7th day Adventist denomination let me give you the backstory of the heated debate. Raised in a home that birthed the righteous and unrighteous, but the holy bible was the law and everything else was secondary. We only had the 66 books of the King James version at the time and there were three dominant images hanging upon the wall, John F Kennedy (murdered 35th US president), Martin Luther King Jr (murdered civil rights activist), and Jesus Christ (Warner Sallman Rendition of murdered messiah).

My brother and I had to read at least two pages from the Britannica Encyclopedia and several paragraphs of the bible every day and be ready to give an oral response of what we read to our aunt who my grandmother named Sista. We found out early that Sista was not a person you would lie to or did not appreciate my brother and I wasting her time, not fully engulfed with educational studies. My grandparents attended separate religious congregations, but they never wavered when it came to Sunday services or punished us for not paying attention during bible class or while the minister was at the pulpit. I take the message of the scriptures to heart as a pre-teen and undoubtedly believe that Satan, demons, angels, and YHWH dwell in the heavens and among us as either protectors or antagonists.

The guests tried to imply on the air that the sons of Elohim were mortal men that were deeply religious. By using the biblical Concordance, they interpreted passages that gave their arguments weight exploring theories that the sons of Elohim were Seth's ungodly children who married women who were wicked and sinful. From my estimation, it was the work of the supernatural that beguiled Chuah to forsake the warning of A'dam to stay obedient to the commandments of YHWH. Cain warned verbally by the Creator that sin was at his door, and he must not answer it. Angels both righteous and unrighteous were giving instructions to the seeds of man how to build and destroy so not farfetched to believe angels worshiped and became manipulative in their interactions with humanity. And to Seth, to him also there was born a son; and he called his name Enosh: then began men to call upon the name of Yahweh. BERE'SHIYTH (GENESIS) 4:26 את CEPHER. Both the Iviry and Yavaniym books of the Bible are saturated with stories of sons of A'dam being tyrants and worshiped as a demigod of their generation and within close-knit societies in ours. We all have read the mythology of Nimrod to the military superiority of Alexander the great. The book of Genesis highlights Nimrod briefly as well as the unknown writers of Apocrypha books which are biblical or related writings not forming part of the accepted canon of Scripture, but no equivalent of the name found in the Babylonian or other cuneiform records. In character, there is a certain resemblance between Nimrod and the Mesopotamian epic hero Gilgamesh written on Akkadian-language tablets found at Nineveh in the library of the Assyrian king Ashurbanipal whose generation was from 668–627 BCE.

The traditional tale found in the Apocrypha books of YASHAR (Jasher) Kush is the son of Cham, the son of Noach, took a woman in those days in his old age, and she bore a son, and they called his name Nimrod, saying, At that time the sons of men again began to rebel and transgress against Elohim, and the child grew up, and his father loved him exceedingly, for he was the son of his old age. Many bible scholars have estimated that this would be close to 2096 BC, 6 x 6 x 7 years after the Great Flood. The garments of skin which Elohim made for A'dam and his woman, when they went out of the garden, given to Kush. (Unto A'dam also and to his woman did Yahweh Elohim make coats of skins and clothed them. BERE'SHIYTH (GENESIS) 3:21 את CEPHER) For after the death of A'dam and his woman, the garments given to Chanok, the son of Jered, and when Chanok taken up to Elohim, he gave them to Methushelach, his son. And at the death of Methushelach, Noach took them and brought them to the ark, and they were with him until he went out of the ark. And on their going out, Cham stole those garments from Noach, his father, and he took them and hid them from his brothers. "And Cham, the father of Kenyan, את saw the nakedness of his father, and told his two brethren without. And Shem and Japheth took a garment, and laid it upon both their shoulders, and went backward, and covered the nakedness of their father; and their faces were backward, and they saw not their father's nakedness." BERE'SHIYTH (GENESIS) 9:22-23 את CEPHER)

Could this be the garment that comes into question? Inquiring minds would like to know. And when Cham begat his firstborn Kush, he gave him the garments in secret, and they were with Kush many days. And Kush also concealed them from his sons and brothers, and when Kush had begotten Nimrod, he gave him those garments through his love for him, and Nimrod grew up, and when he was twenty years old, he put on those garments. And Nimrod became strong when he put on the garments, and Elohim gave him might and strength, and he was a mighty hunter in the earth, yes, he was a mighty hunter in the field, and he hunted the animals and he built altars, and he offered upon them the animals before Yahweh. "And Kush begat Nimrod: he began to be a warrior and hunter in the earth. He was a warrior and a hunter before Yahweh: wherefore Yah said, Even as Nimrod the warrior hunter before Yahweh." BERE'SHIYTH (GENESIS) 10:8-9 את CEPHER

The Book of GENESIS says that Nimrod strengthened himself, but the book of YASHAR writes that Nimrod rose up from amongst his brethren, and he fought the battles of his brethren against all their enemies roundabout. And Yahweh delivered all the enemies of his brethren in his hands, and Elohim prospered from time to time in his battles, and he reigned upon earth. Therefore, it became current in those days, when a man ushered forth those that he had trained up for battle, he would say to them, Like Elohim did to Nimrod, who was a mighty hunter in the earth, and who succeeded in the battles that prevailed against his brethren, that he delivered them from the hands of their enemies, so may Elohim strengthen us and deliver us this day. I began to attribute the guest's theory of sons of Elohim as a human or son of Man who is accorded divine status as someone who has attained the "divine spark" (divine illumination) as a mere mortal being that is born with the frailties of mankind and not an angel that the Bible clearly defined as a son of Elohim. The interpretation of sons of Elohim vs sons of Man found in Genesis would be arduous if you did not fully apply an earnest effort to dissect the interpretation of the phrase "sons of God."

The discussion went back and forth, and we all agreed to make the podcast a two-part series to get further clarification. My concern was the writings found in the Apocrypha and the Bible that mention angels called the Watchers in the second week of the tenth jubilee descending on the earth from the heavenly sanctuary, that they should instruct the children of men, and that they should do judgment and uprightness on the earth. The interaction between sons of Elohim and sons of Man is written in the Torah (and there came two angels to Cedom at even; and Lot sat in the gate of Cedom: and Lot seeing them rose up to meet them; and he bowed himself with his face toward the ground; BERE'SHIYTH (GENESIS) 19:1 את CEPHER) and YAHUSHA spoke of angels (And he said unto him, Amen, Amen, I say unto you, Hereafter ye shall see heaven open, and the angels of Elohim ascending and descending upon the Son of A'dam. YOCHANON (JOHN) 1:51 את CEPHER) The mainstream religious denominations constantly reiterate the Watchers doing righteous services, so I stated, throughout the congregation to include the devil along with Watcher's corrupting humanity in our generation.

Before the birth of Enosh, the sons, and daughters of A'dam began populating the earth in areas around the four rivers flowing out of Eden. The rivers were Pishon in Havilah. Gihon near the land of Kush. The Tigris River and the Euphrates River. The Book of GENESIS detailed the locations of the rivers and the conduct of humankind after A'dam, and Chuah expelled from Eden and began having added children after Cain murdered Abel. Noach before the deluge warned the sons and daughters of Man the wickedness sweeping the earth and the ordinances and commandments of righteousness. He told all three sons and their offspring to bless their Creator, and honor father and mother, and love their neighbor, and guard their souls from fornication and uncleanness and all iniquity. For owing to these three things came the flood upon the earth, namely, owing to the fornication wherein the Watchers against the Torah of their ordinances went whoring after the daughters of men, and took themselves women of all which they chose. The question as to whether the phrase, sons of Elohim refer to human beings or to spiritual beings (demons) debated years before and after our podcast aired on KGM1 radio.

Most religious denominations do not want to include the sexual depravity between angels and humankind but the Bible, Cephar and Koran plead for all parishioners not to be spiritually ignorant but wise and enlightened. NEVUKADNE'TSTSAR, the king of the Babylonian empire, had a dream and only the prophet Daniel could explain the interpretation because of Divine enlightenment said; "This matter is by the decree of the Watchers, and the demand by the word of the holy ones: to the intent that the living may know that El Elyon rules in the kingdom of men, and gives it to whomsoever he will, and sets up over it the basest of men" DANIY'EL (DANIEL) 4:17 את CEPHER.

As a child in Sunday school, this was one of those "WOW" moments because we just learned that a brother killed another brother, and the Devil was an instigator in the problems humankind was dealing with. It would be well after attending many religious denominations that I would learn about the CEPHER and the role that Watchers would play in the disobedience and corruption of all sons and daughters of Man. My opinion to the guests was comparing the generation before Enosh with the spiritual darkness of Revelations that Satan and his cronies will have free reign upon earth to mislead and brutalize all individuals not spiritual literate.

The power of reasoning and understanding the scriptures has always been a tool used by unscrupulous men and women to dominate and control their religious followers. To assign religious manipulation to only the lineage of Japheth misguided and inaccurate since all ethnicities throughout history of humankind have recorded individuals claiming to be the divine reincarnated messiah of Jesus or

Allah, rejecting their status as mere mortals, and playing themselves on an equal autonomy as the Creator leading to greater wickedness. I am not overly criticizing all individuals that have taken the diligence needed to study and research scriptures and manifest qualities that bring them righteousness over wickedness. Sons and daughters of Man claiming divinity base their strongest evidence for their spiritual position to separate from sin with biblical passages "that ye thus requite Yahweh, O foolish people and unwise? Is it not he your father that has bought you? has he not made you, and set up you? Remember the days of old, consider the years of many generations: ask your father, and he will show you; your elders, and they will tell you. When El Elyon divided the nations by their inheritance, when he separated the sons of men, he set the bounds of the people according to the number of the children of Yashar'el. DEVARIYM (DEUTERONOMY) 32:6-8 את CEPHER".

In the scriptures, the sons of Elohim and sons of Man defined so the students of theology can make a correct interpretation of what the writer has chronicled. King Shalomah (Solomon) from every aspect concerning intelligence and Chokmah (Wisdom) never put himself on the same level as a son of Elohim or questioned the sovereignty of the creator. The twelve recognized Iviry tribes were going through turmoil from outside agitators seeking to take away their land rights in the Mediterranean region by warfare and feuding between the sons and wives of king David for the throne. King Shalomah stood before the altar of Yahweh in the presence of all the assembly of Yashar'el, and spread forth his hands toward heaven, he was displaying humbleness and respectful conduct to the Creator of all creation. He was the judge over the rights of all those within his kingdom. The one-man jury who decided the innocence and guilt of all citizens. The executioner that either pardoned or put to death anyone that he chose. When he stood before the people and said, Yahweh Elohai of Yashar'el, there is no Elohim like you, in heaven above, or on earth beneath, who guards the covenant and has mercy with your servants that walk before you with all their heart, he had solidified his place as not an equal or son of Elohim but mortal servant placed in position by the grace of YHWH.

The mentality of sons and daughters of Man is to be their own sovereignty and only accountable to themselves. Forensic scientists and psychologists are still trying to understand why humankind behaves the way they do and why individuals push aside conventional reasoning to fulfill the desires of the heart and worry about the consequences later. These are the sons and daughters of Seth who derive from all ethnicities that call themselves gods and goddesses that claim to have unlocked the mystery of the heavens and solved the puzzle that constructs the spiritual laws that have shaped every generation since the beginning of time.

In fact, the 12 Halakha of the universe that they have mastered and manifest in their daily lives are universal truths from the collective consciousness of the Creator himself. I am a simple-minded person, and I have always believed that too much power corrupts, and vanity does not align you as a son of light but son of darkness. The Creator continues to warn all individuals of self-absorbed vanity with instructions found in the Torah that helps individuals deter from unrighteousness to deceive and power to control others; "Behold, the man has become as one of us, to know good and evil. The innocence as children we all experienced at one time instantly warped into their consciousness, quickly manifesting the reasoning and responsibilities of adults. A'dam and Chuah "eyes of them both opened, and they knew that they were naked; and they sewed fig leaves together and made themselves aprons" BERE'SHIYTH (GENESIS) 3:7 את CEPHER," behold they no longer had a spiritual body but became participants of disobedience and turned a blessing into a curse with physical embodiment, forever restricted in putting forth their hand, and taking also of the tree of life, and eat, and live forever.

This was my opinion I offered in the podcast as to why sons of Man could not have identified as sons of Elohim in Genesis, "For if Elohim spared not the angels that sinned, but cast them down to Sheol, and delivered them into chains of darkness, to be watched unto the judgment of anguish; And spared not the old world, but saved Noach the eighth person, a preacher of righteousness, bringing in the flood upon the world of the wicked; And turning the cities of Cedom and Amorah into ashes condemned them with an overthrow, making them an example unto those that after should live in wickedness" KEPHA SHENIY (2 PETER) 2:4-6 את CEPHER".

For all those that continue to deceive humankind with the reasoning used by the serpent in beguiling Chuah who coerced A'dam to forsake righteousness, do not let your crimes go impenitent. Many have mistakenly allowed an adamant ruach to inflame their ego and suddenly death had opened the pit of SHE'OL for their arrival. Where was their foresight when the green horse was galloping on their heels? Did they not buy from the gatekeepers the knowledge and Chokmah that YHWH and the Watchers have? King Shalomah was correct when he said, the heart of him that has understanding seeks knowledge: but the mouth of fool's feeds on foolishness. All the days of the afflicted are evil: but he that is of a merry heart has a continual feast. Better is little with the fear of Yahweh than great treasure and trouble therewith. This statement rings true today as it did in the generation of Shalomah because it continues to amaze me how individuals conceived through coitus and lived an unrepentant lifestyle before spending time at prison, allowing themselves to believe after consuming hours of theological study that they are gods or reincarnated deities. They have exploited the basic needs of the people who are searching for salvation and purpose, namely L. Ron

Hubbard, author of Battlefield Earth and founder of the Scientology religion. I do not like putting an individual on blast because they are not here to offer a rebuttal, but he reported to have said, "If a man wants to make a million dollars, the best way would be to start his own religion." He also reportedly said, "You do not get rich writing science fiction. If you want to get rich, you start a religion." Two years after saying the latter, Hubbard started his own religion.

I have researched many religious organizations set up in the late 18th century after the Civil War and in the early 19th century during racial unrest in America, and many of the founders and leaders displayed a narcissistic personality disorder complex. Flamboyant characters with larger-than-life personalities that have manifested unbridled power over their congregation because of showmanship and mannerism.

No other religious icon was as bold and unwavering in their convictions like Father Divine aka Reverend M. J. Divine aka Reverend Major Jealous Divine Aka the Messenger. Claiming to be the incarnate god, his International Peace Mission movement expanded quickly from a small minority congregation into a multiracial and international church. I just happened to come across his name and evangelism while watching Lawrence Fishbourne "Hoodlum" and it sparked interest since never encountering an individual who possessed a god complex working at Kgm1 radio but have read about men and women across the religious spectrum that believe they are ordained with great spiritual ability, able to beguile even the devil into salvation. These people intoxicated off their own Kool-Aid if they think they can go toe to toe with the prince of iniquity that orchestrated an army of angels to defy the Highest Elohim to impregnate daughters of Man while introducing corruption upon the earth. The seeds of the Naphaliym written extensively within the Torah thought to be still active among the elites of humanity.

These are rumored to be the gatekeepers who have made a Faustian bargain with top tier entertainers, politicians, athletes, corporate CEOs, and media moguls.

According to rumors and YouTube podcasters that have known someone or enlightened as a member, sworn to secrecy and take a solemn oath before trading your soul for favors, which include knowledge, wealth, fame, and power. Just the thought of kissing the pinky ring like Keanu Reeves who played Kevin Lomax did in the movie Devil's Advocate, gives me the shakes, but that is their prerogative as Bobby Brown would say. They should have known who they were dealing with because the Torah describes Watcher's offspring as warriors and tyrants which were from everlasting, mortal men of the name. Have you not seen President Clinton wearing a blue dress and red high heels displayed on the wall in Jeff Epstein's mansion? How many heads of state or prominent celebrities photographed or filmed in compromising situations later used against them as evidence to keep secrets?

Lately I have seen popular celebrities and athletes confess about their treatment in the industry, but this is after they have reaped the benefits of the darkness and want to now dwell in the light. This is the problem also with so-called ministers of light that like to jump back and forth into darkness to become adulterer, sodomite, or criminal when temptations over power their ruach. It is exceedingly difficult to still be steadfast in the faith when your eyes bombarded with erotic and salacious pop-up images on social media. Pastors and priests have received flirtatious remarks from women and men parishioners because of their position in the congregation before and after the ministry of YAHUSHA. The power of materialism and the allure of wealth generated within the Christian and Gospel industry is why religious sects and cults are surpassing traditional devotional denominations worldwide. In our generation, politicians appeared as conservative Christians or liberal Baptists endorsing candidates who are unrepentant racists and habitual fabricators of the truth. The pre warnings chronicled in the books of the Cepher placed there so you cannot claim ignorance like those that transgressed in antediluvian times who did not put on the whole armor of Elohim.

We can only imagine through our imagination and the writings from antiquity seen among early humankind that did not have the Canonical and Apocrypha books to help them stand against the wiles of the devil. "For we wrestle not against flesh and blood that are the sons and daughters of humankind that bleed like we do but against principalities, against powers, against the rulers of the darkness of this world, against spiritual wickedness in high places" EPH'SIYM (EPHESIANS) 6:11-12 את CEPHER. These rulers that once ruled in darkness exposed because of the courage of individuals not afraid to enlighten theology students with the laws of the universe, once reserved for the elites.

I discovered the life of a man that claimed to be Allah but died from complications of the Covid virus through a google search. *Was it Divine intervention or simply health complications that ended the illustrious career of a delusional man who cast a stone high upon his own head?* The government had an eight-million-dollar judgment against him for forced labor compensation that exemplifies that a deceitful stroke shall make wounds. He that works mischief, it shall fall upon him, and he shall not know whence it comes. Malice and wrath, even these are abominations; and the sinful man shall have them both. All the hours spent on learning the laws of the universe did not add time to his life span or deter a financial judgment against him that could have helped his wives and children after his premature death. *What good is it for anyone to study the laws of the universe if they are not going to apply them correctly?* Since the Watchers came to earth to teach the sons of Man the secrets of the universe, all mayhem has broken loose upon generation after generation.

Let us examine the twelve halakha of the Universe beginning with the halakha of Divine Oneness. The fundamental basis of all humanity is to achieve unity and tranquility, but this seems like a daunting task when antipathy and racism keeps individuals with moral understanding prohibited from abiding by the law of divine oneness. Even nations that used to be the pillar for democracy and justice, are experiencing a surge in political unrest and human rights violations. The halakha of divine oneness goes beyond laws created by man because the offspring of humankind are created through iniquity and prone to narcissistic behavior whose actions profoundly influence the world around us. Divine halakha superseded by manufactured halakha severely altered to appease political correctness lobbied by civic organizations in the 19th and 20th century. Divine halakha is a controversial issue, since adhering to the halakha means the extreme assumption that their source transcends human knowledge and human reason. "Who will rise for me against the evildoers? or who will stand up for me against the workers of iniquity? Unless Yahweh had been my help, my soul had almost dwelt in silence. When I said, my foot slips; your mercy, O Yahweh, held me up. In the multitude of my thoughts within me, your comforts delight my soul. Shall the throne of iniquity have fellowship with you, which frames mischief by a law"? TEHILLIYM (PSALMS) 94:16-20 את CEPHER.

The halakha of Vibration is the result of the energy that you put out into the world related to your thoughts and emotions and how this energy influences your interactions with others. The halakha of Vibration is a fundamental halakha of the universe that says that everything in existence vibrates at a certain frequency. Take for instance music and the instruments that move the listener to either behave radically or be serene. The halakha of Vibration suggests that when you emit positive energy you become hypersensitive to your mental productivity, harnessing the power of the prefrontal cortex (PFC) found within your brain. If early humanity equipped with the research tools at our disposal today instead of being on the destructive tail end of the fallen angels and their offspring, the halakha of Vibration could have helped them capitalize on their mortal strengths. This same halakha deeply undermines the negative effects of post-depression and systematic issues involving economics, education, ethnicity, gender through creative processing techniques to conquer arduous problems and situations from a logical perspective. "The heart is deceitful above all things, and desperately wicked: who can know it? I, Yahweh search the heart, I try the mind, even to give every man according to his ways, and according to the fruit of his doings. As the partridge sits on eggs, and hatches them not; so, he that gets riches, and not by right, shall leave them during his days, and at his end shall be a fool" YIRMEYAHU (JEREMIAH) 17:9-11 את CEPHER.

Taught as a child that the energy you release is the same energy you attract from the world. The halakha of Action requires that you become proactive to manifest the things you want. Yes, it is that literal! This halakha states that you cannot manifest the things you want without becoming a live wire as in an electrical wire to get something going, or better said, without putting your thoughts into action. The idea is that by believing you can do something and focusing your thoughts and energy in that direction, you can make it happen. Our thoughts are incredibly powerful and can play a significant role in deciding the course of our lives. Having a positive attitude can help you overcome your worries and fears, so you can reach for what you want. "And let the counsel of your own heart stand: for there is no man more faithful unto you than it. For a man's mind is sometimes wont to tell him more than seven Natsariym (watchmen) that sit above in a high tower. And above all this pray to

El Elyon, that he will direct your way in truth. Let reason go before every enterprise, and counsel before every action" SIRACH (ECCLESIASTICUS) 37:13-16 את CEPHER.

The halakha of Correspondence states that what happens around us, is a direct reflection of what is happening within us; Our internal environments decide our external environment which is vital part of our moral and spiritual growth. The way that we prioritize daily situations reflects on the many factors that are present within our waking hours and can affect how our laws of oneness work or what values we assign to our laws of action. The opposite of this concept is the external environment that consists of factors such as economic, legal, social, or global factors, which can influence the difference between necessity and miscellaneous. My grandmother would reprimand me for procrastinating and not seeing everything to completion. I would tell her that none of us were born with everything figured out, but it was truly one of my pet peeves that kept me from hitting the mark. Before my motorcycle accident, I continued to slow walk projects and tasks repeatedly until I realized I had to end the cycle and set finish dates. I had to grow up and let the ruach take charge from within, something we all need to recognize and learn from, to end the pattern and manifest the halakha of Correspondence. This level of awareness allows us to make a conscious change and gives us enlightenment over our own destinies. Be open to allowing the law to work through you instead of against you and see what changes. "Make no tarrying to turn to Yahweh and put not off from day to day: for suddenly shall the wrath of Yahweh come forth, and in your security, you shall be destroyed and perish in the day of vengeance. Set not your heart upon goods unjustly gotten, for they shall not profit you on the day of calamity. Winnow not with every wind and go not into every way: for so does the sinner that has a double tongue. Be steadfast in your understanding; and let your words be the same. Be swift to hear; and let your life be sincere; and with patience give answers. If you have understanding, answer your neighbor; if not, lay your hand upon your mouth" SIRACH (ECCLESIASTICUS) 5:7-12 את CEPHER.

The halakha of Cause-and-Effect states that for every action there is a reaction and has a consequence for the action. This halakha is based on the Chokmah that everything in the universe is interrelated and seen among the youth in urban areas where many have been victims to violence or slain because an individual felt disrespected by another which increases conflict and tension. We must fully adhere to the halakha of Cause and Effect in our lives, we must take responsibility for our actions and understand that there are consequences for our positive and negative behavior. Too many individuals have suffered when they have chosen to make intentional choices that lead to negative outcomes that have been detrimental to themselves, and others compared to those who have avoided choices that may have negative consequences. "Restore the earth, which the angels have corrupted; and announce life to it, that I may revive it. All the sons of men shall not perish in consequence of every secret, by which the Watchers have destroyed, and which they have taught, their offspring. All the earth has been corrupted by the effects of the teaching of Aza'zel. To him therefore ascribe the whole crime" CHANOK (ENOCH) 10:10-12 את CEPHER.

The halakha of Attraction is a theory used by successful individuals that believe that optimistic thinking can breed positive results, which is a philosophy that energy precedes manifestation. This idealism is a positive mental attitude with confidence in your abilities to reach success that can shape your future. Optimists tend to view hardships as learning experiences or temporary setbacks that drive an individual to reflect on life's pitfalls and continue to move forward. Many will tell you that the halakha of Attraction generated by anyone that is willing to unlearn factors that play a role that beget defeatism. These factors hamper individuals from reaching their full potential in life such as genetics, environmental influences, and socioeconomic status. When we realize that all factors which perceived negatively that minimize growth can be a useful technique to help you focus on what matters in the present and not dwell on things you cannot control. If your consciousness trained to prioritize issues and circumstances within your ability to guarantee success, it would become less stressful to unlearn negative past experiences or serious contemplation about upcoming events. This allows you to feel more appreciative of what you have now and less consumed with regrets and anxieties. "Therefore, take no thought, saying, what shall we eat? or, what shall we drink? or, where shall we be clothed? (For after all these things do the other nations seek:) for your heavenly Father knows that ye have need of all these things. But seek ye first the Kingdom of Elohim, and his righteousness; and all these things shall be added unto you. Take therefore no thought for the morrow: for the morrow shall take thought for the things of itself. Sufficient unto the day is the evil thereof" MATTITHYAHU (MATTHEW) 6:31-34 את CEPHER.

The halakha of Compensation is the theory that everyone compensated for what he or she has contributed. The phrase a dollar saved is a dollar earned reversed to a dollar earned is a dollar saved. If you fill your consciousness with thoughts, visions and ideas of success, happiness, and optimism, compensated by those positive experiences in your daily activities. I have learned that once something is moving upward it will continue moving in the same manner unless, of course, we alter that movement or stop it with pessimistic thinking. Manifesting the Law of Compensation requires always being ready to implement the halakha of Action by clearing your path of all obstacles and negativity. The manifestation comes from understanding your consciousness and creating short term goals that translate into success and prosperity. One of your main responsibilities in life is to align yourself and your activities with righteousness and morality, accepting that it is an enduring theory that always works, whether anyone is looking or not. "Treasures of wickedness profit nothing: but righteousness delivers from death. Yahweh will not suffer the soul of the righteous to famish but he casts away the substance of the wicked. He becomes poor and deals with a slack hand: but the hand of the diligent makes rich. He that gathers in summer is a wise son: but he that sleeps in harvest is a son that causes shame" MISHLEI (PROVERBS) 10:2-5 את CEPHER.

The halakha of Perpetual Transmutation of Energy states that energy is constantly moving, transmuting, or transferring, and it is always in motion (hence the word perpetual!). Everything is always changing and nothing stays constant. Training your consciousness to accept the positive energy found in uprightness while rejecting negative thoughts and disassociation of individuals whose aura screams unrighteousness can also transmute your own energy to manifest things you want. If energy is always in motion, you can use this knowledge to move through the different forms of energy to your benefit. Applying this law to your life means that you have the power to change the conditions of your life. Life does not happen by chance; it happens by choice, by change. "According as his divine power has given unto us all things את that pertain unto life and holiness, through the knowledge of him that has called us to glory and virtue: Whereby are given unto us exceeding great and precious promises: that by these ye might be partakers of the divine nature, having escaped the corruption that is in the world through lust. And beside this, giving all diligence, add to your faith virtue; and to virtue knowledge; And to knowledge temperance; and to temperance patience; and to patience holiness; And to holiness, brotherly kindness; and to brotherly kindness, love. For if these things be in you, and abound, they make you that ye shall neither be barren nor unfruitful in the knowledge of our Adonai Yahusha Ha'Mashiach" KEPHA SHENIY (2 PETER) 1:3-8 את CEPHER.

The halakha of Relativity states that every person will experience challenges in their lifespan and unforeseen circumstances occur to all of us but if we apply the above laws effectively, we can use these challenges as an opportunity for growth, to strengthen our characters. When we begin to understand the challenges thrown our way and we overcome them, we can become fully prepared to successfully conquer more extreme versions of adversity. I have heard from many individuals that blame Elohim for tragedy and sudden death when it happens and slows their upward movements, but the halakha of Relativity are not about good or bad, it is about the manifestation of growth. Unforeseen circumstances allow us to develop our consciousness and strengthen our character, so we can continue our upward movement to achieve our purpose with sustainable reasoning. When tested with adversity that will come throughout your life, never allow yourself to sink down to a level that leaves you conquered and stagnant. Who has gone through their daily life up to this point without feeling a level of depression and anxiety? As a child we were immune to the challenges of a teenager but as we mature, we begin to experience challenges to our character, integrity, spirituality, and morality. By understanding the reasoning behind the adversity principle, anyone can increase their knowledge and defeat challenges so they can experience the effects of relativity. "Now all these things happened unto them as examples: and they are written for our admonition, upon whom the ends of the world come. Wherefore let him that thinks he stands take heed lest he fall. There is no temptation taken upon you, but such as is common to man: but Elohim is faithful, who will not suffer you to be tempted above that ye are able; but will with the temptation also make a way to escape, that ye may be able to bear it" QORINTIYM RI'SHON (1 CORINTHIANS) 10:11-13 את CEPHER.

The halakha of Polarity is a simple explanation that there are two sides to every story which is a concept derived from the Hermetic principles, that everything has its opposite, and that opposites are the same thing differing only in degree. This principle of spiritual philosophy dates back as early as the first century A.D. outlined by famed author Hermes Trismegistus, believed to have written the Emerald Tablet and the Corpus Hermeticum (two highly influential, ancient teachings). This is the theory that there cannot be good in the world without evil and all humans own two-character traits displayed depending on the circumstances now. One emotion is non-resistant to conflict and aggression. Maintaining a calm energy while being receptive to the attitudes and negative conduct of others. The other emotional character is a high voltage live wire, repulsive, and in principle, hard to handle. There is an opposite for everything in our world; this is necessary for balance within our Universe. Everything has a duality and a built-in opposite that cannot exist without the other. If one side (of anything) has the potential to exist, by the halakha of polarity, the opposite expression must exist also.

In academics, the computation of Mathematics says the polarity of a number says whether it is positive or negative. Numbers bigger than zero are positive, those less than zero are negative. In Quantum physics, polarized electrons are more stable and less likely to undergo spontaneous decay than unpolarized electrons. When we acknowledge and respect the polarity of all things, we understand that one cannot exist without the other, and polarity and duality as fundamental laws to aid us in our spiritual evolution. Everything has its pair of opposites; like and unlike are the same; opposites are identical in nature but different in degree; extremes meet; all truths are but half-truths; all paradoxes reconciled. Let not sin therefore reign in your mortal body, that ye should obey it in the lusts thereof. "Neither yield ye your members as instruments of unrighteousness unto sin: but yield yourselves unto Elohim, as those that are alive from the dead, and your members as instruments of righteousness unto Elohim. For sin does not have dominion over you: for ye are not under the Law, but under grace. What then? shall we sin, because we are not under the Law, but under grace? Never. Know ye not, that to whom ye yield yourselves servants to obey, his servants ye are to whom ye obey, whether of sin unto death, or of obedience unto righteousness? But Elohim be thanked, that ye were the servants of sin, but ye have obeyed from the heart that form of doctrine which was delivered to you. Being then made free from sin, ye became the servants of righteousness." ROMAIN (ROMANS) 6:22-18 את CEPHER.

The halakha of Gender states that we all have the potential to express both feminine and masculine energy; both found within us, regardless of our sex. This is the halakha of the yin and the yang that all things exist as inseparable and contradictory opposite forces such as female-male, dark-light, and old-young. The pairs of equal opposites both attract and complement each other. Neither energy is superior to the other and, as an increase in one brings a corresponding decrease in the other, a correct balance between the two energies reached to achieve harmony. We must all have an equal balance if feminine energy were the seed, then masculine energy would be the pollen. The feminine, the seed (or the idea), needs fertilization by the masculine, the pollen (or the action). A seed cannot come into fruition without fertilization, and pollen is useless without a seed to pollinate. The halakha of Gender is a representation of the two opposing types of energy, one that nurtures and one that drives. One energy of mankind's behavior overemphasizes our masculine energy to express foremost governance, gallantry, and intelligence while those skilled in harnessing the beauty of the halakha of Gender can tap into more feminine qualities within their energy to display transparency, accountability, empathy, communication, and social empowerment.

Balancing our masculine and feminine within society will allow us to tie into our spiritual ruach, better communicators, loving individuals, and be successful in our endeavors as a result. 'Wisdom is glorious, and never fades away: yea, she is easily seen by those that love her, and fond of such as seek her. 'She prevents them that desire her, in making herself first known unto them. 'Whoso seeks her early shall have no great travail: for he shall find her sitting at his doors. To think therefore upon her is perfection of wisdom: and whoso watches for her shall quickly be without care. For she goes about seeking such as are worthy of her, shows herself favorably unto them in the ways, and meets them in every thought. 'For the very true beginning of her is the desire for discipline; and the care of discipline is love. 'And love is the keeping of her Torah; and the giving heed unto her Torah is the assurance of incorruption; 'And incorruption makes us near unto Elohim: 'Therefore the desire of wisdom brings to a kingdom. 'If your delight be then in thrones and scepters, O ye kings of the people, honor wisdom, that ye may reign forevermore. 'As for wisdom, what she is, and how she came up, I will tell you and will not hide mysteries from you: but will seek her out from the beginning of her nativity, and bring the knowledge of her into light, and will not pass over the Truth. 'Neither will I go with consuming envy; for such a man shall have no fellowship with wisdom" CHOKMAH SHALOMAH (WISDOM OF SOLOMON) 6:12-23 את CEPHER.

The halakha of Rhythm adapts to our upward movement and guarantees that transfiguration is always on the horizon. This halakha is one of the necessary procedures that is an eventuality as we journey through various phases in life or experiencing seasons of change. This halakha governs everything that all ethnicities experience including faith, nutrition, economics, family, association, and social class. The phrase "what goes up" will eventually experience a degree of de-escalating. However, instead of scrutinizing this "drop" as something being wrong with you, recognize this abate period as change we must all go through. Then by halakha and nature you accumulate an elevation that was previously held. Know that they are coming in cycles or in a rhythm. For if there were this life only, which belongs to all men, nothing could be more bitter than this. "For what profit is strength that turns to sickness, or fullness of food that turns to famine, or beauty that turns to ugliness. For the nature of man is always changeable. For what we were formerly now we no longer are, and what we now are we shall not afterwards remain. For if a consummation had not been prepared for all, in vain would have been their beginning. But regarding everything that comes from you, do inform me, and regarding everything about which I ask you, do enlighten me. How long will that which is corruptible remain, and how long will the time of mortals prosper, and until what time will those who transgress in the world be polluted with much wickedness? Command therefore in mercy and accomplish all that you said you would bring, that you might be made known to those who think that your long suffering is weakness" BARUK SHENIY (2 BARUK) 21:13-20 את CEPHER.

The sons and daughters of Man keened to spiritual enlightenment and recognize the importance of religion. This acknowledges that angels and higher deities play a role in their successes and failures. Since my adolescent years up to now, I often wondered how long that which is corruptible continues to have precedent over humanity, and how long will the world pollute with much wickedness? The Humans that walk on two feet or creatures that use all four are the creation of the creator spoken of in the Torah, the Bible, and the Quran. I have read several writings within all three publications that seem over exaggerated and more myth and less reality allowing atheists and non-believers opportunities to refute the Creator sovereignty and supernatural power. The big bang theory is still a debatable issue; but what scientists cannot refute is that humans and creatures are so unique and like each other, but unlike creatures, humans know they are going to die. This inevitable fact may seem dubious during infancy or as adolescents, but as teenagers, our intelligence begins to mature, and the cessation of life becomes a reality.

As a teenager I had many friends that developed deep feelings of anxiety and considered suicide while other friends pushed it to the limit and began living life to their full potential. I don't fully know the outcome of the lives of many of my childhood associates after leaving elementary and middle school, but teenagers go through high-school and college with the same mindset they developed as teenagers; but by their late forties, their health and economic status becomes a factor and a lot of them are not happy about it. When I was approaching my mid-thirties, I began to realize after the death of my brother that the party was ending and weekend activities that were priorities in our twenties and early thirties were now being reconsidered to ideas of modern science, which indicates various ways in which diet, and lifestyle can increase human longevity. A death in the family or close friendship can make you reconsider your own lifestyle and the people in your circle. This may be difficult to accept and even more difficult for me to utter, but for many, puberty means that mental and physical growth is on the horizon where you begin to develop and mature.

In the beginning of this chapter, I listed BERE'SHIYTH chapter six since the verses one through five have always puzzled me. How did sons of Elohim interpreted as angels, procreate with daughters of men, were they created with genitals like sons of A'dam? The verses say they saw the daughters of A'dam and took all those they chose. *Were they created with lustful emotions like all ethnicities?* If angels that created without blemish and saw the generations of A'dam and Chuah expand across the earth, what power does a mere child have during puberty or adults lacking enlightenment? I had so many questions growing up in church that went unresolved and had to learn on my own through trials and tribulations. The pastor will quote a snippet from the scriptures saying, "Yahweh knows how to deliver his most holy out of temptations, and to reserve the unjust unto the day of judgment."

As a teenager, it never resonated with me that I would create a moral burden hard to erase while living a carefree lifestyle by walking after the flesh in the lust of uncleanness. At the time, I was enthralled within the entertainment industry and all the benefits that go along with it. Every day was like a party, and I became haughty in character and like so many young people caught up with the glamor and bright lights, I was knee deep in the matrix. "But if a man lives many years and rejoice in them all; yet let him remember the days of darkness; for they shall be many. All that comes is vanity. Rejoice, O young man, in your youth; and let your heart cheer you in the days of your youth, and walk in the ways of your heart, and in the sight of your eyes: but know you, that for all these things Elohim will bring you into judgment. Therefore, remove sorrow from your heart, and put away evil from your flesh: for childhood and youth are vanity" QOHELETH (ECCLESIASTES) 11:8-10 את CEPHER

SONS OF ELOHIM LINKS

Demigod/ Seventh-day Adventists/ God Complex: What It Means and Why People Have Them/ Deal_with_the_Devil/ Stress signaling pathways that impair prefrontal cortex structure and function

MIGRATION OR CAPTIVITY

" **A**nd they will eat and be satisfied, and they will turn to strange Elohim, to Elohim which cannot deliver them from out of their tribulation: and this witness heard for a witness against them. For they will forget all my commandments, even all that I command them, and they will walk after the other nations, and after their uncleanness, and after their shame, and will serve their Elohim, and these will prove unto them an offense, a tribulation, an affliction, and a snare. And many will perish and they will be taken captive, and will fall into the hands of the enemy, because they have forsaken my ordinances and my commandments, and the feasts of my covenant, and my Sabbaths, and my holy place which I have sanctified for myself in their midst, and my Tabernacle, and my sanctuary, which I have sanctified for myself in the midst of the land, that I should set my name upon it, and that it should dwell there. And they will make to themselves high places and Asherah poles and graven images, and they will worship, each his own graven image, to go astray, and they will sacrifice their children to devils, and to all the works of the error of their hearts. And I will send witnesses unto them, that I may see against them, but they will not hear, and will slay the witnesses also, and they will persecute those who seek the Torah, and they will abrogate and change everything to work evil before my eyes. And I will hide my face from them, and I will deliver them into the hands of the other nations for captivity, and for prey, and for devouring, and I will remove them from the midst of the land, and I will scatter them amongst the other nations" YOVHELIYM (JUBILEES) 1:9-14 את CEPHER.

In America, the divide between ethnicities seen during every election cycle when both parties try to persuade specific ethnic groups to choose either democratic or republican party. For me to make sense of it and understand the issues that continue to plague certain ethnicities generation after generation, I will examine within this chapter the offspring of Noach's son Shem according to what the scriptures refer to as exiles. The following paragraphs will be controversial because of long held beliefs about lineage of Noachian tribes and how they make up the various nations and religions of our generation. An opportunity for me to do research on the migration of the sons and daughters of Noach and the many kingdoms and tribal groups enslaved or forced into exile. No other nation from antiquity up to my generation has dealt with adversity because of their own disobedience like the seed of Avraham scattered across the four corners of the world than the children of the sanctified Ya`aqov. Since receiving the covenant between the progenitor Avraham and YHWH, the progeny of Sarah who are many like the grains of sand have been wandering the earth. Stripped of their sanctified inheritance because of their tolerance for idolatry and worship of foreign deities, their continuous rebelling ruach were destroyed or treated harshly as strangers in a strange land. YA'AQOV (Jacob) son YOCEPH (Joseph) experienced the hospitality of Pharaoh and prosperity blossomed for the Iviry nation in the towns around Goshen, believed to stretch north of Cairo in a rough triangle around the modern town of Zagazig, and along the fringe where the delta farmland meets the eastern desert. They were able to build and maintain communities within the Mistrayim political and military power structures until YA'AQOV sons, daughters, and grandchildren generations died off and another generation matured that the Mitsrayim nation distrusted around 1550 B.C, and either made the Iviry elders kiss the pinky ring or broke up the leadership and subjugated the remaining Semitic tribes, under Pharaohs Seti I (13131292 B.C.) and Rameses forced labor to build two store-cities, Pithom and Raamses near the present small town of Tel el Kebir in the northeastern delta, about 20 miles east of Zagazig.

Fourteen generations held as servants of Pharaoh, and the Mitsrayim elite that worshiped deities Osiris, God of the underworld. The Egyptian nation symbolized his power with death, resurrection, and the cycle of Nile floods that Mitsrayim needed for agriculture. Isis worshiped for the safe passage and rites for the newly deceased. In the Greco-Roman period, they gave her a new spin with the name goddess Aphrodite spreading her Hellenistic idolatry as far west as Great Britain in Europe and as far east as Afghanistan. Many biblical scholars have made striking comparisons of Isis with the infant Horus with the Christian imagery of Mary and the infant Jesus. Horus shaped by man in artwork and figurines as a man with a falcon's head, whose embodiment is associated with war and hunting. He was also the embodiment of a divine kingship, between sons of A'dam and sons of Elohim that many kingdoms after the fall of Egypt latched onto.

The deity Seth's power attributed to chaos, violence, deserts, and storms. Depicted as an animal or as a human with the head of an animal with a long snout and long squared ears at the tips. In his fully animal form, he has a thin doglike body and a straight tail with a tuft on the end. Many scholars now believe that no such animal ever existed, and that the Seth animal is some sort of mythical composite. Ptah was the head of a triad of gods along with the lion-headed goddess Sekhmet, and the god Nefertem. Ptah's original association seems to have been with craftsmen and builders. The 4th-dynasty architect Imhotep deified after his death as a son of Ptah. Scholars have suggested that the Greek word *Aiguptos*—the source of the name Egypt—may have started as a corruption of Hwt-Ka-Ptah, the name of one of Ptah's shrines. The goddess Hathor was depicted as a cow, as a woman with the head of a cow, or as a woman with cow's ears. Hathor who embodied motherhood and fertility believed that she protected women in childbirth. She also had a role in the burial ritual, being known as "the lady of the west." (Tombs built on the west bank of the Nile.) In some traditions, she would welcome the setting sun every night; living people welcomed into the afterlife in the same way. Anubis attributed to burial rituals and the care of the dead. Represented as a jackal or as a man with the head of a jackal. The association of jackals with death and funerals arose because Egyptians would have seen jackals scavenging around cemeteries. In the Old Kingdom (c. 2575–2130 BCE), before Osiris rose to prominence as the lord of the underworld, Anubis considered the principal god of the dead and became the patron god for embalmers.

Thoth, the god of writing and wisdom, depicted in the form of a baboon or a sacred ibis or as a man with the head of an ibis. Believed to have invented language and the hieroglyphic script. As the god of wisdom, Thoth was said to own knowledge of magic and secrets unavailable to the other gods. Bastet was represented as a woman with the head of a lion or a wild cat. She took the less ferocious form of a domestic cat in the first millennium BCE. In later periods she was represented as a regal-looking seated cat, sometimes wearing rings in her ears or nose. In the Ptolemaic period she came to be associated with the Greek goddess Artemis, the divine hunter and goddess of the moon. From 1539–1292 BCE, the deity Amon worshiped as a god of the air, and the name means the "Hidden One." Represented as a man wearing a crown with two vertical plumes. His animal symbols were the ram and the goose.

After the rulers of Thebes rebelled against a dynasty of foreign rulers known as the Hyksos and re-established native Egyptian rule throughout Egypt, Amon received credit for their victory. Today the massive temple complex devoted to Amon-Re at Karnak is one of the most visited monuments in Egypt. As you travel during the winter and summer, take notice if these deities appear as statues or artwork in America or abroad. Idolatry never stops pushing an agenda prescribed by the Watchers but reinvents itself with generations that become complacent with the Torah illiterate religious congregations and loud sounding tongue of their priests and ministers. Thank your Jewish nation for your active participation in the distribution of the Cepher and the Torah to all seeds of Avraham scattered across the globe. Your European converts from the loins of Japheth are like the converts of the Christian denominations that choose YHWH and the ministry of YAHUSHA over the other deities worshiped by humanity. Before the internet and research tools were available in public libraries and online search engines, millions were in the dark about the power of repentance and mercy available for the exiles and converts of Yashar'el, and now we are seeing a diverse multitude from the seeds of Noach enlisted in YAHUAH proud army fleeing idolatry.

History has chronicled many nations of antiquity and in the earlier generations denied the children of Avraham mercy and civility upon foreign soil. Bamboozled with propaganda that inadvertently aligns with prophecies becoming reality. He has said, which heard the words of El, and knew the knowledge of El Elyon, which saw the vision of El Shaddai, falling into a trance, but having his eyes open: I shall see him, but not now: I shall behold him, but not nigh: there shall come a star out of Ya`aqov, and a scepter shall rise out of Yashar'el, and shall smite the corners of Moab, and destroy all the children of Seth. And Edom shall be a possession, Se'iyr also shall be a possession for his enemies; and Yashar'el shall do valiantly. Out of Ya`aqov shall come he that shall have dominion and shall destroy him that stays of the city. And when he looked at Amaleq, he took up his parable, and said, "Amaleq was the first of the nations; but his latter end shall be that he perishes forever. And he looked on the Qeyniyiym, and took up his parable, and said, Strong is your dwelling place, and you put your nest in a rock. Nevertheless, the Qayiniy shall be wasted, until Ashshur shall carry you away captive. And he took up his parable, and said, Alas, who shall live when El does this! And ships shall come from the coast of Kittiym, and shall afflict Ashshur, and shall afflict Eber, and he also shall perish forever" BEMIDBAR (NUMBERS) 24:16-24 את CEPHER.

One of the greatest weapons used on exiles and captives is mind manipulation designed to influence or control another, usually in an underhanded manner, which helps a strategic agenda. Methods used to distort the individual's sense of reality may include seduction, suggestion, persuasion, and blackmail to induce submission. Usage of the term varies depending on which behavior was included, whether referring to the general population or used in clinical contexts. Manipulation was considered a dishonest form of social influence used at the expense of others. While researching brainwashing and mind-controlling techniques used to control captives throughout the history of humanity, I stumbled upon the BITE technique. Defined as Behavior Control, Information Control, Thought Control, and Emotional Control. Numerous writers claim that religious denominations have mastered the technique with ability and now have the power of controlling the minds of parishioners with behavior control. With this control, congregations have implemented clothing and apparel restrictions, mandated policies on sexuality and gender-neutral doctrines.

The Catholic church bans priests and nuns from marriage and exploits parishioners financially with Information Control. Other congregations I know are deliberately withholding and distorting information about ministers' misconduct, while forbidding you from speaking with ex-members and critics. Network television Evangelists utter the anti-semitism word loosely to generate sympathies for their cause and use propaganda extensively. White Evangelicals continue to instill Black vs. white hatred during election time, while network news pushes the conservative good vs. liberal evil divide among constituencies stirring up the political violence in America. Urban denominations use excessive singing, and theatrics to replace sermons of moral accountability and repentance.

Even today, so-called leaders instill fears from the era of slavery and Jim Crow upon the people, while not orchestrating an escape plan to erase high unemployment, the wealth gap and violence in their communities. Bill Cosby and Kanye West were ridiculed for saying the thoughts that so many wished they could, but this did not sit well with some that let their emotions outweigh reasoning. We have given too much power to worldly desires, sinful temptations, or immoral ambitions. Help sponsor and support feelings of guilt, shame, & unworthiness, because of the color of skin and ethnic background. The covenant of Avraham depends on parishioners rising from the forced religions of the 1800s created from western philosophy and idolatry. During Sunday school, the Assyrian siege of Jerusalem (circa 701 BC), then capital of the Kingdom of Judah, never discussed because from my estimation, it did not fit the agenda of the church doctrines. *Why are ministers in urban denominations only referencing the YAVINIYM (Greek) scriptures without the IVRIYM (Hebrew) books?*

Just because most of the European slave ships picked up bodies in Cushite lands does not mean the entire cargo was from the seed of Cham. In 721 B.C. Ashshur (Assyria) (Iran) swept out of the north, captured the Northern Kingdom of Israel, and took the ten tribes into captivity. From there they became lost to history. "The wrath of Elohim came upon them, and slew the fattest of them, and smote down the chosen men of Yashar'el. For all this they sinned still and believed not for his wondrous works. Therefore, their days did he consume in vanity, and their years in trouble. When he slew them, then they sought him: and they returned and inquired early after El. And they remembered that Elohim was their Rock, and El Elyon their Redeemer. Nevertheless, they did flatter him with their mouth, and they lied unto him with their tongues. For their heart was not right with him, neither were they steadfast in his covenant. But he, being full of compassion, forgave their iniquity, and destroyed them not: yes, many a time turned his anger away, and did not stir up all his wrath. For he remembered that they were but flesh; a wind that passes away and comes not again. How oft did they provoke him in the wilderness and grieve him in the desert! Yes, they turned back and tempted El and limited the Holy One of Yashar'el. They remembered not his hand, nor the day when he delivered them from the enemy" TEHILLIYM (PSALMS) 78:31-42 את CEPHER.

Many of the captives that did not flee to the mountains or into Cushite territories became exiles in Assyria, named for the god Ashur found in the Mesopotamian plain. Borderline on the west by the Syrian desert, on the south by Babylonia, and on the north and east by the Persian and Urartian hills. The Ashur empire was without doubt the most feared kingdom in the Mediterranean or Near Eastern world; only Hammurabi and Thutmose III had approached it, and Persia alone would equal it before the rise of Alexander the Great and the YAVINIYM empire. I do not want to offend anyone reading this chapter, but I must put this out there, that America was not the first place where the sons and daughters of Yashar'el held in bondage. In Sunday school, I learned the lineage of Japheth which has come to be known as the European nations, fought alongside the sons of Cham to defeat and conquer the sons of Shem, more importantly the nation of Yashar'el. The first prophecy directed towards the lineage of YA'AQOV going into captivity revealed to Abram; and, lo, a horror of great darkness fell upon him. And he said unto Abram, know of a surety that your seed shall be a stranger in a land that is not theirs, and shall serve them; and they shall afflict them four hundred years; And, that nation, whom they shall serve, will I judge: and afterward shall they come out with great substance.

I do not want to appear as a conspiracy theorist, but weren't the captives of American slavery in bondage for four hundred years as well as the IVRIYM nation? If I can go further as a conspiracy theorist, the sons, and daughters of Japheth after the Greeks and Roman conquered and subdued African nations, worked alongside the sons and daughters of Cham in the land of Kush to bring the lineage of Shem to distant lands far away in bondage. The similarities of both the generations of YECHEZQ'EL (Ezekiel) and this generation are inscrutable beyond any means that one could imagine. In the last twenty plus years, religious denominations have been in the spotlight for their clergy committing hypocrisy, child molestation, fraud, heresy, and Debauchery.

YHWH addressed the nation of Israel with similar accusations against the shepherds of Yashar'el that do feed themselves without feeding the flocks spiritually and morally. He laid their crimes out to YECHEZQ'EL that they eat the fat, and clothe themselves in the finest of wool, and pronounced judgment on the rich fed: but ye feed not the flock. The diseased have ye not strengthened, neither have ye healed that which was sick, neither have ye bound up that which broken, neither have ye brought again that which was driven away, neither have looked for that which was lost; but with force and with cruelty have ye ruled them. And they scattered, because there was no shepherd: and they became food for all the beasts of the field when scattered. My sheep wandered through all the mountains, and upon every high hill: yes, my flock scattered upon all the face of the earth, and none did search or look for them. Therefore, ye shepherds, hear the Word of Yahuah; As I live, says Adonai Yahweh, surely because my flock became a prey, and my flock became food for every beast of the field, because there was no shepherd, neither did my shepherds search for my flock, but the shepherds fed themselves, and fed not my flock; Therefore, O ye shepherds, hear the Word of Yahweh; Thus says Adonai Yahweh; Behold, I am against the shepherds; and I will require my flock at their hand, and cause them to cease from feeding the flock; neither shall the shepherds feed themselves anymore; for I will deliver my flock from their mouth, that they may not be food for them. For thus says Adonai Yahweh; Behold, I, even I, will both search my sheep, and seek them out. As a shepherd seeks out his flock on the day that he is among his sheep scattered; so, will I seek out my sheep, and will deliver them out of all places where they scattered in the cloudy and dreary day. And I will bring them out from the people, and gather them from the countries, and will bring them to their own land, and feed them upon the mountains of Yashar'el by the rivers, and in all the inhabited places of the country.

The exile and captivity of the sons and daughters of Noach has been in existence since the Exodus of Moshe and has continued in the 20th century. There have been countless debates regarding the authentic proof that the ark of Noach ever existed, but the proof of Noach existence is found within the Table of Nations which chronicles the genealogy of the sons and daughters of Noach, according to the Torah in the book of BERE'SHIYTH (Genesis 10:9), and their migration or exile into many lands. "The duty of the historian not only to record the events of their narratives with the causes and consequences, but to skctch the attending scenes and circumstances as to present a clear and living picture of the whole 'Lyman Coleman 1855.

The Sons and daughters of Japheth are nations in Asia Minor, the Aegean Sea (Greeks), and beyond. *Javan* (*Yawan*) Hebrew, i.e., "Ionians" *Gomer* = Gimmirray in Akkadian; "Cimmerians" in Greek, *Ashkenazi* (*Ashguza*) in Akkadian "Scythians" *Elisha* (*Alashiya*) in Akkadian "Cyprus" *Kittim* is the Greek *Kition*, modern Larnaka in Cyprus. Sons of Ham: races found around Mitzrayim (Egypt). *Cush*, aka Ethiopia or as in Genesis 2:13 the land of the Kassites, in Mesopotamia. *Put*, is Punt, or Libya. *Canaan*, Canaanites, later called Phoenicians. Note that Canaan's first-born son is *Sidon*, a city in Phoenicia (and modern-day Lebanon). *Babel* = Babylon; *Erech* = Uruk; *Shinar* = Sumer. Nineveh and Calah are both Assyrian cities, the latter built in the thirteenth century B.C. *Caphtorim*, inhabitants of Crete. *Jebusites*, Hurrians who ruled Jerusalem around 1400 B.C. Sons of Shem: Semites, or people speaking Semitic languages. However, Semitic-speaking enemies of the Hebrews (Canaanite and Mesopotamian peoples) are classed under Cham. *Eber* = eponymous ancestor of the Hebrews, *Elam* = Elamites, non-Semitic speakers, but "neighbor and traditional rival of Mesopotamian states" *Aram* = eponymous ancestor of the Aramaens, the most widespread of all Semitic groups. Aramaic later replaced Hebrew as the commonly spoken language of Israel. Joktan's sons are "various Arabian tribes."

I have researched the names of the founders of the nations and discovered that most of these nations worshiped many deities that Israel was forbidden from mixing in with them, but they continued to build alliances with Gog, the land of Magog, the chief prince of Meshek that many reference books since Flavius Josephus generally identify in Ezekiel's generation as an area in modern Turkey and Tubal, that is traditionally, considered to be the father of the Caucasian Iberians (ancestors of the Georgians).

Iberia was also known as the Georgian kingdom of Kartli during Classical Antiquity and the Early Middle Ages was a significant monarchy in the Caucasus, either as an independent state or as a dependent of larger empires, notably the Sassanid and Roman empires. Iberia, centered on present-day Eastern Georgia, bordered by Colchis in the west, Caucasian Albania in the east and Armenia in the south. Prophesy against him, And say, Thus says Adonai Yahweh; Behold, I am against you, O Gog, the chief prince of Meshek and Tubal: And I will turn you back, and put hooks into your jaws, and I will bring you forth, and all your army, horses and horsemen, all of them clothed with all sorts of armor, even a great company with bucklers and shields, all of them handling swords. The nations that made alliances with Gog included Persia that renamed Iran, officially the Islamic Republic of Iran is a country in West Asia. It borders Turkey to the northwest and Iraq to the west, Azerbaijan, Armenia, the Caspian Sea and Turkmenistan to the north, Afghanistan to the east, Pakistan to the southeast, the Gulf of Oman, and the Persian Gulf to the south. Kush referred to as the nation of Ethiopia is in the upper Nile region of Sudan, areas south of the Sahara, and certain areas in Asia found near the Red Sea, and Libya which is a nation in the Maghreb region of North Africa.

Libya borders the Mediterranean Sea to the north, Mitsrayim (Egypt) to the east, Sudan to the southeast, Chad to the south, Niger to the southwest, Algeria to the west, and Tunisia to the northwest, as well as maritime borders with Greece, Italy, and Malta to the north, with them; all of them with shield and helmet. Gomer (Gimer) father of Ashkenazi, associated with the Scythian cultures of Sarmatians (not to be confused with the Semite Samaritans) were a large confederation of ancient Iranian equestrian nomadic peoples who dominated the Pontic steppe from about the 3rd century BC to the 4th century AD then later with the Slavic territories, and, from the 11th century onwards, with Germany that is a nation in Central Europe and northern Europe, or the Indo-European people, in a manner similar to Tzarfat or Sefarad.

Riphath, and Togarmah, and all his bands; the house of Togarmah of the north quarters, and all his bands: and many people with you. Gimer (Gomer), and Magog, and Madai, Javan, Tubal, and Meshek, and Thiyrac. And the sons of Gimer; Ashkenazi, and Riyphath, and Togarmah. And the sons of Javan; Eliyshah, and Tarshiysh, Kittiym, and Dodaniym. The sons of Cham; Kush, and Mitsrayim, Put, and Kenyan. And the sons of Kush; Ceva, and Chaviylah, and Cavta, and Ra`amah, and Cavteka. And the sons of Ra`amah; Sheva, and Dedan. And Kush begat Nimrod: he began to be mighty upon the earth. And Mitsrayim begat Ludiy, and Anamiym, and Lehaviym, and Naphtuchiym, And Pathruciym, and Kacluchiym, (of whom came the Pelishtiym,) and Kaphtoriym. And Kenyan begat Tsiydon his firstborn, and Cheth, The Yevuciy also, and the Emoriy, and the Girgashiy, And the Chivviy, and the Arqiy, and the Ciynai, And the Arvadiy, and the Tsemariy, and the Chamathiy.

The sons of Shem; Elam, and Ashshur, and Arpakshad, and Ludiy, and Aram, and Uts, and Chul, and Gether, and Meshek. And Arpakshad begat Shelach, and Shelach begat Eber. And unto Eber were born two sons: the name of the one was Peleg; because in his days the earth divided: and his brother's name was Yoqtan. And

Yoqtan begat Almodad, and Sheleph, and Chatsarmaveth, and Yerach, Hadoram also, and Uzal, and Diqlah, And Eyval, and Aviyma'el, and Sheva, in BABEL (Babylon), MITSRAYIM (Egypt), KUSH (Africa). Ramesses II (c. 1279–1213 BC) or Ramesses the Great, is the Exodus pharaoh mentioned in the Bible as enslaving the Yashar'el nation.

Under bondage with the Egyptian nation, the sons, and daughters of YA'AQOV tested with idolatry and all the practices that YHWH would condemn as abominations. When I examine the father Avraham do I attach him to the Israelites since what came first, the egg or the chicken? And what religious denomination did he adhere to since his generation came before Judaism, Islam, and Christianity? Only two facts that are for certain, YHWH spoke to Avraham about a covenant that his sons and daughters will be innumerable like the grains of sand on the beach and Avraham spoke the IVIRY dialect. The language passed on to his sons YISHMA'EL (Ishmael) whose mother was HA'GER, an Egyptian from lineage of CHAM. "And Sarai Abram's woman took Ha'ger the Mitsriy, after Abram had dwelt ten years in the land of Kena`and gave her to her man Abram to be his woman. And he went in unto Ha'ger, and she conceived: and when she saw that she had conceived, her mistress despised in her eyes" BERE'SHIYTH (GENESIS) 16:3-4 את CEPHER.

YITSCHAQ (Isaac) whose mother was SARAH, an Assyrian from the lineage of SHEM. ZIMRAN, YOQSHAN (Jokshan) MEDAN, MIDYAN (Midian) YISHBAQ (Ishbak) SHUACH (Shuah) six sons whose mother was QETURAH (Keturah) a Kenyan from the lineage of CHAM. "And it was at that time that Avraham again took a woman in his old age, and her name was Qeturah, from the land of Kenyan" YASHAR (JASHER) 25:1 את CEPHER. We also know that ÀVRAHAM sons passed the IVIRY language to their sons and daughters that spread across the land and built nations and kingdoms "The sons of Avraham; Yitschaq, and Yishma'el. These are their generations: The firstborn of Yishma'el, Nevayoth; then Qedar, and Adbe'el, and Mivsam, Mishma, and Dumah, Massa, Chadad, and Teyma, Yetur, Naphiysh, and Qedemah. These are the sons of Yishma'el. Now the sons of Qeturah, Avraham's concubine: she bore Zimran, and Yoqshan, and Medan, and Midyan, and Yishbaq, and Shuach. And the sons of Yoqshan; Sheva, and Dedan. And the sons of Midyan; Eyphah, and Epher, and Chanok, and Aviyda, and Elda`ah.

All these are the sons of Qeturah. And Avraham begat Yitschaq. The sons of Yitschaq; Esau and Yashar'el. The sons of Esau; Eliyphaz, Re'u'el, and Ye`iysh, and Ya`alam, and Qorach. The sons of Eliyphaz; Teyman, and Omar, Tsepho, and Ga'tam, Qenaz, and Timna, and Amaleq. The sons of Re'u'el; Nachath, Zerach, Shammah, and Mizzah. And the sons of Se'iyr; Lotan, and Shoval, and Tsiv'on, and Anah, and Diyshon, and Etser, and Diyshan. And the sons of Lotan; Choriy, and Homam: and Timna was Lotan's sister. The sons of Shoval; Alyan, and Manachath, and Eyval, Shephiy, and Onam. And the sons of Tsiv'on; Ayah, and Anah. The sons of Anah; Diyshon. And the sons of Diyshon; Amram, and Eshban, and Yithran, and Cheran. The sons of Etser; Bilhan, and Za`avan, and Ya`aqan. The sons of Diyshan; Uts, and Aran. Now these are the kings that reigned in the land of Edom before any king reigned over the children of Yashar'el; Bela the son of Be'or: and the name of his city was Dinhabah." DIVREI HAYAMIYM RI'SHON (1 CHRONICLES) 1:28-43 את CEPHER.

Fully engaged in Mitsrayim society as house servants or slaves for agriculture and infrastructure duties, religious practices of the Egyptians clung onto the people after being freed from hardship and labor. Evident throughout the generations of Moshe up to king Jehoiachin, son of King Jehoiakim, the king of Judah. He came to the throne at the age of 18 during the Chaldean invasion of Judah and reigned for three months. Forced to surrender to Nebuchadnezzar II and taken to Babylon (597 BC), along with 10,000 of his subjects. 40 years later Nebuchadnezzar died, and his successor released Jehoiachin. The Assyrians conquered the northern kingdom of Israel in 722 B.C.E. and deported the Israelites, the "Ten Lost Tribes never heard from again until the emergence of the Jewish Nation during the Romaiym (Roman) empire. "And the children of Eliyshah are the Almaniym, and they also went and built themselves cities; those are the cities situated between the mountains of Iyov and Shivathmo; and of them were the people of Lumbardiy who dwell opposite the mountains of Iyov and Shivathmo, and they conquered the land of Italia and remained there unto this day. And the children of Kittiym are the Romaiym who dwell in the valley of Kanopia by the river Tibreu. And the children of Dodaniym are those who dwell in the cities of the sea Giychon, in the land of Bordna. These are the families of the children of Japheth according to their cities and languages, when scattered after the tower, and they called their cities after their names and occurrences; and these are the names of all their cities according to their families, which they built in those days after the tower" YASHAR (JASHER) 10:15-18 את CEPHER.

The demise of the northern kingdom of Israel was a longish affair, lasting from 734 B.C.E. to the conquest of the capital at Samaria in 722 B.C.E. and its reconquest in 720 B.C.E. And, though the deportation of the Israelites began with the early Assyrian campaigns in 734–732 B.C.E. it continued until at least 715 B.C.E. With the Israelites being in exile and enslaved by so many different nations and tongues, what happened to their original Iviry language that is a Northwest Semitic language within the Afroasiatic language of 400 languages spoken in West Asia, North Africa, the Horn of Africa, and parts of the Sahara and Sahel? "Our father Avraham dwelled with Terach his father who is from the lineage of Shem. Terach took Abram his son, and Lot the son of Haran his son's son, and Sarai his daughter in law, his son Abram's woman; and they went forth with them from Ur of the Kasdiym, to go into the land of Kenyan; and they came unto Haran and dwelt there" BERE'SHIYTH (GENESIS) 11:31 את CEPHER.

Hebrew is a regional dialect of the Canaanite languages, natively spoken by the Israelites and remained in regular use as a first language until after 200 CE and is the only Canaanite language, as well as one of only two Northwest Semitic languages, with the other being Aramaic, still spoken today. It is truthful to say that the Avraham lineage spoke the IVIRY language and was able to blend in with many kingdoms around Kush, the Mediterranean, East Asia because they understood the dialect. I encourage everyone to begin researching for themselves beyond the historical footprints of European and Western cultures taught from grades k-12 in the public educational school system. It is the benefit of individuals to suppress the truth of the existence of the sons and daughters of YA'AQOV traveling to America before the voyages of Columbus and as captives during the Transatlantic Slave Trade between the 16th and 19th centuries. Taught at an early age to look an individual of all ethnicities in the eyes when discussing a matter and to always give thanks to Yahweh before bedtime, before leaving home, and throughout the entire day. YHWH as long as I could remember was my go-to person, and this may sound like a cliche, but since my birth he has protected me from death on many occasions. I called upon Yah in distress and when something went as planned and the assignment carried out. Yah answered me in my sleep and set me down and disciplined me more than once for disobedience. I truly understand that we should never forget about millions of Chamites and Semites brought to America in fetters and chains, but Yahweh is on my side and has been with me from day one and I will not fear speaking what I learned from the Torah and leaving the past about slavery and Jim crow behind me so what can man do unto me?

What I fear is closing my eyes in death and not fully carrying out the assignments taught through divine intervention, in particular exploring and sharing the migration of my ancestral Semite tribe over two continents, the continent of Kush and the Asia Pacific continent. This is not to take away from the accomplishments of the other tribes of Noach, but we all need to reinforce our commitment to bridging ethnic divides that continue to separate ethnicities based on skin pigment to overcome divisions that increase racism and racial discrimination. For me to fully understand beyond the smoking mirrors and distractions that followed me throughout my teenage and adult years, in learning about my ancestors whose migration started in the land of Kemet and may have lived in the Asia Pacific region since at least the 7th century, I need to explore more about the Siddis in India, the Sheedis in Pakistan and the Kaffirs in Sri Lanka who are among the largest of Chamites and Semites descent. This unspoken truth not considered in public educational school doctrines because they give added evidence of the theory of Black Indians in America. The United Nations on Human Rights share these issues of pervasive racial prejudices against people of African descent and members of Asian and Pacific societies.

I have long ago shifted away from the legacies and education of colonialism and enslavement, which have kept millions of individuals from past and present generations in mental, financial, and spiritual bondage. America is not the home of my ancestral tribe, but it is the land I call home like every ethnic tribe that has come from Asia through the Bering land bridge between 30,000–12,000 years before the population of the tribes of Japheth. Little historical facts are beginning to emerge regarding Indians that were here before Columbus set his feet on American shores but Angela Walton-Raji for nearly 20 years has taken up the baton to research the Cherokee, Chickasaw, Choctaw, Creek and Seminole Nations before the U.S. Congress created the Dawes Commission, which was charged with dissolving collective tribal land ownership and allotting land to individual tribal members. In 1920, Carter G. Woodson argued the following in the Journal of Negro History: "One of the longest unwritten chapters of the history of the United States is that treating of the relations of the Negroes and the Indians." Historians have tried to write that chapter, particularly over the last five decades. Their efforts have paralleled the formation of an identity category informed by, reflective of, and at times defiant of this complex history.

While researching my family history derived from my mother's lineage I discovered many startling truths about the Indian population. The Seminole tribe roamed the territories of Florida in the 18th century, and now make up the Seminole Nation of Oklahoma, the Seminole Tribe of Florida, and the Miccosukee Tribe of Indians of Florida, as well as independent groups. The Seminole people appeared in a process of ethnogenesis who settled in the early 1700s, most significantly northern Muscogee Creeks from what are now Georgia and Alabama. The word "Seminole" derived from the Creek word *simanó-li*. This translated as "frontiersman", "outcast", "runaway", "separatist." The Seminole identify as *yat'siminoli* or "free people" because for centuries their ancestors had successfully resisted efforts to subdue or convert them to Roman Catholicism. They signed several treaties with the U.S. government, including the Treaty of Moultrie Creek, and the Treaty of Paynes Landing.

As a producer of both music and film, I have found myself discouraged with Hollywood and funding available to produce projects beyond slavery themes or civil rights films currently licensed to Black film directors. We can easily produce storylines of the African guides and translators of the colonial era who became valued contacts with Indigenous peoples, while we change the narrative of Black history. Take for example the African and Indian alliance known as the Pueblo revolt of 1680 that ended Spain's rule of the southwest for a dozen years and shed light on Francisco Menendez and the 1738 Black Indian community that defended its liberty in Florida against British incursions and describes the Lowry Gang in North Carolina that fought the Civil War Confederacy and then battled the KKK. History defined as his-story and many times not factual when it comes to the lineage of tribes from the Cham and Semite kingdoms. Our migration and exile from our place of origin began with disobedience and idolatry but does not have to continue via ignorance. Since the Proclamation of Emancipation, we have expired the chains and fetters from around the necks and feet of individuals, but the disparities exist. Today, millions are still in poverty and hopelessness while religious denominations pray to a deity that will not rescue or lift them from idolatrous practices. Every year the murder, drug addiction, and prison incarceration rate increase while babies are born and educated under the exact circumstances as their parents.

As a parent and grandparent of beautiful children that deserve an opportunity to experience a life full of righteousness and unity, I must continue to seek redemption for all the children of patriarch Avraham. "Then hear from the heavens, even from your dwelling place, and do according to all that the stranger calls to you for; that all people of the earth may know your name, and fear you, as do your people, Yashar'el, and may know that this house which I have built is called by your name. If your people go out to war against their enemies that you shall send them, and they pray unto you toward this city which you have chosen, and the house which I have built for your name; Then hear from the heavens their prayer and their supplication and support their cause. If they sin against you, (for there is no man which sins not,) and you be angry with them, and deliver them over before their enemies, and they carry them away captives unto a land far off or near; Yet if they bethink themselves in the land whither they are carried captive, and turn and pray unto you in the land of their captivity, saying, We have sinned, we have done amiss, and have dealt wickedly; If they return to you with all their heart and with all their soul in the land of their captivity, whither they have carried them captives, and pray toward their land, which you gave unto their fathers, and toward the city which you have chosen, and toward the house which I have built for your name" DIVREI HAYAMIYM SHENIY (2 CHRONICLES) 6:33-38 את CEPHER

MIGRATION OR CAPTIVITY LINKS

ready-for-a-linguistic-controversy-say-mhmm/ Generations_of_Noah/ *Historical Textbook and Atlas of Biblical Geography* by Lyman Coleman/ egyptian-gods-and-goddesses/ study/manual/old-testament-student-manual-kings-malachi/enrichment/ people-african-descent-asia-and-pacific/ /an-ancestry-of-african-native-americans/ history-identity-theory

NOTES:

OFFERINGS AND ASCENDING SMOKE

"There I beheld the Ancient of Days, whose head was like white wool, and with him another, whose countenance resembled that of man. His countenance was full of grace, like one of the holy angels. Then I inquired of one of the angels, who went with me, and who showed me every secret thing, concerning this Son of A'dam; who he was; whence he was and why he went with the Ancient of

Days. He answered and said to me: This is the Son of A'dam, to whom righteousness belongs; with whom righteousness has dwelt; and who will reveal all the treasures of that concealed: for Yahweh Tseva'oth has chosen him; and his part has surpassed all before Yahweh Tseva'oth in everlasting uprightness. This Son of A'dam, whom you behold, shall raise up kings and the mighty from their dwelling places, and the powerful from their thrones; shall loosen the bridles of the powerful, and break in pieces the teeth of sinners. He shall hurl kings from their thrones and their dominions; because they will not exalt and praise him, nor humble themselves before him, by whom their kingdoms granted to them. The countenance likewise of the mighty shall he cast down, filling them with confusion. Darkness shall be their habitation, and worms shall be their bed; nor from that their bed shall they hope raised, because they exalted not the name of Yahweh Tseva'oth. They shall condemn the stars of heaven, shall lift their hands against El Elyon, shall tread upon and inhabit the earth, showing all their acts of iniquity, even their works of iniquity. Their strength shall be in their riches, and their faith in the Elohim whom they have formed with their own hands. They shall deny the name of Yahweh Tseva'oth and driven from the houses of his assembly, and of the faithful who suffer in the name of Yahweh Tseva'oth" CHANOK 46:1-6

If you are still with me and beginning to have questions about what you have read up to this point? Thank you. This book titled "Let It Make Sense" was written to spark the fuse within your cerebellum to hit the clutch and put your reasoning in second gear so you can distance yourself and your kinfolks far from the fallacy that continues to empower network news outlets, and mainstream theology. This has been a journey of enlightenment that has increased harmonic balance within my life, family structure, and overall rectitude that was once moving in contradiction and idiocy.

This chapter, I must admit, gave me pause, but only for a moment, because loyalty is the highest level from the laws of the universe that someone can achieve upon their journey of enlightenment. Loyalty defines your integrity, steadfastness, values, and dauntlessness. We can effectuate affection and benevolence towards individuals depending upon our mood swings, but loyalty is instinctive within our ruach. During my teenage years, my allegiance tested when law enforcement was locking individuals up under the Rico act. Tried during the preliminary stages of us setting up our independent recording company. With every opportunity presented, it meant defying the Torah and cutting a covenant with individuals who became a snare and distraction at the time. Even the religious denominations that require your devotion to ideologies of Neoplatonism set up by Western culture and influenced by the Roman Empire in the late 4th century are in stark contrast with Monotheism. The hustle game wanted me to get rich while corrupting my community with narcotics and criminal activities. The entertainment industry wanted us to glorify the hustle game with music and videos that are degrading to women and increase stereotypes that are harmful to residents in urban communities. Even religion muted when musicians within the hip hop and rock genre have displayed Hellenistic altars, sacrilegious images, and props like Asherah poles. Let us be candid, the entertainment industry demands loyalty from those upgraded like major figures in the streets.

Conspiracy theorists believe that the world economy, media, and politics controlled by only a few families who communicate through secret signs and mainstream music and movies. The YouTube and Instagram platforms are inundated with theorists who say that members of secret political and religious organizations communicate through song lyrics and hand signals to relay secret messages. They reiterate that the fallen ruachoth with various names in religion like The Devil, Satan, Lucifer, Beelzebub, Mephistopheles is in control because of the bible passages like "Therefore rejoice, ye heavens, and ye that dwell in them. Woe to the inhibitors of the earth and of the sea! for the devil has come down unto you, having great wrath, because he knows that he has but a brief time. And when the dragon saw cast unto the earth, he persecuted the woman which brought forth the male child. And to the woman given two wings of a great eagle, that she might fly into the wilderness, into her place, nourished for a time, and times, and half a time, from the face of the serpent" Chizayon (Revelation) 12:12-14.

They honestly believe that Satan appears often as a character in literature and various other media, beginning in the 6th century when the Council of Constantinople officially recognized Satan as part of their belief system. These conspiracy theorists who are constantly on social media platforms highlighting superstars such as Beyoncé, Black Sabbath, Madonna, Zeppelin guitarist, Jimmy Page, Doja Cat, Lil Nas X, three 6 Mafia, Lil Uzi Vert, and Playboi Carti, are trying to create a new world order by brainwashing new generations. The singer, Beyonce's song that was meant to address female empowerment was a recruitment call of action to join dark forces many have said. "Let me upgrade you, flip a new page, introduce you to some new things, and upgrade you, I can (up), can I? (Up), let me, upgrade you, Partner, let me upgrade you, upgrade you."

In my opinion, the song pleads for allegiance between a man and women but the Torah says For you shall worship no other El, for Yahweh Qanna is my name, he is a jealous El, Lest you cut a covenant with the inhabitants of the land, and they go a whoring after their Elohim, and do sacrifice unto their Elohim, and one call you, and you eat of his sacrifice, And take of their daughters unto your sons, and their daughters go a whoring after their Elohim, and make your sons go a whoring after their Elohim. King Shalomah warned about shifting his allegiance from the creator to other deities and the Bible chronicles the outcome of his shift. You cannot buy loyalty or put it on or take it off as you would do a jacket when the weather changes.

Children's attachment is towards our maternal parents, especially mothers that fed and cared for us during our infancy stage, but it is our dad who had the duty of training, protecting, and molding our psyche to be prepared for the next phase of our growth. Though my mother did the best she could while fleeing from an abusive relationship, it was my grandmother that introduced my brother and me to the Bible and this is where the story begins. Children's thoughts of loyalty and fortitude were never imagined and after stumbles and setbacks during my life, to now being able to talk about fidelity without fear and boundaries is therapeutic. To have this opportunity through my writings to declare the episodes of my defiance created by the harsh reality of rebellion that was volitional.

Since I began working on this book, I must be transparent of my enthusiastic pursuit of gratifications of the flesh during a period that saw urban and suburban youth murdered and incarcerated during the crack cocaine epidemic. My allegiance shifted, after seeing the other side of the perspective not spoken of in prior church sermons. Taught that Yahweh Elohim formed the man of the dust of the ground and breathed into his nostrils the breath of life, and the man became a living soul, but the homily that temptations were constantly knocking at the door waiting on the theocratic benighted to open was never a recurring theme. I never imagined that I would fall victim to smoking mirrors and illusions of grandeur from the tree of unrighteousness and offering myself as a willing participant in the garden created by the serpent. It was the spiraling effect of a downward trajectory that many experienced during that era. The offerings and pleasures of insurgency during my youth faded expeditiously, which left memories of regret and chastity destroyed. And Yahweh Elohim commanded the man, saying, of every tree of the garden you may freely eat, but of the tree of the knowledge of good and evil, you shall not eat of it, for in the day that you eat thereof you shall surely die, and I have witnessed disillusionment while reaching for the stars while dwelling in Sheol.

I can say that the tower of Babel that is yet discovered by archeology, was rightly displayed since the founding of Antebellum America, on the currency emboldened with the aphorism, "In God We Trust". During the Civil War, however, in response to increased religious fervor, Congress passed legislation to allow for the motto used on coins. The Church which is meant to be the embodiment of Chokmah (wisdom), integrity, faith, and reasoning, staying upright as ambassadors of theology to teach humanity that there exists in pleasure a malicious disposition, which is the most multiform of all the affections. "In the soul it is arrogance, and love of money, and vaingloriousness, and contention, and faithlessness, and the evil eye. In the body it is greediness and gormandizing, and solitary gluttony. As pleasure and pain are, therefore, two growths of the body and the soul, so there are many offshoots of these passions" Reviy`iy (4 Maccabees) 1:25-28.

In my estimation, the church has chosen the riches of the world, since the separation of British rule and have pledged allegiance to money that creates idolatry over the duties as priests of the Ha' Mashiach. Beloved, when I gave all diligence to write unto you of the common salvation, it was needful for me to write unto you and exhort you that ye should earnestly contend for the faith delivered unto the qodeshiym. For there are certain men crept in unawares, who were before of old ordained to this condemnation, wicked men, turning the grace of our Elohim into lasciviousness, and denying the only Adonai Elohim, and our Adonai Yahusha Ha'Mashiach. "I will therefore put you in remembrance, though ye once knew this, how that Yahuah, having saved the people out of the land of Mitsrayim, afterward destroyed them that believed not. And the angels which did not guard their first estate, but left their own habitation, he has reserved in everlasting chains under darkness unto the judgment of the momentous day.

Even Cedom and Amorah, and the cities about them in like manner, giving themselves over to fornication, and going after strange flesh, are set forth for an example, suffering the vengeance of eternal fire" Yahudah (Jude) 1:3-7. I am speaking now to all parishioners and believers of an unseen spiritual power greater than the offerings and ascending smoke of humankind. Evaluate your loyalty, which is not the riches and fame that become void when you leave this earth, but the redemption of your soul measured against the trust of the god of this world. You will find that your soul is worth more than the currency that the mint could print up. "My own feeling in the matter is due to my very firm conviction that to put such a motto on coins, or to use it in any kindred manner, not only does no good, but does positive harm, and is in effect irreverence, which comes dangerously close to sacrilege. Any use which tends to cheapen it, and any use which tends to secure treated in a spirit of levity, is from every standpoint profoundly regretted. It seems to me eminently unwise to cheapen such a motto by use on coins. In all my life I have never heard any human being speak reverently of this motto on the coins or show any signs of its having appealed to any high emotion in him, but I have, hundreds of times, heard it used as an occasion of and incitement to sneering. Everyone must remember the innumerable cartoons and articles based on phrases like 'In God we trust for the 8 cents,' Surely, I am well within bounds when I say that a use of the phrase which invites constant levity of this type is most undesirable." - President Theodore Roosevelt, 13 November 1907.

Trust, and its enduring companion, loyalty, give us strength when we are feeling down and motivate us to stick to the causes and by the people that matter most. We are going to continue this chapter, which examines the definition of loyalty and the offerings and ascending smoke that many have knowingly or unconsciously enslaved themselves to idolatry. Out of love for the ruach within each man and woman that pleads to breathe and not suffocate from the corrupt teachings of the Watchers. The brother or sister who peers beyond skin pigment but trapped in the traditions and separatism of the world. The religious convert whose faith tested daily within their own household, place of work, and congregation. "When I was a child, I spoke as a child, I understood as a child, I thought as a child: but when I became a man, I put away childish things. For now, we see through a glass, darkly; but then face to face: now I know in part; but then shall I know even as also I am known. And now abides faith, hope, love, these three; but the greatest of these is love" Qorintiym Ri'shon (1 Corinthians) 13:11-13.

My career as longshoreman, requires an oath when I reached A status to uphold the union standards of brotherhood and labor. The concept of loyalty is an unbreakable bond set between two people or more that signifies allegiance, commitment, constancy, dedication, devotedness, faith, and steadfastness, by offering your energy, time, and resources to fulfill an oath or pledge in exchange for spiritual enlightenment, career ascent, or financial prosperity. Many have executed all the qualities of loyalty that either used for dwelling in the light or tiptoeing in the darkness. My allegiance during my swearing in was to a specific organization or group to advance the goals and agenda of said group, which equates to my unwavering efforts to accomplish the goal of Daniel J. Keefe, a tugboat worker on the West Coast that founded a longshore union on the Great Lakes in 1877 and served as president of the International Longshoremen's Association (ILA) from 1892 to 1909. In 1933, Harry Bridges, an Australian-born American union leader, considered a founder of longshore unions, led the formation of the ILA to unionize West Coast dockworkers.

In 1937, he helped set up the International Longshore and Warehouse Union (ILWU) by merging several chapters of the ILA, expanding membership to include warehouse workers. Bridges served as president of the ILWU from 1937 until his retirement in 1977. He was a prominent labor leader who influenced US trade unionism but was often at odds with conservatives in the labor movement and criticized by employers and government officials. Bridges was also a Marxist and ardent supporter of the Soviet Union. He died in San Francisco in 1990 at the age of 88, this was six years before I entered the industry. Before joining ILWU Local 10, it was all about me and what I was going through. I went from hustling as a street pharmacist to having a career with excellent benefits and I still was unsatisfied.

Whoever said money brings happiness was either born into extreme wealth or just saying that to push their own narrative. When accustomed to setting your own rules and not being accountable to anyone but yourself, there is a transition period where you either adjust to fit the strategy or cause disruption and disqualify yourself from reaching a higher status. I chose to do it my way like Frank Sinatra and for fifteen years, it was a rocky road of self-inflicted wounds because I continued fostering the rebellious mindset that I had during my youth. My Solipsistic and assumptive behavior before the accident was appalling because it was either my way or letting the back door hit you where YHWH split you. This is the sole reason I passed up on career promotions, membership with industry groups, and incessant invites to parties and exclusives. I did not fit in with their agenda because my ruach was priceless and sodomy was out of the question. *Was I apoplectic?* I could not party like a rock star. Hell to the naw, naw, naw.

After the motorcycle accident, I have been on a continuous introspection, taking heed to the ruach for tutelage of the enigmas of the universe. Now I have come to realize that the journey can be daunting at times trying to reach enlightenment while rebranding myself. My wife still sees the old Gabriel and character flaws that altered my paths while loyal to disobedience, but now I can look back over the years at previous setbacks, and sing the Kenny Rogers lyrics "If I knew then what I know now, If I knew then, you'd be here right now, I'd trade the world and its gold, to have and to hold, The one thing in life I love. If I knew then, oh, what I know now, we would never have drifted apart. If I had only taken your dream and made it part of mine, If I knew then, oh, what I know now."

My redemption was not derived from the words or the offerings of man but from the divine intervention of the creator of the universe. Many that survived urban warfare, both physical and psychological, know what I am talking about. Once the memories have cleared away and the trials and tribulations are in the rear view, you can begin to reflect on the life you have created for yourself.

I have lived life like a Donald Goines novel, a Martin Scorsese film, and a TBN special. I must pay homage to West Coast rap lyrics for keeping me grounded. Artists that kept it real like 2pac, NWA, Too Short, E-40, Infamou$, Digital Underground, Master P, Spice 1, MC Hammer, Richie Rich, RBL Posse, Mac Dre, Mr. Fab, and Keek da Sneak. These are the artists not compromised or hijacked in secret meetings and freak-offs. I am still breathing and climbing because of my urban training in both Oakland, California and Houston, Texas. While many have thrown shade at the genre, because of the bubble gum lyrics, and questionable sexuality of rappers today, this was the music of the nineties on the west coast, speaking to a generation of teenagers harassed daily by law enforcement, while attending funerals of friends and family murdered by gang violence and calamitous crack cocaine wars. Unlike the early days of the Italian Mafia that controlled the underworld with an iron fist and put loyalty as their number one code of ethics for survival, many individuals in urban areas were treacherous among their peers and only allegiance was to vendors and law enforcement as confidential informants. Like the civil rights movement of the sixties, people were on the government payroll and doing more harm than good. As a teenager, enthralled with the gifts received for shedding the blood of man, working stealthily to increase impunity for my activities, not considering that even Baphomet lives without judgment.

This is the era that DMX released "It's Dark and Hell is Hot " and the whole album was bananas. I kept this album in the CD player the entire summer because the lyrics to Damien spoke to the vibe that my brother and I were experiencing trying to get a break in the music industry. "Why is it every move I make turns out to be a bad one? Where is my guardian angel? Need one, wish I had one" Everyone has choices from the time they begin to learn right from wrong and the moves we were making to push our records were not always legal in any sense of the word. There were several occasions while getting No Mercy Entertainment off the ground floor, that we ignored the principle of the law by claiming we were in ignorance of the law. We knew that our actions are not an excuse for evil or improper behavior, or a defense to many of the situations we were involved in. I have sat many times in the courtroom and listened to defendants plead that they did not know their actions were illegal, even if they were honestly unaware that they were breaking the law. I was inadvertently pledging allegiance with culture vultures in the entertainment industry and wholesale market whose deities did not align with the deity I have come to know as the Creator of all humanity and the giver of righteousness and reasoning.

We were independently pushing a hard line, making all the wrong moves, trying to make a million dollars, while swimming upstream among a school of piranha feasting on minnows and guppies. I have seen people run out of boardrooms with pants around their ankles from thinking these sons and daughters of Japheth were soft. Musicians and most independent companies producing and distributing projects causing the earth to sin, found themselves dropped and discarded because loyalty is like contracts from major recording labels, improvident and worthless. When I say that loyalty to the Alpha and Omega is not always easy, and we make daily offerings unbeknownst to various demons, principalities and Western esoteric traditions is an understatement. Our team would rather earn a hard nickel than an easy dollar by taking presents or gifts for the sacrifice of a son or daughter of A'dam in an industry that requires devotedness, and blood for blood.

People on social media are now telling horror stories about the music industry, both secular and religious, because they both intertwine on various levels. Few people that have signed up and whose escapades videotaped as insurance for their silence will ever stop walking in idolatry because they have grown accustomed to the pleasures and lifestyle of Dionysus. It is almost impossible to ask a teenager or young adult that has all the trappings of Baphomet to follow sound reasoning of the Cepher when it is not profitable, and tangible compared to the offerings given by the gatekeepers of the world. You will get better results striking a peace deal between Palestinians and Ashkenazi Jews for eternity. They do not want to hear from the hypocrites who preach to them that darkness will never prevail over light and that Jesus may save you from every kind of death. Any rapper hitting the charts knows the power of a PR campaign and how alcohol and women will make men of understanding fall away. Married couples and entertainment are strange bed partners and those that cleave to harlots will become impudent.

How many celebrities in your generation have suddenly perished or died from drugs and now moths and worms shall have them to heritage? Nobody is immune from controversy while throwing criticism at elites and a bold man or woman taken away or silenced. Loyal friend is rare in the entertainment business, since loyalty is very shallow, and individuals are hasty to give credit and light-minded because their own indiscretions and sins shall offend their own soul. From charges of pedophilia to the Me-Too Movement, whoso takes pleasure in wickedness condemned, but he that resists pleasures crowns his life. There are levels in both corridors of righteousness and unrighteousness and those that can rule their tongue shall live without strife, and those that hate babbling shall have less evil. This is the commandment I learned early but these new industry plants do not have elders; but have PR firms and found themselves in constant turmoil because of their lyrics and antics. Whether it be to friend or foe, talk not of other men's lives; and if you can without offense, reveal them not. For he heard and saw you, and when time comes, he will hate you. People love to hear gossip and watch a train wreck unfold. If you have heard a word, let it die with you, and be bold, it will not burst you.

I have often wondered who raised these new gangster rappers that indict themselves in felonies during studio sessions. There is a fool that travails with a word, as a woman in labor of a child. As an arrow that sticks in a man's thigh, so is a word within a fool's belly. The world has turned into a dog-eat-dog world that has lost the moral compass of its ancestors, and now humanity has become less sensitive to the moral breakdown of western society. Examine the major network news pundits and how they throw colleagues under the bus for a news scoop or interview. Politicians who were once members or leaders of the clergy seen within a political party corrupted the most. Admonish a friend, he has not done it, and if he has done it, that he does it no more. Admonish your friend, for he has not said it, and if he has, that he speaks it not again. Admonish a friend, for many times it is a slander and not believe every tale. There is one that slips in his speech, but not from his heart, and who are they who has not offended with their tongue? The urban parable "Game is told and not sold" speaks volumes to living a life beyond the smoking mirrors and paparazzi cameras.

Raised in Oakland, Ca where young hyenas are born daily, it has always been my character to stay in my own lane. Admonish your neighbor before you threaten him, and not being angry, give place to the Torah of El Elyon. The fear of Yahuah is the first step accepted by him, and wisdom obtains his love. The knowledge of the commandments of Yahuah is the doctrine of life, and those that do things that please him shall receive the fruit of the tree of immortality. We are now living in the matrix controlled by families that have an agenda of control and manipulation. Every few years they show how they will disrupt the system via banking, health, education, government, and entertainment. During the Covid epidemic, people lived in fear from a worldwide plague broadcasted daily on every news channel. The worst of an individual's character exposed when banned from their daily activities that seemed un-American. These individuals rebelled against the government for banning their interstate travel or indulging in recreational activities with their family. These law-abiding citizens that mocked the rights of individuals outside their political party, were now acting in disobedience to the law and order they vowed to live by. Fueled by school closures, potential stock market crash, increase within urban voting districts, pandemonium unleashed, and the state Capitol breached. The same individuals who voted for strict prison sentences for Black and brown citizens, were now feeling the unequal rights that millions of Americans were dealing with daily. While citizens in urban communities were already grappling with unemployment for decades and exuberant interest rates, the Covid pandemic brought systematic racism to the front door of middle-class America.

Churches were no longer worshiping in their denominations but via Skype and social media. Patriotism tested and the fear of violations to the constitution was on the rise. Though uncertainty was sweeping across the entire world, the fear of Yahuah is all wisdom, and in all wisdom is the performance of the Torah, and the knowledge of his omnipotence. Raised in both the church and the underworld of criminality, my offerings are the words that I speak, and the actions implemented from my heart. If I profess to be an emissary of the Most High El and say to my adoniy, I will not do as it dis-pleases you, though afterward I do it, I stand in contrite of my pledge and angers him that nourishes me. The knowledge of wickedness is not wisdom if I prolong in wickedness, neither at any time the counsel of sinners, prudence if I listen to them. There is wickedness in disloyalty, and the same an abomination, and there is a fool wanting in wisdom. He that has small understanding, and fears Elohim, is better than one that has much wisdom, and transgresses the Torah of El Elyon. SIRACH 19:2-24.

There is an undeniable contradiction with pledging allegiance to the world and most discourses heard every Sunday in religious denominations. The first contradiction I hear spewed from the mouth of most Evangelicals and pulpit preachers is the ministry of prosperity, and it is better to give a love offering blessed for your generosity, than have the house of God dwell in poverty. How many times did you see the ushers collect the tithes and offerings, and you had second thoughts of giving all you had for the week? How many times did you feel it was your duty to give a sin offering to the church because the preacher compelled you to do so? How much better is it to get wisdom than gold! and to get understanding rather than silver! The creator of the heavens does not need wealth created by man, but wealth built by wisdom, devotion, love, unity, and uprightness.

The highway of the Yashariym is to leave from evil, he that keeps his way guards his soul. There are charlatans and wolves taking courses in public speaking and psychology to deceive parishioners by using scripted messages and memorized bible scriptures. They shall condemn the stars of heaven, who lift their hands against El Elyon, shall tread upon and inhabit the earth, showing all their acts of iniquity, even their works of iniquity. Their strength shall be in their riches, and their faith in the Elohim whom they have formed with their own hands. They shall deny the name of Yahuah Tseva'oth and driven from the houses of his assembly, and of the faithful who suffer in the name of Yahuah Tseva'oth. Chanok (Enoch) 46:5-6.

We have discussed topics ranging from alliances to patriotism. I wrote about the offerings given to individuals that seek fame and prestige in industries known to create egotistical behavior. We saw the blatant hypocrisy of religious denominations and how they align themselves with politics and secular entertainment. The inspiration for this chapter derived from me looking at TV programs, and being outside among the public and thinking, I cannot be the only one seeing this craziness. Throughout my experiences and journeys around righteous and unrighteous circles I have been steadfast in my beliefs that never compromise your integrity, there is no turning back. Beware that you forget not Yahuah Elohayka, in not guarding his commandments, and his judgments, and his statutes, while you are chasing that all mighty dollar. It may have the inscription "In god we trust" but to whom are you coveting and giving adulation? The ministry that delivers the sermon of opulence and supporting an autonomous ruach, or the ministry that warns you about not trading your morality for the treasures of the world.

The difficulty of not conforming to this world is the temptations and pleasures bombarded with daily. The erotic pictures and videos of women popping up on social media. The music and movies with

Debauchery, carnage, acquisitiveness that alters the mind of youth from all ethnicities. From the time of my youth, I have seen disillusionment take shape within the business of spirituality. Along with the continuous reminiscence of slavery that reminds Black people they are second class citizens in America, the theology created to control captives under Japheth oppression has not made urban communities safe. The religious denominations that demand parishioners to pledge allegiance to Jesus, Jehovah, or a deity created from the Roman diocese considered to have been founded by Jesus Christ around 30 A.D. Mainstream religious denominations' principal ideologies and hierarchy can be traced back to Emperor Constantine who established the church's rights and became the official religion of the Roman Empire. The church's position defined during the Council of Trent (1545–63) when the Church of England forced by its monarchs and elites to break away from the authority of the pope and the Catholic Church. These events were part of the religious and political movement that affected the practice of Christianity in Western and Central Europe.

To control constituents from thoughts of uprisings and Exodus, the Negro Bible distributed among the *British West-India Islands* in 1807 from passages of 1611 King James Rendition. The Roman Empire and lineage of Japheth has broken away from the Noachian theory of theology to set up a kingdom with domination in 2024 of over 1.39 billion baptized parishioners worldwide. With Bishops acting like kings within their territory with wealth and influence, I saw satanic imprints that have not transformed the renewing of the mind, that parishioners may prove what is good, and acceptable, and perfect, will of Elohim. Instead, politicians and the clergy have allowed every man that is among you, to think of himself more highly than he ought to think. How can a convert think soberly, as Elohim has dealt to every man the measure of faith, when religious denominations have allowed satanic principles and corruption to infiltrate their membership. For as we have many members in one body that attempts to restore the Avraham covenant, and all members have not the same office that brings all converts to repentance, so we, being many, are one body in Mashiach, and everyone has a duty as members to heal one of another of unrighteousness. Having then gifts differing according to the grace given to us, whether prophecy, let us prophesy according to the proportion of faith, or ministry, let us build on our ministering effectively, or he that teaches, on teaching that differs from the fleshly reasoning of the world.

The scriptures do not restrict him from ruling, if it is with diligence, and to show mercy, with cheerfulness. Let love be without dissimulation. Abhor that which is evil, cleave to that which is good. Be kindly affectioned one to another with brotherly love, in honor preferring one another. Not slothful in business, fervent in the ruach, serving Yahuah. In God we trust have dissipated those illiterates in theology to display loyalty when they have eaten and are full of offerings of unrighteous smoke, and have built goodly houses, and dwelt there. If your congregation does not warn parishioners to be on guard when their silver and gold multiplied, and all that you have multiplied, flee from the grips of the kingdom of Babylon. Then your heart lifted, and you forget Yahuah Elohayka, which brought you forth out of the land of Mitsrayim, from the house of bondage, both spiritual and physical. Who led you through that great and terrible wilderness, wherein were fiery serpents that try to poison the word of YHWH, and scorpions that pierce through the heart and mind of converts, and droughts that have left billions of parishioners dying of moral and spiritual thirsts.

Where there was no water because of idolatry that makes you forget who brought you forth water out of the rock of flint. Who fed you in the wilderness with manna, which your fathers knew not, that he might humble you, and that he might prove you, to do you good at your latter end. Wealth has opportunities to enrich and save those in need but warn individuals to never say in your heart, my power and the might of my hand has gotten me this wealth. "But you shall remember Yahuah Elohayka, for it is he who gives you power to get wealth, that he may set up his covenant, which he swore seven oaths unto your fathers, as it is this day. And it shall be, if you do at all forget Yahuah Elohayka, and walk after other Elohim, and serve them, and worship them, I testify against you this day that ye shall surely perish. As the nations which Yahuah destroys before your face, so shall ye perish, because ye would not be obedient unto the voice of Yahuah Elohaykem. Pride goes before destruction, and a haughty ruach before a fall. Better it is to be of a humble ruach with the lowly, than to divide the spoil with the proud" Mishlei (Proverbs) 16:15-19.

Poverty has transformed many to become beasts preying on the misfortunes of others. Wealth has proved a mindset of superiority and separation from faith that builds strong moral and upright reasoning. By keeping your eyes wide open and fixated on truth instead of smoking mirrors is important to name the extremes. The Iviry scriptures chronicled the lineage of Avraham having financial means proven from faith and loyalty, but there is a poverty mindset that believes Christians should be poor. This has affected converts in urban communities who have a poverty mindset set up by bishops with wealth and influence. Too many parishioners rely on sermons that plead for them to wait on a Javan inspired deity to solve their worrisome mental, and improvised state. We listen to conservatives and liberal politicians that are diminishing rights of low- and middle-class citizens who typically end up with too few resources that alter their current lifestyle.

The main motivation behind this gospel is to advance an individual's own will and wellbeing. Money and religion are delicate subjects that many are afraid to discuss, especially individuals taught that the two kept separate. If the creator gives us reasoning to understand the laws of the universe, it makes sense for all to gain Chokmah on allegiance and offerings beneficial for our spiritual well-being. And Yahusha said unto him: "Why do you call me good? None is good, save one, that is, Elohim. You know the commandments, do not break wedlock, do not kill, do not steal, do not bear false witness, Honor your father and your mother. And he said: All these have I kept from my youth up. Now when Yahusha heard these things, he said unto him: Yet lack you one thing: sell all that you have, and distribute unto the poor, and you shall have treasure in heaven: and come, follow me. And when he heard this, he was very sorrowful: for he was extraordinarily rich. And when Yahusha saw that he was very sorrowful, he said: How hardly shall they that have riches enter the Kingdom of Elohim! For it is easier for a rope to go through a needle's eye, than for a rich man to enter the Kingdom of Elohim. And they that heard it said: Who then saved? And he said: The things which are impossible with men are possible with Elohim." LUQAS 18:19-27.

Now this chapter was not to confuse but enlighten you and warn them which cause divisions and offenses loyal only to their check and savings balances. There are many idolatry practices among humankind contrary to the doctrine which ye have learned and avoid them with proper reasoning. To distance themselves from an improvised lifestyle, individuals have pledged allegiance to deities and groups that serve not our Adonai Yahusha Ha'Mashiach, but their own belly. The light has become darkened and by good words and fair speeches deceive the hearts of the simple. The power and influences of satanic principles are clearer on mainstream platforms than ever before and have infiltrated all major industries worldwide. Now longer is the reasoning of uprightness and morality hidden and understood by a few, but the obedience to continue a lifestyle that separates the flesh and ruach has come unto all men. I am glad therefore on your behalf that you have continued to take this journey with us to be wise unto that which is good and reject loyalty concerning evil.

LINKS

celebrities-associated-with-the-occult/

NOTES:

CONTINUOUS SEEDS UPON THE EARTH

"And I will prove my covenant with you; neither shall all flesh be cut off anymore by the waters of a flood; neither shall there anymore be a flood to destroy the earth. And Elohim said, this is the sign of the covenant which I make between me and you and every living creature that is with you, for perpetual generations: I do set my bow in the cloud, and it shall be for a sign of a covenant between me and the earth. And it shall come to pass, when I bring a cloud over the earth, that the bow shall be seen in the cloud: And I will remember my covenant, which is between me and you and every living creature of all flesh; and the waters shall no longer become a flood to destroy all flesh. And the bow shall be in the cloud; and I will look upon it, that I may remember the everlasting covenant between Elohim and every living creature of all flesh that is upon the earth" BERE'SHIYTH (GENESIS) 9:11-16 את CEPHER.

The above scripture is a covenant from the Most High ELOHIM to never get medieval on humanity again and wipe everyone off the soil for evil deeds. This was the climate change the first earth age generated by rebelliousness of both Chauh and A'dam. The Merriam-Webster Dictionary and Thesaurus defines climate; A region of the earth having specified climatic conditions and the prevailing influence or environmental conditions characterizing a group or period. The above account enlightened readers about the atmosphere catalyzed between the forces of light and darkness, culminating in a necessary diagnosis of severe consequences that would forever change the relationship of moral and spiritual beings.

For anyone that ever-attended Sunday School, this was the second most studied story from the Bible. There continues to be speculation on the writing of BERE'SHIYTH between 15th and 13th centuries BCE, while others believe written between 1450 and 1400 BCE. Nous generalities help those who read or study the first chapters of BERE'SHIYTH understand what truth, speculation or myth is. It is our human nature to analyze everything for accuracy and verify if these concepts or theories are foreign to our reasoning. The proverb that "if something sounds too good it might not be" is not always the case in situations when a profound outcome becomes beneficial to your mental, spiritual, physical, and financial prosperity. I have learned to build upon my Faith by not what I can see but the testimony of the before and after. The examination of my earlier lifestyle as a person on trial interrogated and inducted by the lead prosecutor, Aza'zel.

Everything of idolatry or myth contrived or formed by the thoughts or hands of man, but the authentication of the flood verified by the rainbow that appears for all humanity to see. Our awareness of the image of a rainbow denotes good sense because though we cannot touch a rainbow, we perceive that it exists because we can see it. I can gaze at the moon or feel the warmth of the sun, but when I saw a rainbow for the first time, it was breathtaking to see one of the most admired meteorological phenomena that directly points to the existence of a spiritual Creator. My rudimentary understanding while seeing such a phenomenon allowed me to rationally contemplate that there must be some truth in the tale of the Noachian flood. The writers of the bible may have stretched the tale of Samson, but hearing a biblical story of A'dam and Chuah rebellion made me fully engaged in the Torah. It was not until I beheld the visual account of the flood and chronicles of human/ruachoth coitus, that the natural disaster of this size began to register with my consciousness. The impact of death displayed on canvas was more insightful than the sermon preached on TV by the televangelist. This is not to diminish their theories or interpretation of one of the most horrific stories from antiquity, but my understanding and explanation of divine punishment accentuated by the painter's rendition of the holocaust.

Atheists can try to disprove various writings within the scriptures, but rainbows are not from the creation of man but when light from the sun scattered by water droplets through a process called refraction. Refraction occurs when the light from the sun changes direction when passing through a medium denser than air, such as a raindrop. Once the refracted light enters the raindrop, reflected off the back and then refracted again as it exits and travels to our eyes. For me, seeing a phenomenon mentioned in the Torah is a source of knowledge and reasoning opposed to speculation or mythology that I have accepted as truth because of emotion. There are many things from antiquity that are difficult to explain or that science is yet to prove existed, like the Garden of Eden that explorers have yet to find, or the vessel whereabouts that Noach and his family used. There are so many mysterious places and events unexplained in books of the Cepher that had me at one time questioning their accuracy.

Is it a myth that a rebellious cherub used a serpent to beguile Chuah to disobey the command from the Creator to not eat from a certain tree? Do cherubs stay in front of the tree of life guarding against trespassing? Was A'dam and Chuah created in the appearance of angels and thus naked, but their evil deed ushered in pain and suffering and became mortal? From my estimation, the definition of evil must be based on the knowledge that an individual fully can choose right from wrong and understands the consequences of their actions. A'dam and Chuah warned and sinned based on a lie and defied righteous reasoning for companionship. The Concept of sin involves the knowledge of immoral and unrepentant behavior from individuals capable of making independent decisions, which sets up pain and suffering upon yourself or others. When I had inappropriate thoughts or envisioned misfortune on individuals that upset me, I never considered those actions evil. Though I did regret having those inclinations in my head and asked for forgiveness, evil must involve the desire to inflict significant harm mentally, spiritually, or physically on an individual without moral justification.

There were times working on film or music projects that I wanted to dog walk individuals that played with my emotions. I dismissed those acts of retribution from manifesting in my heart quickly because a scheme and plan of action devised to carry out those bad intentions. "For the vile person will speak villainy, and his heart will work iniquity, to practice hypocrisy, and to utter error against El-Yahuah, to empty the soul of the hungry, and he will cause the drink of the thirsty to fail. The instruments also of the churl are evil: he devises wicked devices to destroy the poor with lying words, even when the needy speak right" Yesha'yahu (Isaiah) 32:6-7.

We are once again living under the same circumstances as Noach because the rain is scarce, so the rainbow does not make an appearance to remind us about the depravity, narcissism, sadism, and idolatry that has taken hold of the people. As one of the richest countries in the world, you would think that civility and hospitality would be an overall goal for the multicultural citizens of America. Instead, this melting pot at times governed by politicians and elites with omnipotent characteristics who are passing laws meant to inflict grievous harm on working- and middle-class citizens. I cannot make this up when it comes to the blatant hypocrisy within the technology industry and the homelessness in Metropolitan cities. I saw parents pushing babies in shopping carts through homeless encampments during the winter. It sickened me to watch small children sleeping on cardboard because working parents cannot afford the rent of a two-bedroom apartment. The book of BERE'SHIYTH says the lawlessness before and during the generation of Noach was deliberate because of the actions of Watchers, wicked and terrifying to all those that dared to defy their power.

Like other great Metropolitan cities receiving help from an influx of corporate spending, individuals malevolently motivated are subverting the will of the people for their own agendas and strategies. The Covid epidemic and technology blackouts are just dry runs for more sinister plans in the future. Homelessness in cities where vacant office complexes sit are proof that we have reached a generation that is morally corrupt under the authority of individuals who follow deities not aligned with love and righteousness. "You have been in Eden, the garden of Elohim; every precious stone was your covering, the sardius, topaz, and the diamond, the beryl, the onyx, and the jasper, the sapphire, the emerald, and the carbuncle, and gold: the workmanship of your tabrets and of your pipes was prepared in you in the day that you were created. You are the anointed Keruv that covers; and I have set you so: you were upon the holy mountain of Elohim; you have walked up and down amid the stones of fire. You were perfect in your ways from the day created, till iniquity found in you. By the multitude of your merchandise, they have filled the midst of you with violence, and you have sinned: therefore, I will cast you as profane out of the mountain of Elohim: and I will destroy you, O covering Keruv, from the midst of the stones of fire. Your heart lifted because of your beauty, you have corrupted your wisdom by reason of your brightness: I will cast you to the ground, I will lay you before kings, that they may behold you" Yechezq'el (Ezekiel) 28:13-17.

The Creator has informed us in the iviry and yavaniym besorath that wicked dark forces are active in kingdoms around the world. There is a battle between the supernatural and mortal man first waged in the garden and continued with the birth of the Naphaliym. I have read the tale of A'dam and Chuah from Sunday school to adult theological study and I ask this question; do you think it is purely myth that some fruit after eating made the first mortal couple own chokmah like the Creator? Or was it an examination between the forces of light and dark to discover the true nature of humanity when left to decide their own path? This is the quandary of many of us that succumb to excessive imposition and make hasty decisions that compromise our integrity. Chuach vilified throughout history as the woman who choose death over life and cursed us all for her disobedience. She confessed to the serpent: We may eat of the fruit of the trees of the garden: But of the fruit of the tree, which is amid the garden, Elohim has said: "Ye shall not eat of it, neither shall ye touch it, lest ye die."

Chuah knew the consequences, but out of spite of restriction from the tree, chose to risk it all for the power of independence and her eyes opened. She was alone in her defiance initially, but it was now the nature of independence and self-governed reasoning that she quickly gave to A'dam so he too could also become independent. Even the serpent acknowledged the unyielding insight of the Creator; For Elohim knows that in the day ye eat thereof, then your eyes opened, and ye shall be as Elohim, knowing good and evil. The Creator warned both A'dam and Chuah of the consequences that would befall them for disobedience. A'dam could have pleaded for repentance and quickly changed the judgment of death by telling the Creator; Chuah was weak because of the serpent persuasion but please pardon my woman for her rebellion. Instead of manning up and being the head instead of the tail, A'dam chose to also become disobedient and let the serpent become victorious over the admonishing of the Creator.

This is a cautionary tale, because every man and woman are either struggling or have struggled with trust and equally yoked in their relationship with YHWH. How many times have you warned your mate about an issue or pleaded with them to change course, but they still went ahead, and the outcome had severe consequences? There is always that initiation in your mind that you are approaching imminent danger, or you have crossed the point of no return. There have been many times that my woman has called out my recklessness in the past, but instead of correcting my steps from the word go, I allowed my arrogance to let me play the fool. "The way of man is forward and strange: but as for the pure, his work is right. It is better to dwell in a corner of the housetop, than with a brawling woman in a wide house. The soul of the wicked desires evil: his neighbor finds no favor in his eyes. When the scorner punished, the simple made wise: and when the wise instructed, he receives knowledge. The righteous man wisely considers the house of the wicked: but Elohim overthrows the wicked for their wickedness" Mishlei (Proverbs) 21:8-12.

The cautionary tales we just read are more than spiritual but lifesaving. There is murder and oppression among the offspring of

A'dam and Chuah. Brutality and sexual assault are common in the antediluvian era and committed without remorse. All these crimes committed by humanity chronicled in the first chapters of the book of BERE'SHIYTH. After the destruction in the Noachian era, humankind continued to oppress the weak and slaughter the helpless. Tribes trained in battle and fierce in combat rose up, conquered smaller villages, and held them in bondage. All the men of your confederacy have brought you even to the border: the men that were at peace with you have deceived you and prevailed against you; they that eat your bread have laid a wound under you: there is no understanding in him. Shall I not on that day, says Yahuah, even destroy the wise men out of Edom, and understanding out of the Mount of Esau? And your mighty men, O Teyman, dismayed, to the end that every one of the Mount of Esau cut off by slaughter. For your violence against your brother Ya'aqov shame shall cover you, and you cut off forever.

In the day that you stood on the other side, in the day that the strangers carried away captive his forces, and foreigners entered his gates, and cast lots upon Yerushalayim, even you were as one of them. But you should not have looked on the day of your brother on the day that he became a stranger; neither should you have rejoiced over the children of Yahudah on the day of their destruction; nor should you have spoken proudly on the day of distress. You should not have entered into the gate of my people in the day of their calamity; yea, you should not have looked on their affliction in the day of their calamity, nor have laid hands on their substance in the day of their calamity; Neither should you have stood in the crossway, to cut off those of his that did escape; neither should you have delivered up those of his that did remain in the day of distress. Ovadyahu (Obadiah) 1:7-14.

The annals of antiquity set up around 3000 BCE that the first kingdoms were in Kengir, also known as Sumer, and Kemet, also known as ancient Egypt. These kingdoms had monarchs whose subjects paid taxes for services, and they had the power to create and enforce laws. Sumer found between the Tigris and Euphrates Rivers in what is now Iraq. The Sumerians had their own written language and were known for their construction projects, such as irrigation canals and ziggurats, large temples. There is also evidence that the Sumerians traded and fought with neighboring peoples. The Akkadian Empire, which succeeded Sumer, considered the first known ancient empire of Mesopotamia. King Sargon of Akkad sometimes called the first person in recorded history to rule over an empire, though earlier Sumerian rulers like Lugal-zage-si may have a similar claim.

Only a few know the truth about mankind's history, and if angels really existed. I wonder what cataloged under the Vatican that can enrich the souls of all parishioners instead of keeping millions in spiritual limbo.

Throughout the chapters of this book, I have included links and data to justify my theory of all ethnicities deriving from one gene pool. A'dam and Chuah began to procreate with sons and daughters that eventually migrated by boat or land to islands and territories outside of Eden. There is DNA evidence that Humans are 99.9% identical in their genetic makeup, and new facts about the origin of man discovered through research. The lineage of Noach migration to all four corners of the world is available on the world wide web, and how Cham, Japheth, and Shem set up existing tribes and kingdoms from antiquity whose names changed beginning in the Greco-Roman era. One thing I do not want the reader to be confused about is the difference between Yavaniym mythology and chronicles of early humankind found within IVRIYM Cephers and dead sea scrolls.

Atheists and western religions have tried to discredit the sons of Elohim created before humankind to teach and protect the children of A'dam, but began lustful affairs with the daughters of Man. The stories of Greek and Roman pantheons also include the story of how the world began when Gaia (the Earth) appeared from Chaos or the big bang theory. The earth labeled "she" like how chokmah "labeled" she. Gaia then gave birth to Ouranos (the Sky) and other primordial deities like Pontos (the Sea) and Ourea (the Mountains). Incest occurred between Gaia and Ouranos who had 12 children – known as the Titans – including Cronos and Rhea, Zeus' parents. The Titans rebelled against their father Ouranos, overthrew him, and Cronos became the ruler of the gods until Zeus deposed him to rule over the Olympic gods. These are offspring that wreaked havoc and dominated weaker sons and daughters of Man and this Yavaniym mythology is like the tales of the Naphaliym.

Movies and books are in worldwide circulation promoting idolatry in elementary schools and universities. Yavaniym mythology intertwined in western culture and religions to the point that conspiracy theorists have named families of fame with unmeasurable resources that are lawless and above the recognized elites and consider them to be the offspring of deities. Now you can believe or consider everything you read up to this point as hogwash. But the consequences of a world filled with wickedness, idolatry and supernatural occurrences is reality, but advised to; "Put on the whole armor of Elohiym, that ye may be able to stand against the wiles of the devil. For we wrestle not against flesh and blood, but against principalities, against powers, against the rulers of the darkness of this world, against spiritual wickedness in high places. Wherefore take unto you the whole armor of Elohim, that ye may be able to withstand in the evil day, and having done all, to stand. Stand therefore, having your loins girt about with truth, and having on the breastplate of righteousness; And your feet shod with the preparation of the Besorah of peace" Eph'siym (Ephesians) 6:11-15.

Is it a myth that the Torah describes the anger of the Creator for the wickedness of both the Watchers and the Naphaliym? Noach was a prophet and the first evangelizer given the divine apocalyptic warning to construct a massive floating vessel to house his entire family and hundreds of beasts and animals for a worldwide flood. I also believe that during the construction of the floating vessel, the wickedness of humanity intensified up to the point when the heavens opened and the dam gates with water covered even the highest mountains of the earth. The book of BERE'SHIYTH says all humanity destroyed both righteous and unrighteous, and the Watchers fled the earth back to the heavens but found themselves locked in chains for judgment or exiled back to earth to wreak more havoc. The Sabbath lesson was more intriguing and resonated differently than the other lessons in our study course, because of the implications of coitus between a mortal woman and spiritual demon that I always imagined was impossible because of the holiness factor. In the back of my mind, I knew demon possession was not farfetched, but I still allowed someone to sow seeds of doubt based upon their theories. I accepted that celestial beings created without the gentiles necessary for copulation and procreation, so it was impossible to imply that the sons of Elohim impregnated daughters of men. I needed added evidence from other publications separately from Christianity or Judaism to prove his theory was incorrect, so I researched the Qur'an in the book of Suras.

Muhammad mentions the flood but what I really needed was missing on the Naphaliym, but the prophet writes "And revealed to Noah, none of your people will believe except those who already have. Do not distress by what they have been doing. And build the Ark under Our ʿwatchfulʾ Eyes and directions, and do not plead with Me for those who have done wrong, for they will surely drown. So, he began to build the Ark, and whenever some of the chiefs of his people passed by, they mocked him. He said, if you laugh at us, we will soon' laugh at you similarly. You will soon come to know who visited by a humiliating torment in this life and overwhelmed by an everlasting punishment in the next. And it said, O earth! Swallow up your water. And O sky! Withhold your rain. The floodwater receded and the decree carried out. The Ark rested on Mount Judi, and the water washed away the wrongdoing people! Noah called out to his Lord, saying, My Lord! Certainly, my son is also of my family, your promise is surely true, and You are the most just of all judges! Allah replied, O Noah! He is certainly not your family; he was entirely of unrighteous conduct. So do not ask Me about what you have no knowledge of! "I warn you, so you do not fall into ignorance."

While Judaism and Islam teaches converts to examine every utterance for truth and accuracy, there are stories in the Akkadian tablets discovered in 1849 by archaeologist Austin Henry Layard in the ruins of the library of Ashurbanipal, an ancient Babylonian city found on the lower Euphrates River in southern Mesopotamia in 19th–16th century BC. Babylon chronicled in the Torah as being the location of the tower Babel and functioned as the religious and political hub of an extinct Semitic language spoken in ancient Mesopotamia from the 3rd BC until its gradual replacement of the Aramaic language among Assyrians and Babylonians from the 8th century BC until its decline during the Hellenistic period. The story of Gilgamesh is from ancient Mesopotamia and is the literary five Sumerian poems about Gilgamesh, king of Uruk, some of which may date back to the Third Dynasty of Ur (c. 2100 BC), describing a flood on the Euphrates River. The tale of Atrahasis, which chronicles the story of a huge flood on the Tigris River.

In the Epic of Gilgamesh, the writer warned that a deity plans to destroy the wicked and a prophet is to build a ship to save everyone in his household, including beasts. In the Epic of Atrahasis, a tribal chief and his family survived destruction in a boat that sailed to safety. These stories from four different kingdoms describe a destructive event in the land of Mesopotamia, but was this the only flood that destroyed lives or was there more destruction to come? Many believe that if the flood really occurred, it only covered a small region and not the entire earth. Many atheists believe that not all humankind destroyed but migration was happening before the Epic of Noach ever existed and these individuals escaped to dry land. Their theory is that those that live in the United States, and traveled to cities in the Pacific, you may have never flown over the entire ocean. Your booked flight may have chosen curved routes that fly over the landmass of the Pacific.

The Pacific Ocean is a massive body of water that will require an extremely large amount of fuel to fly across, so it is possible to travel on dry land. Their hypotheses may have merit if there were publications and Cephers from antiquity that traced migration in this region after A'dam and Chuah exiled from Eden. If Chuah could have seen the devil and his entourage have in the works for us, would she have eaten from the tree? If Noach would have only known the trouble that would surround his sons and daughters after migrating to all four corners of the world, he would have never got on that boat. Thank goodness for Enoch for preparing our generation with the books of antiquity that have educated those fleeing the power of the Watchers. Chokmah and reasoning to dig underneath the surface hidden by Satan's army. "Yes, speedily was he taken away, lest that wickedness should alter his understanding, or deceit beguile his soul. For the bewitching of wickedness obscures things that are honest; and the wandering of lustful desire undermines the simple mind. He made perfect in a brief time, fulfilled a long time: For his soul pleased Yahuah: therefore, he hastened to take him away from among the wicked. This the people saw, and understood it not, neither laid they up this in their minds: That his grace and mercy is with his qodeshiym, and that he has respect unto his chosen" Chokmah Shalomah (Wisdom of Solomon) 4:11-15.

When I began drafting this book, I truly made every effort to let the ruach lead me "To let it make sense" and hopefully make it easier for my children and their children to navigate in a world where suppression of moral beliefs and holistic traditions frowned upon.

It just hit me while writing this paragraph that there is a strong probability that the location around Eden and the four rivers that once flowed into the garden may have altered by the deluge. Landmarks once recognizable before the calamity may have destroyed the external layer of the earth, so from my perspective, the Garden of Eden's whereabouts are lost forever.

An overwhelming majority of atheists (94%) say "religion causes division and intolerance", according to a 2023 survey. And 91% say the statement "religion encourages superstition and illogical thinking." Three-quarters (73%) say religion does more harm than good in American society. Nine-in-ten Swedish adults say belief in God is not necessary to be moral and have good values, while 85% in Australia, 80% in the Czech Republic and 77% in France say this. A quarter of French adults (23%) identify as atheists, as do 18% of adults in Sweden, 17% in the Netherlands and 12% in the United Kingdom.

According to the most recent data from the Global Carbon Atlas, the top five countries that have produced in aggregate the most CO_2 since the Industrial Revolution are the United States, China, Russia, Germany, and the United Kingdom. The largest emitters were in China, the U.S., India, Russia, and Japan. Every twenty years humankind faced with a threat to their existence reported by media sources that sends them into a frenzy. This is when all ethnicities and cultures come together singing come by yah and praying for unity and peace. The forties had World War 2 when the president said, "A Day Which Will Live in Infamy". On August 6th and 9th 1945, the United States detonated two atomic bombs over the Japanese cities of Hiroshima and Nagasaki killing between 129,000 and 226,000 people, most of whom were civilians.

The Cepher says the Creator will never again destroy the earth with water because of mankind's wickedness, but humanity is fulfilling prophecy and suffering the same fate of those corrupted by the Watchers from antiquity. The innocence belonging to humanity with ethical fortitude is yielding to evilness and Idolatry that continues to revolve from one decade to the other. Before and after 1999, religious denominations, conspiracy theorists, and your ordinary run of the mill nut jobs, were pushing this end of the world and Armageddon hype. For over 20 years, they have bombarded the internet with illuminati conspiracies, new world order take-over, and government manipulation of climate and medicine. For those who know little about global warming like me, global warming refers to long-term shifts in temperatures and weather patterns. Living in California and on occasion traveling back home to Texas, I welcome the warm sun because it means time in the swimming pool or hours at the beach. Believe me, I'm all for mankind not destroying environments with toxins and pollutants but when former Vice President Al Gore expressed optimism that humanity can still repair the damage to the environment that is causing global warming, I thought to myself, *do they really think the Creator will let the wickedness of mortal man destroy his greatest creation again?* Then he went on to say, "The good news is we can reclaim control of our destiny," but what destiny is he referring to? The destiny of all ethnicities living in peace and harmony or the destiny that evilness and corruption eradicated from all four corners of the world.

Before doing research about this chapter, I was illiterate about global warming, and to be truthful, never gave a second thought about the shifts in nature. In high school, the burning of natural fossil fuels like coal, oil and gas was never an important subject matter to me. If the teacher discussed the harmful effects of refineries, automotive plants, and landfills in science class, I never really paid much attention because my focus was somewhere else. Now global warming has become a crisis on the news and greenhouse gas emissions are a serious threat to humanity. Al Gore went further to demand that the world take immediate action because "This is our moral duty to correct the wrong of previous generations to save the planet for future generations." I have heard the same doomsday rhetoric from religions and politicians turned environmentalists about calamitous events on humanity 's horizon. We have seen winter conditions in the summer and tropical islands evacuated because of flooding. The introduction of artificial intelligence will eventually make humans less self-sufficient and more reliant on technology that can shut down the world with a virus program. Politicians and the media push a hellenistic agenda of women dating women and men married to men, and children are taught LGBT rights in public education.

After the motorcycle accident I began to examine my former lifestyle and individuals I saved in my contact list; and I began removing individuals. I went on an apology campaign to everyone that I had a disagreement with and made a sincere effort to be less domineering to my wife. If I did not fall on my road king and experience the divine intervention that propelled me upon this path, I would still be the butthole that irks everyone. Opinionated, male chauvinistic, hustler. Always on the grind, only concerned with my own survival. And the chief of the ruachoth, Mastema, came and said: Yahuah, Creator, let some of them remain before me, and let them hearken to my voice, and do all that I shall say unto them; for if some of them are not left to me, I shall not be able to execute the power of my will on the sons of men; for these are for corruption and leading astray before my judgment, for great is the wickedness of the sons of men. And he said: Let the tenth part of them remain before him and let nine parts descend into the place of condemnation. And one of us commanded that we should teach Noach all their medicines; for he knew that they would not walk in uprightness, nor strive in righteousness. And we did according to all his words: all the malignant evil ones we bound in the place of condemnation and a tenth part of them we left that they might be subject before Satan on the earth. Yovheliym (Jubilees) 10:8-11.

Every election cycle, liberal or conservative political parties scare voters with threats of global warming, breakdown in law and order, recession or downward economy, and their candidates have the solution to unite the country. All these voters expected to choose the lesser of two evils while religious and political conspiracy theorists believe a secret organization is pulling the strings behind closed doors.

The fifties ushered in the UFO era that began with an unprecedented rash of media attention during the summer of 1952 that culminated with reports of sightings over Washington, D.C. During the sixties, America convoluted in the war with Vietnam. The Civil Rights movement brought to the forefront racial prejudice in the South and North. Music and movies began distributing projects that made people pay attention to life in America. Paul Erlich, a Stanford biologist and end times prophet, preached a starvation gospel in the seventies: "The Green Revolution is going to turn brown. Hundreds of millions of people will starve to death despite any crash programs embarked upon now. At this late date nothing can prevent a substantial increase in the world death rate."

Illegal narcotics were taking hold of Vietnam veterans coming home from the war. Since the seventies, drug overdoses have been growing exponentially long before the fentanyl and prescription opioid epidemic. During the 1980s, AIDS ravaged the United States. Chernobyl nuclear power plant in Ukraine had two massive explosions releasing 400 times more radiation than the atomic bomb dropped on Hiroshima. Two workers in the explosions died, and shortly after, 28 more would be dead by acute radiation exposure, and thousands were diagnosed with cancer.

Researchers studied 57 cities where crack cocaine arrived in 1982 and found the epidemic has a devastating impact on young black teens. The crack epidemic surged in murder rates for all ethnicities, only the rate among black males aged 15–24 did not decline. For young black men, there was also a sharp rise in gun-related murders and gun-related suicides after the arrival of crack, but no corresponding change in murders and suicides without guns. Between 1982 and 1985, the number of cocaine users increased by 1.6 million people. The Reagan era "War on Drugs," included the passing of federal anti-drug laws, increased federal anti-drug funding, the initiation and expansion of prison and police programs. The 100-to-1 ratio between powdered cocaine and crack cocaine used as a guideline for mandatory punishment, with a minimum penalty of 5 years for possession of 5 grams of crack cocaine or 500 grams of powdered cocaine.

In the early 2000s, we glued to our television sets on the terrorist attacks on September 11, 2001. The entire world reacted to the airplanes crashing into the twin towers in NYC and Pentagon in DC with 2,977 murdered and thousands injured at the World Trade Center, the Pentagon, and in Somerset County, Pennsylvania. The apocalypse is tomorrow, and if not, the day after. On March 20, 2023, the United Nations warned of humanity's ticking "time-bomb," released a "report of reports" highlighting a multi-trillion-dollar plan to implement climate policies across the globe. Our world inundated since the forties with religious zealots saying humanity is facing the likelihood of the book of Revelations becoming reality. Through all the events happening, I have always had faith that humankind is unable to destroy the greatest act of the Creator.

The world will continue to support life on earth, though Hollywood is profiting from mankind's hysteria with movies like "The Planet of The Apes," "The Book of Eli," "Legend," and "Terminator." Yahuah has declared that he smelled a sweet savor; and Yahuah said in his heart, I will not again curse the ground anymore for man's sake; for the imagination of man's heart is evil from his youth; neither will I again smite anymore everything living, as I have done. While the earth exists, seedtime and harvest, and cold and heat, summer and winter, and day and night shall not cease. Bere'shiyth (Genesis) 8:21-22.

Former Vice President Al Gore expressed optimism that humanity can still repair the damage to the environment that is causing shifts in the climate. As the world is developing at a drastic rate and innovative technology introduced like electric vehicles, Ai technology and automation, driving a gasoline car or coal for heating a building still pose a threat after releasing carbon dioxide in the atmosphere. I have driven at night on Highway 80 near the Chevron plant and it continues to remind me of a scene from "Mad Max", flames of fire shooting up in the sky in Northern California. The Chevron plant has been sued several times for releasing toxins through a process called flaring, which is a way to safely divert pressurized material and burn it in smokeless flares. They claim these flares convert hydrocarbon vapors into harmless carbon dioxide and water vapor but when things go awry their spokesperson must make a statement that harmful gases accidentally released in the nearby communities.

In 2021, five refineries in Texas exceeded federal pollution limits of the carcinogenic chemical benzene. There is evidence that benzene exposure is associated with damage to reproductive organs and fetuses. I encourage everyone reading this chapter to investigate for themselves the many cancer-causing agents released in their communities. Many people are shocked to learn the pollutants released every year into our air and water system from corporations that never had their workers and nearby residents' best interests. Texas and California or not alone in polluting the earth, a dozen refineries in the U.S. exceeded the EPA's limit on benzene emissions. According to UN climate experts, these emissions have increased sea levels to 15 to 25 cm (six to 10 inches) and the pace of rise is accelerating, especially in some tropical areas. If warming trends continue, the oceans could rise by one added meter (39 inches) around the Pacific and Indian Ocean islands by the end of the century. Salt contamination to water and land will make many atolls uninhabitable long before covered over by the sea.

According to a study cited by the UN's Intergovernmental Panel on Climate Change, five nations (the Maldives, Tuvalu, the Marshall Islands, Nauru, and Kiribati) may become uninhabitable by 2100, creating 600,000 stateless climate refugees. Dozens of cities along the US coastline are sinking at alarming rates, leaving them far more exposed to devastating flooding from sea level rise than previously thought. As oceans rise and the coasts sink, up to 343,000 acres of land exposed to destructive flooding by 2050, from hazards such as hurricanes, coastal storms, and shoreline erosion, according to the study published in the journal Nature. In a worst-case scenario, 1 in 50 people in the 32 cities are exposed to flood.

After researching the failures that have contributed to the dilemmas of the last eighty years, the only conclusion is that the Haves have not fully recognized the plight of the Have-nots. There are many verses where insight is given into the very thoughts of the Creator. The wickedness of humankind has shown itself to be hereditary and passed down from parent to child, but everyone knows the difference between right and wrong and capable of changing the climate around them. The Creator saw the world steering off course and needed to change the entire trajectory; but wickedness, already embedded, was not destroyed. The Sons of Elohim were creating defiance against the creator by teaching men and women to be self-willed and brutes upon the earth. After the deluge, the mindset of disobedience was like an evil plague inflicted on mortal men and women that continues with a higher degree in our generation. These same plagues are embedded within all of us reading this book and will pass along to the next generation if we do not change the way we do things.

You do not have to be spiritually inclined to notice the undertones of wickedness, acquisitiveness, dogmatism being a prime factor in politics, education, media, and religion. This may go over the heads of most atheists, but Aza'zel taught men to make swords, knives, shields, and breastplates, used by all the foes and believers of the Bible. The fabrication of mirrors, the workmanship of bracelets and ornaments, the use of paint, the beautifying of the eyebrows, stones of every valuable and select kind, and all sorts of dyes, that increased vanity and conceit among mankind was introduced by the Watchers so that the world became altered from the original plan established by the Creator. From the gate, adversaries of YHWH have tried to destroy the sovereignty he has over humankind with deception, assault, idolatry, and demonic influence. Noah instructed his sons and daughters the knowledge and reasonings given to him; but impiety increased, fornication multiplied, and his progeny transgressed and corrupted all their ways.

I want to add that it is hard for me to believe that all the Watchers were imprisoned after the Noachian flood. Either books and cephers discovered by children of Shem, Cham, and Japheth that the Watchers left before the flood or rebelliousness is a trait within our DNA that passed on to our children. YHWH continues to warn the elect that children of iniquity will choose death over life and pleasures of sin rather than a lifestyle of morality. Information that was once hidden details the tactics used by demons to enslave followers still pursue the offerings of Amazarak who taught all the sorcerers, and dividers of roots. Armers, the solution of sorcery, and Barkay'al, the observers of the stars. Akiybe'el taught the signs, Tamiy'el taught astronomy, And Asarad'el taught the motion of the moon. The apocrypha go into detail about how the Watchers have never left the earth after the deluge but continue to build alliances with mortals, passing on generational curses more destructive than natural catastrophes. "The men destroyed, cried out; and their voices reached to heaven" Chanok (Enoch) 8:1-9.

The global atmosphere after the Noachian flood plagued with one tragedy after another. I would love to sugarcoat the future of humanity, but I am afraid that people would rather follow lies and attach themselves to violence and barbarian conduct instead of living in unity. The Creator made the decision to never again destroy every living thing because of wickedness, but the scriptures tell the enlightened that permission given to Watchers to wreak havoc once again upon Noah's family. To mislead those that are lukewarm in their beliefs and sign all those up ready to bypass the reasoning of YHWH. I am not trying to make anyone think that the world is ending but being in the entertainment and media industry that has an enormous influence on people makes me recognize the reality of human nature and Satan's influence. The music that was once uplifting has been replaced with spiritism, substance abuse, sodomy, and murder. Death, fornication, and illiteracy pushed on a younger generation that no longer prescribes to the morality that increases theocratic stability.

You conjugate teenagers and young adults owning military grade weapons in a city like Oakland, Ca, and you will get a murder rate averaging over two hundred lives annually and it is not hard to believe that the imagination of man's heart is evil from his youth. We have bypassed all pleasantries to appease individuals whose lifestyle morally conflicts with our ancestral values. We must get beyond race issues or giving people passes with identical skin pigment and hold them accountable for their actions. Several years back, the comedian and activist Bill Cosby who donated millions to the HBCU angered individuals by giving it to them raw and in your face. The mainstream media overhyped the comment when Mr. Cosby told a room full of activists that too many Black men are beating their wives while their children run around not knowing how to read or write. "They think they are hip; they cannot read, they cannot write. They are laughing and giggling, and they are going nowhere." Now you know that people were highly inflamed with his comments because he was talking about private matters in public and confirming many of the stereotypes within the Black community. Cosby is at a time in his life where he is not trying to win any People's Choice awards or become mayor of Philadelphia, so he has been gassing Black parents and the youth population. Mr. Cosby has spent his whole life uplifting the Black race through entertainment and education and, he is telling the truths that most Black people and religious organizations are afraid to admit. I am putting a twenty on a ten and including my own observation that "We cannot simply blame Caucasians for problems such as murder rate increases, teen pregnancy, and high school dropout rates because our ancestors were once in bondage." The Creator resolved to never again destroy the people and creatures of the earth with a flood, but we sacrifice ourselves daily to idolatry, diseases, illiteracy, savagery, and self-destructive behavior passed on from earlier generations. Not all Black people are identical; but like all ethnicities, many share character traits, culture ideas and identify with individuals with matching skin tones while a cloud of suspicion hangs over the head of outsiders.

All the health and mental issues derive from a lack of education, employment, security, medical, and air quality regulations affect northern Blacks, southern whites, documented Hispanics, Chinese immigrants, and Middle East citizens. The problems of one ethnic group will eventually spill into the neighborhood of another group if a concentrated effort of deterrence not applied. Raised to believe that your moral conduct and theological beliefs superseded your skin pigmentation. We must be on similar wavelengths for me to truly call you my brother or sister. I have traveled outside of California and experienced southern hospitality from whites and redneck bigotry from Blacks.

Do you think global warming causes climate change in urban communities while not affecting the suburban and gated communities? Unfortunately, and I say this with sarcasm, in the United States, the wealthy must eventually meet the homeless family. Housing prices have tripled in affordability from greedy developers and corrupt politicians catering to the tech industry until the bubble burst and now we have foreclosures and abandoned homes. Political parties blame each other over food prices, immigration, inflation while politicians are immune to all the problems their constituents deal with daily.

LINKS

Nous/ Theodicy/ children-reflect-parental-behavior/ crack-epidemic/ literacy-by-any-means-necessary-the-history-of-anti-literacy-laws-in-the-u-s/ five-texas-refineries-polluted-above-federal-limit-on-cancer-causing-benzene-last-year-report-found

CORRUPTING POWER

“And Kush begat Nimrod: he began to be a warrior and hunter on the earth. He was a warrior and a hunter before Yahuah: wherefore said, Even as Nimrod the warrior hunter before Yahuah. And the beginning of his kingdom was Babel, and Erek, and Akkad, and Kalneh, in the land of Shin'ar. Out of that land went forth Ashshur, and built Nineveh, and the city Rechovoth, and Kelach, And Recen between Nineveh and Kelach: the same is a great city”

BERE'SHIYTH (GENESIS) 10:8-12 את CEPHER. "And Kush begat Nimrod: he began to be a warrior and hunter on the earth. He was a warrior and a hunter before Yahuah: wherefore said, Even as Nimrod the warrior hunter before Yahuah. And the beginning of his kingdom was Babel, and Erek, and Akkad, and Kalneh, in the land of Shin'ar. Out of that land went forth Ashshur, and built Nineveh, and the city Rechovoth, and Kelach, And Recen between Nineveh and Kelach: the same is a great city" BERE'SHIYTH (GENESIS) 10:8-12 את CEPHER.

Since I could remember, history has always fascinated me, especially individuals that have kicked it up a notch and taken their game plan to a new level. Warriors that fought for their tribe. Kings that marched in front of the battle line and conquered entire kingdoms. Women that stood side by side never flinching in the battle. History details the past so in the present we can shape our future. In elementary up to college, I bought into the propaganda that Blacks in America lived in the jungle and were uncivilized. This was pure ignorance that I later rectified after learning that Aram Naharayim (Mesopotamia) identified as the cradle of civilization and introduced codes in the areas of law, writing, religion, and mathematics. King Hammurabi reigned from 1792 to 1750 B.C. along the Euphrates River and formed 282 laws for commercial trading to the requirements for civil obedience. These codes enforced within the empires of the Ashshuriym, Mitsriym, Babylonians, and Phoenicians, that were later adapted into Western culture.

The Torah highlights fabled cities, including Mitsrayim, Babel, Edom, and Yerushalayim that spawned eastern cultures, theological traditions, and innovations in architecture and holistic medicine. It is a plus that writers from antiquity never included ethnicity but kingdoms, as they leave breadcrumbs that spark readers to dig deeper into civilizations of their ancestors. For instance, the Torah outlined

Avraham marrying Sarah "And in the fortieth jubilee, in the second week, in the seventh year thereof, Abram took to himself a woman, and her name was Sarai, the daughter of his father, and she became his woman" Yovheliym (Jubilees) 12:9. Avraham also had two women besides Sarai discussed in the Bible and Apocrypha as Ha'ger "Now Sarai, Abram's woman bore him no children: and she had a handmaid, a Mitsriy, whose name was Ha'ger" Bere'shiyth (Genesis) 16:1. Mitsriy in English pronounced Egypt is in the northeast corner of Africa and the Sinai Peninsula in Asia. The Mediterranean and Red Sea borders it. The countries near Mitsriy borders are Sudan, Libya, Gaza Strip, Israel, and the Gulf of Aqaba, which separates Egypt from Jordan and Saudi Arabia. Keturah was Avraham's last wife, and she was from the land of Kenyan pronounced Canaan and described in the Bible as being in the southern Levant, which is the area that includes modern-day Israel, the West Bank, Gaza, Jordan, and parts of Syria and Lebanon."

And Avraham took to himself a third woman, and her name was Qeturah, from among the daughters of his household servants, for Ha'ger had died before Sarah" Yovheliym (Jubilees) 19:11 Avraham's father's name was Terach, and doing my research it was common to marry a sister or brother. Terrach did not choose a wife outside of his tribe but married a woman named Edna, the daughter of his father's sister. Their tribe was from Ur of the Kasdiym and the term that appears in the books of the bible as Kasdiym pronounced Chaldees in English. Their history traced back over 5,500 years to ancient Mesopotamia, which is present-day Iraq. Mesopotamia is in the Middle East in Western Asia and North Africa region and situated on the same latitude as the southern United States, 6,326 miles by boat. In the tablets of Tell-el-Amarna, Amenophis III and IV, set up an empire that made kingdoms pay tribute that were under their control. From 1580 to 1350 b.c. Mitsrayim nation reigned throughout the entire region followed by the Ramessid dynasty, 1319-1200 b.c.

The Creation of humanity measures the successes and failures of rulers and kingdoms that either choose to dominate or liberate citizens with the Code of Hammurabi. It was the book of BERE'SHIYTH that inspired me to dig deeper into history and uncover truths before European chattel in America. I owed this to my children and their children to combat the continued stigma of the system of enslavement and ownership of humans and their offspring as property. During my elementary through college academia years, my family never allowed the narrative set up by western educational curriculum that over-emphasizes the accomplishments of Japheth citizenship while Chamite and Semite perspective begins with chattel slavery. It also embeds within young minds the European superiority complex that completely ignores the advancements contributed to western society from inventors, educators, soldiers, and politicians with black or brown pigmentation. Early Mesopotamian societies (present day Iraq) discussed as the benchmark for kingdoms in eastern Europe, northern Europe, southern Europe, Central Europe, and the British Isles. All nations have engaged in either covert intelligence or destruction of their enemy's infrastructure and historical artifacts.

The first nation that comes to mind is the Yashar'el nation that beseech the Creator for favors in military campaigns. Neither was Yahuah passive or forgiving when authorizing his chosen people to vanquish his adversaries. "And when King Arad the Kena'aniy, which dwelt in the Negev, heard tell that Yashar'el came via the spies; then he fought against Yashar'el, and took some of them prisoners. And Yashar'el vowed a vow unto Yahuah and said: If you will indeed deliver these people into my hand, then I will destroy their cities. And Yahuah hearkened to the voice of Yashar'el and delivered up the Kena'aniym; and they destroyed them and their cities: and he called the name of the place Chormah" Bemidbar (Numbers) 21:1-3 Annuals from antiquity shed light on the use of espionage to further advance the engineering and assets of kingdoms. In the 4th century

BC, Sun Tzu, a theorist in ancient China influenced by the book "Art of War." Quoted as saying "One who knows the enemy and knows himself will not be endangered in a hundred engagements." He stressed the need to understand yourself and your enemy to gain the upper hand. After researching his thoughts on the informant's role in disruption of an organization's agenda, it calls to mind the efforts of individuals in the Civil Rights Movement on the government's payroll. The clandestine agent who becomes a major figure in the underworld as a kingpin, but secretly leads a double life as an informer for law enforcement. The industry plant" who receives financial and material support from entertainment and media elites to influence followers down a path of misinformation and debasement. The Mitsrayim kingdom studied by archaeologists since the eighteenth hoped to discover pyramid construction and agriculture.

One aspect overlooked in public education textbooks is their developed system for the acquisition of intelligence needed for the security of their growing empire. The ruler Thutmose I (1525-ca. 1512 b.c.) military campaign was extensive and was victorious in conquering the kingdom of Aram (Syria) "And it was in those days that there was a great war between the children of Kush and the children of the East and Aram, and they rebelled against the king of Kush in whose hands they were. So Kikianus, king of Kush, went forth with all the children of Kush, a people many as the sand, and he went to fight against Aram and the children of the East, to bring them under subjection. And when Kikianus went out, he left Bil'am the magician, with his two sons, to guard the city, and the lowest sort of the people of the land. So Kikianus went forth to Aram and the children of the East, and he fought against them and smote them, and they all fell down wounded before Kikianus and his people. And he took many of them captives and he brought them under subjection as at first, and he encamped upon their land to take tribute from them as usual" Yashar (Jasher) 72:1-5.

The Yavaniym nation considered by many to be one of the most important cultural transplants providing the Greek alphabet that later evolved into the Latin alphabet, which became the most widely used alphabet in the world. "And the children of Javan are the Yavaniym who dwell in the land of Macedonia, and the children of Madai are the Orelum that dwell in the land of Curson, and the children of Tubal are those that dwell in the land of Tuskanah by the river Pasha. And the children of Meshek are the Shivnashniy and the children of Thiyrac are Rushash, Kushniy, and Ongolis; all these built themselves cities; those are the cities that are situate by the sea Yevuc by the river Cura, which empties itself in the river Tragan. And the children of Eliyshah are the Almaniym, and they also went and built themselves cities; those are the cities situated between the mountains of Iyov and Shivathmo; and of them were the people of Lumbardiy who dwell opposite the mountains of Iyov and Shivathmo, and they conquered the land of Italia and remained there unto this day. And the children of Kittiym are the Romaiym who dwell in the valley of Kanopia by the river Tibreu. And the children of Dodaniym are those who dwell in the cities of the sea Giychon, in the land of Bordna. These are the families of the children of Japheth according to their cities and languages, when they scattered after the tower, and they called their cities after their names and occurrences; and these are the names of all their cities according to their families, which they built in those days after the tower" Yashar (Jasher) 10:13-18.

Now as we fast forward to European domination in the 1500s, following prince Henry the Navigator's discovery of Africa (1418) and Christopher Columbus' exploration of America (1492). We will never know the hidden artifacts and cephers in ancient kingdoms along the Mediterranean coasts and African countries that tell the true history of the people since A'dam and Chuah. Most of the art relics and writings of ancient civilizations are either destroyed or placed in museums in Russia, Portugal, Asia, Spain, France, Rome, and

England. These kingdoms have colonized parts of Alkebulan and the Mediterranean to drain their resources and spread westernized religious philosophy and culture.

During the 8th through 6th centuries b.c, the Yavaniym (Greek) nation stormed across the Mediterranean and Black Sea to reap the benefits of fertile soil because their growing kingdom became overpopulated. The territories and the citizens displayed hospitality like the native Americans in the Columbus era, but these native tribes quickly found themselves displaced by Yavaniym colonies who pillaged their lands for economic growth. Colonizer's set up seaports to conduct trade, transport military personnel, and political communication, which became useful for the expansion of Greek culture, and influence. The Yavaniym nation set up schools wiping out ancient native dialects for the Greek language and replacing long held traditional values with its religious rites, forcing mandatory adaptations to Yavaniym traditions within independent polis (cities). The introduction to a Hellenic civilization swept across the land that would later intermingle with the native Italic civilizations. The Yavaniym nation would set up kingdoms throughout the Caucasus to southern Spain, and from southern Russia to northern Egypt. The Greek universities of antiquity beginning in the 5th century all had a standardized theme of education considered essential for participation in Greek culture.

While doing research on Yavaniym culture, I came across striking similarities that would later be adapted into American culture. These similar adaptations in education based on class and were either formal or informal. Formal education taught in a public setting with hired sophists and intellectuals in Athens and other Greek cities. Informal education provided by an unpaid teacher and occurred in a non-public setting like home schooling that many individuals have committed to during American slavery. Education was an essential part of a person's identity, but basic and higher were founded on the fundamentals of sexism and bigotry for Greek education which was primarily for males and non-slaves. Ripe fruit never grown from a diseased tree, and European immigrants in America adapted similar laws from Greek antiquity to prohibit the education of slaves. Since elementary grade taught that my ancestors were slaves, and the deity Jesus Christ was my only hope for salvation.

Throughout the years, the history of Chamite and Semite people told with struggle and strife in the form of Jim Crow, systemic racism, illiteracy, unemployment, prison incarceration, and debilitating diseases. My grandfather always instilled in my brother and me the strength in knowing where you came from so no man can dictate where you are going. The history of a nation and their children shipped to hostile foreign lands is a fulfillment of prophecy. The breadcrumbs of learning my identity of being the son of Avraham replaced with falsehoods from both theocratic doctrines and propaganda. Religious denominations and the Negro Bible created during slavery to keep individuals held as chattel is still in effect today. We are seeing in my generation, a nation that has been struggling both internally and externally with the problems of unhinged reasoning which needs addressing. It has been well documented that the Catholic church between 1095 and 1270 a.d (Anno Domini, which is Latin for "in the year of our Lord".) orchestrated religious crusades that were nothing more than military campaigns that waged war on the Muslim population and to occupy Yerushalayim. There were many military campaigns between Christianity and Islam based on religion and economics. These battles from the First Crusade to what is happening now in Palestine and Egypt are millennium wars that will never see an end.

There are too many factions within the middle east that will continue to evolve if nations continue to force the colonization of foreign lands.

I will never during my lifetime become educated or understand the beliefs held by the Shi'ite Fatimids, who had Palestine at the time the First Crusade arrived. Political science was never interesting to me until I began watching CNN, Fox News, and Al Jazeera Television during the Bush family presidency. Like millions of Americans glued to their television sets, we saw the US-led invasion of Iraq in 2003, and the reports of American soldiers and their allies destroying thousands of antiquities from museums and archaeological sites. News commentators were reporting damage done to the Iraq National Library and Archive and over 15,000 objects stolen from the National Museum of Iraq in April 2003, including artifacts thousands of years old. Archaeological sites looted and plundered, and this is the reason a majority of Chamites and Semites living in America do not know their true history.

The movie "Roots' tried to shed light on the dilemma but had more questions than answers. In the sixties, many Blacks began discussing their native American heritage and changing the narrative that all Blacks living in America were in fact not slaves, but here before Christopher Columbus. A dear friend began tracing her family tree and uncovered information hidden from many individuals. With her constant perturbation, we began researching the information of my grandparents' ancestral backgrounds and found we both derived from native American tribes. I knew my grandmother Cassie May was Indian, but never researched what tribe she derived from. I informed Ms. Williams and after further research we discovered the Dawes Act of 1887. The Federal Indian policy focused specifically on granting land allotments to Native Americans that embedded European American culture, like the slaves that had to abolish their African culture for the culture of their slave masters.

Senator Henry Dawes of Massachusetts, authorized President Grover Cleveland to break up reservation land and register Native Americans on a tribal roll. My coworker informed me that certain Indian tribes excluded from receiving land that they once occupied with the passing of the Dawes Act. Cherokees, Creeks, Choctaws, Chickasaws, Seminoles, Osage, Miamies, Peorias, Sacs and Foxes. In 1893, President Grover Cleveland appointed the Dawes Commission to negotiate with the Cherokees, Creeks, Choctaws, Chickasaws, and Seminoles, who were known as the Five Civilized Tribes. Many Native American tribes lived in the southeastern United States, from North Carolina to the Gulf of Mexico, including Chickasaw, A Muskogean tribe that originally lived in northern Mississippi and Alabama, and believed to have migrated from the West. Choctaw, A tribe with ancestral lands in central and southern Mississippi, eastern Louisiana, and western Alabama, known for being skilled traders, farmers, and warriors. Atakapa, Karankawa, Mariame, and Akokisa are semi-nomadic tribes that live on the Texas Gulf Coast and are skilled in fishing, hunting, and gathering. Miccosukee, A tribe in south Florida officially recognized by the federal government in 1962. Acolapissa, tribe that moved to Bayou Castine on Lake Pontchartrain in 1702, and then across the Mississippi near New Orleans around 1719. Other tribes in the southeast include the Creek, Cherokee, and Seminole. Europeans first arrived, the southeast was one of the most densely populated areas of native North America, with most groups living in the piedmont to take advantage of the game, plants, and arable land.

I hope that readers share this information with family members who live or migrated from the Southern United States that includes the states south of the Mason-Dixon Line, the Ohio River, and South Atlantic States including Delaware, Florida, Georgia, Maryland, North Carolina, South Carolina, Virginia, and West Virginia. East South-Central States: Alabama, Kentucky, Mississippi, and Tennessee. West South-Central States: Arkansas, Louisiana, Oklahoma, and Texas. As a result of these negotiations, several acts passed that allotted a share of common property to members of the Five Civilized Tribes in exchange for abolishing their tribal governments and recognizing state and federal laws. To receive the allotted land, members were to enroll with the Office of Indian Affairs (later renamed the Bureau of Indian Affairs [BIA]). Once enrolled, the individual's name went on the "Dawes Rolls." This process aided the BIA and the Secretary of the Interior in deciding the eligibility of individual members for land distribution. The welfare act and the Dawes Act of 1887 stood in comparison because of racial bigotry in both cases. Government aided programs helped European immigrants who married tribal members that later birthed biracial children. The government always discouraged marriages between Black and white people before and during the Jim Crow era, but politicians seemed to change course hoping Native Americans would assimilate into white American society.

Some white settlers believed that Native American traditions were barbaric and intolerable, and that only by abandoning their spiritual traditions and accepting Christianity salvation afforded to them. This same bigoted philosophy was instrumental in introducing slaves to Jesus Christ. Religious organizations believed that assimilation was the only way for Native Americans to coexist with white people. Social reformers also supported the act, believing that it would help Native Americans overcome poverty. The Dawes Act was effective in breaking up Native tribes and resulted in Native Americans losing 62% of their land holdings. Land has always been the cause of many wars and battles between the Native Americans and European settlers depicted in most American westerns. This was pure propaganda like war movies with over emphasis on American prowess and others as villains. For Native Americans and freed slaves, there seems to have been an organized effort from 1890 to our generation to dismantle the family structure. Watching cowboy movies as a kid, I never imagined my indoctrination to view Indians as savages and murderers while praising Caucasian cowboys as heroes. As a kid, my dad was an enthusiastic fan of western movies, but I never saw Black cowboys in Hollywood productions until the comedy movie "Blazing Saddles."

When I began asking for enlightenment to write this chapter on "Corrupting Power" I did not know what direction to go. I knew I wanted to address all the problems facing urban communities and how the deteriorating factors via morality, religious and secular literacy, employment, marriage, and civility spoken of throughout the scriptures. I began seeing the breakdown of the family after watching the movie "Claudine" and how the federal government was forcing women to bypass marriage for welfare benefits. "Therefore, take heed lest you should forget Yahuah Elohayka and all his ways in the land to which you go and should connect with the people of the land and pursue vanity and forsake Yahuah Elohayka. But when you come to the land serve there Yahuah, do not turn to the right or to the left from the way which I commanded you and which you did learn. And may El Shaddai grant you favor in the sight of the people of the earth, that you may take there a woman according to your choice; one who is good and upright in the ways of Yahuah. And may Elohim give unto you and your seed the blessing of your father Avraham, and make you fruitful and multiply you, and may you become a multitude of people in the land whither you go and may Elohim cause you to return to this land, the land of your father's dwelling, with children and with great riches, with joy and with pleasure. Yashar (Jasher) 29:26-29".

Now let us break down some interesting statistics that I hope to change the narrative with the fact that Black women had a higher marriage rate than white women. This is contrary to American advertising that highlights happy European families buying homes while Black families are non-existent. By the 80s, prison incarceration was higher for Blacks than other ethnicities. The crack epidemic exploded in urban communities and the high school dropout rate increased. Guns and military grade weapons flooded improvised communities, and the homicide rate began being headlines in mainstream media. Today, a rife has been torn in the fabric of the American family with only 44% of Black children with a male dominant father figure in the household. With a domineering dad out of the home and women relying on a savior for salvation, the rate of Black out-of-wedlock births went from 24.5% in 1964 to 70.7% by 1994, roughly where it stands today. With the political agenda constantly attacking Blacks on welfare, little spoken of the poor and working-class white families that are surpassing Black households. Under President Johnson's administration in 1964, benefits skyrocketed and came under greater scrutiny within the federal government. The movie "Claudine" has become a cult classic in our household, and I encourage readers to examine the welfare program's disparaging outlook on marriage that went to mothers without a male in the household.

I often wondered if the same intrusive investigation applied to all ethnicities or only penalized Black households. The reasoning of most Western governments was to encourage non-westerners to abandon their culture and traditions of their ancestors for Christianity and economic stability. The reasoning of this chapter is for readers to unlock the history of their ancestors not taught in public education. What the movie "Roots" carried out in the seventies with the chronicles of an African family locked in American bondage, I hope to recapture with this book "Let It Make Sense." No longer will I accept the excuses uttered by individuals that the history of Black Americans lost forever, or public education has failed our children. The presumptuous pleasures of wealth and living the American dream have made individuals including myself, to abandon faith taught to us as children. The prospect of getting out of their improvised communities plagued with barbarity and depravity has forced many to forsake education at an early age and risk it all for illegal compensation. I cannot blame anyone but myself for choosing street life at the age of fifteen to pursue the lifestyle of a street pharmacist. I was not born in poverty or denied opportunities to excel because of my ethnicity. Motivated by the lifestyle of my uncles that lived life to the fullest with beautiful women in attendance. This is my cautionary tale to young people who become swept up with smoking mirrors and journey down a road with devastating consequences. "For the temperate mind has power to conquer the pressure of the passions, and to quench the fires of excitement, and to wrestle down the pains of the body, however excessive; and, through the excellency of reasoning, to abominate all the assaults of the passions. But the occasion now invites us to give an illustration of temperate reasoning from history. For at a time when our fathers were in possession of undisturbed peace through obedience to the Torah, and were prosperous, so that Seleucus Nicanor, the king of Asia, both assigned them money for divine service, and accepted their form of government, then certain persons, bringing in new things contrary to the general unanimity, in various ways fell into calamities" Makkabiym Reviy`iy (4 Maccabees) 3:17-21.

The slogan "Make America Great Again" was conceived by a few individuals that want to manipulate and suppress many. It has always been strategic like the colors and pieces on the chess board that the more skilled player yells checkmate against those illiterates to the game. I ask that we call a truce among all ethnicities and seek Chokmah instead of becoming mesmerized by the smoking mirrors that once redirected sons to not walk in his ways, but turned aside after lucre, and took bribes, and perverted judgment. Then all the elders of Yashar'el gathered themselves together, and came to El-Shemu'el unto Ramah, and said unto him: Behold, you are old, and your sons walk not in your ways: now make us a king to judge us like all the nations. But the thing displeased Shemu'el when they said: Give us a king to judge us. And Shemu'el prayed unto Yahuah. And

Yahuah said unto El-Shemu'el: Hearken unto the voice of the people in all that they say unto you: for they have not rejected you, but they have rejected me, that I should not reign over them. According to all the works which they have done since the day that I brought them up out of Mitsrayim even unto this day, wherewith they have forsaken me, and served other Elohim, so do they also unto you. Now therefore hearken unto their voice: howbeit yet protest solemnly unto them and show them the manner of the king that shall reign over them. And Shemu'el told את all the words of Yahuah unto the people that asked of him a king. And he said: This will be the manner of the king that shall reign over you: He will take your sons, and appoint them for himself, for his chariots, and to be his horsemen; and some shall run before his chariots. And he will appoint him captains over thousands, and captains over fifties; and will set them to ear his ground, and to reap his harvest, and to make his instruments of war, and instruments of his chariots. And he will take your daughters to confectioneries, and to be cooks, and to be bakers. And he will take your fields, and your vineyards, and your olive yards, even the best of them, and give them to his servants. And he will take the tenth of your seed, and of your vineyards, and give to his officers, and to his servants. And he will take your menservants, and your maidservants, and your goodliest young men, and your asses, and put them to his work. He will take the tenth of your sheep: and ye shall be his servants. And ye shall cry out on that day because of your king which ye shall have chosen you; and Yahuah will not hear you on that day. Nevertheless, the people refused to obey the voice of Shemu'el; and they said, Nay; but we will have a king over us; That we also may be like all the nations; and that our king may judge us, and go out before us, and fight our battles.

This is the dilemma that continues to plague the sons and daughters of Noach and will forever separate them, which is the true intention of the serpent in the garden. The adversaries of righteousness have stored up the knowledge of antiquity to keep the pawns from ever realizing that they are mere disposable pieces for the queen. All that one achieves, legitimate or illegal, altered because of the skills of the chess master. Not everyone can be saved, but everyone has the power to change the game. If you are breathing and still on the board then you have an opportunity to redeem yourself. Examine those of great wealth and fame that have come out into the light to expose the darkness. While they enjoyed the pleasures of this world, the harp, and the viol, the tabret, and pipe, and wine, in their feasts: but they regard not את the work of Yahuah, neither consider the operation of his hands. Therefore, my people are gone into captivity, because they have no knowledge: and their honorable men famished, and their multitude dried up with thirst. Therefore, Sheol has enlarged herself and opened her mouth without measure: and their glory, and their multitude, and their pomp, and he that rejoices, shall descend into it. And the mean man brought down, and the mighty man humbled, and the eyes of the lofty humbled: But Yahuah Tseva'oth exalted in judgment, and El that is holy sanctified in righteousness. Yesha'yahu (Isaiah) 5:12-16.

Long live the king" is a traditional proclamation that refers to the heir who takes the throne after the death of a monarch. The phrase originated from the law of le mort saisit le vif, which says that sovereignty is at once transferred when the earlier monarch dies. "The king is dead" announces the death of the monarch, while "long live the king" refers to the heir who succeeds them. The tradition dates to England in 1272, when Henry III died while his son, Edward I, was away fighting in the Crusades. "Long live the king" used as an expression of support for a person, group, or plan. For example, "long live the Queen" or "long may it continue" can express support for someone or something and the hope that they will last a long time.

LINKS

ancient-middle-east-hammurabi/ Colonisation_of_Africa/ milestone-documents/dawes-act/ family-breakdown-and-americas-welfare-system/ trust-us-were-government-aclu-looks-domestic-surveillance-and-need-watch-watchers/ Intelligence in the Ancient Near East/ Western-colonialism/ Crusades/

NOTES:

____

____

____

____

____

____

____

____

____

____

____

____

____

____

NOTES:

____

SEXUAL DEBAUCHERY

" **A**nd Lot went up out of Tso'ar, and dwelt in the mountain, and his two daughters with him; for he feared to dwell in Tso'ar: and he dwelt in a cave, he and his two daughters. And the firstborn said unto the younger, our father is old, and there is not a man in the earth to come in unto us after the manner of all the earth: Come, let us make our father drink wine, and we will lie with him, that we may preserve seed of our father. And they made their father drink wine that night: and the firstborn went in and lay with her father; and he perceived not when she lay down, nor when she arose. And it happened on the morrow, that the firstborn said unto the younger, Behold, I lay yesternight with my father: let us make him drink wine this night also; and go in, and lie with him, that we may preserve seed of our father. And they made their father drink wine that night also: and the younger arose and lay with him; and he perceived not when she lay down, nor when she arose" BERE'SHIYTH (GENESIS) 19:30-35 את CEPHER.

I want to give a warning to all the readers that this is the last chapter of this book and will be very candid. This chapter designed by chronicle order beginning with the existence of humankind to the nature of both man and women. As I continue this journey of enlightenment seeking divine interpretation from the ruach to unlock the revelatory epistles found in the Cepher, I can only reflect on my tendencies to envisage copulation as a youth. I would wake up from a wet dream and stuff my underwear in the bottom of the clothes basket feeling contrite and bewildered on this continuous occurrence. The chimera was too embarrassing and made it difficult to speak to anyone or seek counseling from my pastor.

When I read the book of Ivriym for the first time in my youth, the reasoning of the saying "Wherefore, seeing we also are compassed about with so great a cloud of witnesses, let us lay aside every weight, and the sin which does so easily beset us, and let us run with patience the race that is set before us" Ivriym (Hebrews) 12:1 went over my head and out the window. The sermons on Yoceph (Joseph) and his defiance to stand firm in his adoniy's house not to succumb to Zelikah, his adoniy's woman who enticed Yoceph daily and lusted after his beauty in her heart, designed to warn us not to engage in fornication and adultery. We advised to "Put on the whole armor of Elohim, that ye may be able to stand against the wiles of the devil" Eph'siym (Ephesians) 6:1 My sexual hormones were ragging because of the frequent wet dreams.

The heavyweight boxing champion Mike Tyson made quotes that resonated with me throughout the years. Mike's words hit like a ton of bricks and made me realize that "Everybody has plans until they get hit for the first time." What the champion uttered so eloquently coincides with the saying "no plan survives first contact with the enemy." This was the reality of my current situation on the unpredictability of life and the importance of resilience when bombarded with temptations. The battle was too strong to fight when I began indulging in self-gratification and coitus during my teenage years. Instantly mesmerized with pornographic content, which made me guilty of lustful enticement which carries the idea of being guilty, exposed, and vulnerable to YHWH judgment. The nakedness I am speaking of is contrary to the wise counsel to clothe yourself in the full suit of righteous armor.

I knowingly took a stroll on the Wild side and stayed there on an extended vacation because of the erotic visualization. I did not realize that I was building a decadent disposition at an early age that I could have easily avoided by being truthful about my moral imperfections to my youth spiritual counselor. Till this day, I regret not informing my mother of the concupiscence of the female teenagers that robbed me of my innocence and through their actions, propelled me on a journey to quench an unquenchable thirst of sexual dehydration. Never truly able to recapture the purity of abstinence christened on my wedding day. If only I would have known then what I know now, I would have attached a tassel to my genitals as a reminder to guard against the beguiling ways of the strange woman. I thank the Creator of earth and every living thing upon this planet that YHWH has bestowed Chokmah upon, to let repentance and redemption be tsiytsith upon their consciousness throughout their generations, and that they attach upon the tsiytsith, the fortitude of courage and strength. "And it shall be unto you a mental and spiritual tsiytsith, that ye may be encouraged, and remember all the commandments of Yahuah, and do them; and that ye seek not after your own heart and your own eyes, after which ye use to go a whoring: That ye may remember, and do all my commandments, and be holy unto your Elohim. I am Yahuah Elohaykem, which brought you out of the land of Mitsrayim, to be your Elohim: I am Yahuah Elohaykem" Bemidbar (Numbers) 15:38-41.

I warn every male and female that the power of the male and female genitals is known to make individuals succumb to lunacy and Irrational behavior. There have been many occasions under the influence of alcoholic beverages that I have experienced heartbeat acceleration during mental arousal before coitus was engaged upon. I have been with my woman since our teenage years and an erection still occurs when she comes out of the shower and my penis fills with blood, causing it to expand and become firm. I tell her constantly that it is mental not physical, and I might have an erection if I feel sexually aroused, so she must play her position.

Husbands or wives must keep the exact energy they have while dating their mate, active in their marriage. The courtship, intimacy, communication, and compassion should not cease after the victory of a marriage certificate achieved. I have heard too many husbands complain that copulation and home cooked meals are sporadic, and in the words of the late BB King "The Thrill Is Gone." This also is the complaint of wives with unemployed men and stay-at-home dads. The Victoria Secret collection replaced with flannel pajamas and hair bonnets to seem unattractive because you want to control him with the vagina. Men, please keep your women satisfied and auspicious because I have seen marriages end first with separation then divorce with a disenchanted mate taking a celibate and indolent position. Never give an opportunity for your mate to say that you drove them into the arms of another man or that they seek the counsel of a female friend to understand his wife's mood swings. That man or woman outside the marriage who has the ear of your mate can easily become a sexual partner in a matter of no time, wreaking havoc in an already volatile situation. For in many things, tempted by our fleshly desires and without a strong moral foundation we can easily succumb to temptations and sink in quicksand.

I have always regretted letting my concupiscence inclinations overthrow my sensibilities when it comes to women. I put in jeopardy the love of my soulmate for desires that I only regret later because I was not strong enough to stand upright against seduction. I only hope that my past indiscretions can serve as a reminder to always stay ten toes down when it comes to marriage. If you currently have a beautiful and capable mate that has your best interests at heart, do not jeopardize what you have for a maybe or what if. I have known that any offense that is not encumbering upon your spiritual, physical, and psychological wellness, resolved through open and truthful dialogue. I have always known that a lack of honest communication can build a barricade of incertitude that only cultivates mendacity. I have been extremely fortunate to recover from the miscalculations of my past via spiritual enlightenment and introspection to love thyself and bridle the whole body. My strength did not derive from my loins but unity among the brethren, the love of family, a commitment of understanding so my woman and I can agree together. Three sorts of nature my soul hates, and I hope not to offend anyone, but I must be open. A poor person that is proud, a rich person that is a liar, and an old adulterer that dotes. If you have gathered nothing in your youth, how can you find anything in your old age? O how comely a thing is judgment for gray hairs, and for ancient humankind to know counsel! O how comely is the wisdom of the aged and understanding and counsel to individuals of honor. Much experience is the crown of the aged, and the fear of Elohim is their glory.

There are nine things which I have judged in my heart to be happy, and the tenth I will utter with my tongue: A person that has joy in his children, and individuals that live to see the fall of their enemy. Well, is those that dwell with a mate of understanding, and that has not slipped with their tongue, and that has not served a mate more unworthy than themselves. Well, it is those that have found prudence, and those that speak in their ears of them that will hear, O how great is individuals that find wisdom! Yet is there none above him that fears Yahuah. The ultimate character flaw for all humanity is not being able to control their inhibitions. So many times, have I overestimated the power of allurement when dealing with the opposite gender. No one wants to contemplate defeat by not fully understanding the two greatest gifts given to our genitors in the garden of Eden. The competency to commune with each other and unconditional love between the male and female species. I have seen both the kingfish and idealists get companionship and because of their own insecurities lose love without ever truly knowing what love is. This cycle continues over and over in relationships because many cannot fathom the burdensome loneliness. We all at one time during our companionship, too immature to stay in a bond of unity for superficial reasoning. Blessed is the man or woman that has a virtuous mate, that gives balance and increases Chokmah within the relationship.

All jokes aside, I have always recommended to friends that they should know the actual appearance of a woman without makeup. How many times have you heard men say "deceived by the woman they thought they married to the woman they got. She does not cook, clean the house, or hang out partying all night." I have always subscribed to the notion that men who look for a trophy wife will be the biggest loser in the end. You should never expect more from a woman if you only seek sensual pleasure without inquiring about the sustainable qualities needed from a prospective mate. The same applied to a woman that notices the red flags of a man but dismisses the warning signs and risks it all in the hopes of finding love.

The BIBLE (Basic Instructions Before Leaving Earth) is a great educational manual when we truly adhere to the philosophical reasoning passed down from humankind of antiquity. The story of Dinah, who intermingled outside the nation of Yashar'el raped because of her beauty. The tale of Samson, who trusted his woman that would deceive him thrice before his enemies blinded him. Then the queen of the Yashar'el nation, who corrupted a king using her sexuality, and who's name will forever attached to any woman suspected of being a harlot. "And when Yahoo came to Yizre'el, Iyzebel heard of it; and she painted her face, and tired her head, and looked out at a window. Melekiym Sheniy (2 Kings) 9:30".

The question I pose to all the men is, who does not want a virtuous woman? that rejoices with her man and adds years to his life in peace. Are you a woman that seeks an able man to be her durable foundation, that will walk with her in integrity and compassion? A mate is someone that knows the heart and feelings of his man or woman, which given as insight because they follow the counsel of Yahuah.

I have a pet peeve with too many individuals measuring their commitment inside a relationship based upon financial and social status. Whether a person is rich or poor, does not increase or disqualify them from matrimony but examine their morality and reasoning. Life filled with temptations and devils, so are they aligned with Yahuah to make them able to sustain the complexities of marriage? There are three things that my heart feared before I put full trust in the Cepher. I was sorely afraid of my past relationships causing a riff in my marriage. A scorned ex-lover slandering me. The grief and scourge of the tongue of a woman that is jealous over another woman. While I was slipping and sliding, I met an evil woman that was difficult to shake. There was another lady that seemed like she had the best intentions until her sting was as deadly as a scorpion. The drunken woman with great anger after too much tequila, bringing shame to herself and me. The adulterous affairs of a woman exposed to the public while in a monogamous relationship.

The hardest pill to swallow for me was forgiveness, and trying to control suspicion, which will always cast doubt on the unfaithful spouse's repentance. Too many individuals have pleaded for forgiveness only to become repeat offenders. I was shameless and continued an unrepentant lifestyle that caused infidelity, taking great liberties of my woman's kindness. The guilty conscience is a scarlet letter reminding you constantly about the mistakes you made that your mate will never forget. She will open her mouth with kind words but deep inside is animosity brewing that awaits the next disappointment. The grace of a woman delights her man, and her discretion will fatten his bones. A silent and loving woman is a gift of Yahuah, that can understand the shortcomings of the nefarious nature of humanity.

Now I want to erase the myth that all men are dogs, because women also have a little alley cat in them that roams the streets from time to time. So, whoever started labeling virile males as hounds on the prowl forgot that men also have been the victim of a promiscuous and perfidious woman. For me not to acknowledge the woman's role in destroying the love of her man or children, for an adulterous affair is ludicrous. We cannot blame the one without taking a strong look at the other. There was a time when men would do the running but, in our generation, women are abandoning the kids and the dog. Becoming female cougars stalking young boys is a midlife crisis that men go through. I commend all the reformed cheaters that decided to grow up and beat back temptations that have enslaved them. As the sun rises and makes all those rejoice because of temperament, so is the beauty of a faithful mate in the ordering of their household. These are unlearned life lessons before my motorcycle accident, that would have kept the flowers blooming during winter seasons, and my vitality away from strangers. To be honest with ourselves is the first step to conquering the disobedience brewing within incarnate humans. Always searching for perfection in others when they must examine their own flaws initially. Forsaking a fruitful possession in their own field, becoming a sharecropper sowing seeds, trusting in the goodness of the neighbor's stock. "A harlot accounted as spittle; but a married woman is a tower against death to her man. A wicked woman given to a wicked man: but a righteous woman given to him that fears Yahuah. A dishonest woman condemned to shame: but an honest woman will reverence her man. A shameless woman counted as a dog; but she that is shamefaced will fear Yahuah. A woman that honors her man judged wise of all; but she that dishonors him in her pride counted wicked of all" Sirach (Ecclesiasticus) 26:1-26.

I have only myself to blame for past indiscretions, because neither was I forced or in a comatose state when behaving foul. No one else can improve upon their own decision-making or influenced by unscrupulous individuals until they decide enough is enough. I embarked on this journey towards better awareness and maturity for the sake of my own sanity. There is the inevitable that we all must wrap our minds around, leaving our mortal shells since birth and taking a journey no longer in the present. The dynamism we perceived in our prime became less important as geriatric pushes us closer to the hereafter. The young man I looked at so many times in the mirror began aging and memories of foolishness counted among the simple ones. The wealth accumulated or gifts given cannot buy me one second more from the place called hades. In my youth, I tried to speed up my journey to the corridors of darkness with asinine reasoning and endeavors, a young man once voids of understanding, and behaving without guidance seeking pleasure over prudence.

What would they say about you during your eulogy if honesty and truth were the only words uttered? Would someone approach the podium and say in the twilight, in the evening, in the black and dark night, were women with the attire of a harlot, and subtle of heart. She is loud and stubborn, but our brother found comfort in her house. A man devoted to church on Sunday, but in the darkness of the streets, disguised himself to wait at every corner. So, she caught him, and kissed him, and with an impudent face said unto him. I have peace offerings with me; this day I have paid my vows. She knew his pleasures and came forth to meet him, diligently seeking his face, and found him in want. Our brother knew the consequences of visiting such places, but the scent of her perfume captivated his manly nature. Come, let us take our fill of love until the morning and let us solace ourselves with love. For my husband is not at home, he has gone and left me lonely and in want. With her painted lips and words filled with erotica, she caused the brother to yield. A man married for over twenty years; captivated like so many men who let a strange woman with flattering lips seduce them. Hearken unto me now and do not walk the path of the wayward soul. The speaker has everyone gasping from the straightway remarks about the departed, but all are at full attention to the words of his mouth. The speaker closes the eulogy asking the audience not to let their morality decline or go astray as both the man and woman. "For she has cast down her net and many were wounded. Many strong men slain by their fleshly desires and ignorance. Her house is the way to Sheol, going down to the chambers of death. *Would a eulogy like this make you reconsider fornication and take control of your members?* If my heart has been deceived by a stranger, or if my woman was in need at my neighbor's door, please do not count this against us. If I continue to play the fool after pleading for mercy, then let my woman grind unto another, and let others bow down upon her. For this is a heinous crime; yes, it is an iniquity punished by the judges. For it is a fire that consumes destruction and would root out all my increase" Iyov (Job) 31:9-12.

I have referenced the scriptures throughout this entire book starting with chapter one, because I can be truthful to myself and say I fell off the path into the ditch of darkness and despair. The ruach has grown weak and my faith unstable, with episodes of disobedience and shame. I thought it would only be fitting to bring closure to this chapter with a message of hope and reasoning, that hopefully someone will take my confessions to heart and avoid the pitfalls in matrimony. My goal is to inspire individuals contemplating marriage or currently dating to avoid many mistakes that beget transgressions conducted in my youth in a state of lasciviousness. I can never replace the years squandered on immaturity, but I can rectify the now and hereafter with common sense. How many husbands or wives can be truthful and say where your treasure is, there will be your heart also. Did the secret affairs and flings that caught your eye make you regret that you broke your spouse's heart? The light of the body is the eye; if therefore your eye is blind to enticement, your whole body shall be full of light. I have always abhorred the notion that all men are scoundrels when both women and men have a tendency of letting their eyes be reckless, sparking the hypothalamus within the cerebrum that controls lust. I also must strike down the stereotypical fabrication that Black men and women are by nature born with extreme libidinous. This theory created by unintelligent and racist men who were concerned about the wandering eyes of their women.

King Shalomah shed light on the nature of humanity that most individuals should heed. "For honorable age is not that which stands in length of time, nor measured by number of years. But wisdom is the gray hair unto men, and an unspotted life is old age. He pleased Elohim and was beloved of him: so that living among sinners translated. Yes, speedily was he taken away, lest that wickedness should alter his understanding, or deceit beguile his soul. For the bewitching of wickedness obscures things that are honest; and the wandering of lustful desire undermines the simple mind" hokmah Shalomah (Wisdom of Solomon) 4:8-12.

This is only the beginning of a long journey to transform my entire body that was once full of darkness, into a creation that was meant to be a holy temple. If therefore, you strive to gain the light that is to shine out of the darkness, how great is that darkness, and who holds the power to turn on the switch? Let us all set out "To Let It Make Sense" before we reach a point that our next breath will be our last.

LINKS

erectile-dysfunction/ how-an-erection-occurs/ 42-restraint-bias-explained-why-we-succumb-temptations

ABOUT THE AUTHOR

I did not author this book as a self-help manual or to direct the reader to convert to the Iviry theocratic study, but to share memories from my youth to adulthood, while trying to expound on family, morality, financial independence, and ancestral values.

Several years ago, I broke both legs in separate motorcycle accidents that forced me to evaluate my reasoning and spirituality. I went into a deep depression and began to question why this was happening to me while hospitalized at a rehabilitation facility in Alameda, CA, from April to December 2023. During that period, I began prioritizing my obligations while confined to a hospital bed from the immobilization of two surgeries on my right leg.

The irony of the situation is breaking my left leg from riding my Harley Road King in the exact month, time, and area in 2022. I have come to the assumption that the incidents were a blessing and chastisement, in which I had to disassociate myself mentally and emotionally from several lucrative projects currently in production. We are truly tested like the prophet Job, and I was at my snapping point contemplating if the consequences outweighed the offense. I truly believe without the Divine intervention while in my unconscious state at night, I would never manifest my dreams into reality during the day in my conscious state without the discipline, sacrifice, determination, and courage needed to evolve.

The accident aided my recollection of my teen years during the MTV and BET era that consumed enormous hours watching music videos, that I would assimilate while I slept. Every fantasy I would envision was the total opposite of my current reality. From imitating the pop star, Michael Jackson, to the flamboyant lifestyle and dynamic flair of Hugh Hefner. Before the accidents, our positioning from creation to end comes in behavioral patterns like the four seasons that are either righteous or unrighteous while on Earth.

I truly want to thank Yahuah Assembly for weekly Sabbath discourses online and at the Oakland, CA congregation on Parker Avenue. I strongly believe that my lineage derived from the Iviry people discussed in the spiritual precepts which are an accursed people. Since my birth, I truly believe death and Hades are on my heels, but it is Elohim that keeps them at bay. It has been the Sunday school teachings that have kept me from being fully engulfed in fellowship and rituals that the entertainment industry fully endorses and condones. Too many individuals reared in Christian denominations have succumbed to kissing the pinky ring and signed oaths of alliance to gain success in a world of illusion, smoking mirrors, and carnage. This has been my Achilles since my aunt dropped me from a one-story flight of stairs on my head as an infant and survived. I have survived pain and trauma only to regroup and this inclines me to be reminiscent of my journey and share with you now!

Let It Make Sense is Gabriel Solomon's first published book.

For Donations and Speaking Engagements, please Contact:

GABRIEL SOLOMON

tpngmediainfo@gmail.com

REFERENCES

Maps and locations from Hebrew to English pronunciation/ Cities near the 4 rivers flowing from Eden/ Hebrew Calendar displaying months and jubilees/ Hebrew Feasts of the Torah/Hebrew basic language/ migration maps and cities of Cham, Shem, Yapheth/ slavery maps/ certificate of marriages throughout generations/ pictures of idols, Asherah poles, pillar of stones/ pictures of angels in museums/ pictures of Noach and the flood/ map of mount Hermon/ explanation of pagan Christian holidays and rituals/ updated names of cities and towns in Cepher/Heathen Nations that conquered and took captive the Iviry nation/ Beautiful men and women of Shem and Cham Nation dressed in ancient attire.

Reference sites: Museum of Cario/ Brain genetics/ Mind manipulation/ Sexual behavior/ Origin of paganism/ Slavery and Christianity/ Marriage equality

NAMES AND PLACES

CHUAH(Eve)/ AVEL(Abel)/ QAYIN(Cain)/ CHANOK(Enoch)/
LYRAD(Irad) LEMEK(Lamech)/ AVRAHAM(Abraham)/
YISHMA'EL(Ishmael)/ Aharon(Aaron)/ YITSCHAQ(Isaac)/
YA'AQOV(Jacob/ YASHAR'EL(Israel)/ KENA'AN(Canaan)/
YOCEPH(Joseph)/ MATTITHYAHU(Matthew)/ LUQAS(Luke)/
TSILLAH(Zillah) /YAVAL(Jabal)/ YUVAL(Jubal)/ TUBAL
QAYIN(Tubal Cain)/ NA'AMEL(Naamah)/ SHETH(Seth)/ ENOSH
QEYNAN(Kenan)/ MAHALA'EL/ YERED(Jared)/
METHUSHELACH(Methuselah)/ LEMAK(Lamech)/
NOACH(Noah)/ SHEM(Cham) CHAM(HAM)/
YAPHETH(Japheth)/ RIVQAH(Rebecca)/ LAVAN(Laban)/
RE'UVEN(Reuben)/ SHIM'ON(Simeon)/ LEVIY(Levi)/
YAHUDAH(Judah)/ NAPHTALILY(Naphtali)/
YISSHAKAR(Issachar)/ DIYNAH(Dinah)/ YOCEPH(Joseph)/
BINYAMIYN(Benjamin)/ EPHRAYIM(Ephraim)/
MENASHSHEH(Manasseh)/ MAKPELAH(Machpelah)/
DAVIYD(David) YECHIZQIYAHU(Hezekiah)/
NEVUKADNE'TSTSAR(Nebuchadnezzar)/ DANIY"EL(Daniel)/
SHALOMAH(Solomon) YAHUYAKIYN(Jehoiachin)/
TSIDQIYAHU(Zedekiah)/ KORESH(Cyrus)/
ZERUBBAVEL(Zerubbabel)/ ZEVULUN(Zebulun)/
MIDDIYN(Middin)/ MASHIACH(Messiah) RUACH(Spirit)/
Tephillah(Pray)/ YAHUDIY(Jew)/ YAVAN(Greece)/
Yavaniy(Greek) Yavaniym(Greeks)/ ARAV(Arab)/
PECACH(Passover)/ KASHER(Fit)/ KERUV(Cherub)/
KERUVIYM(Cherubs)/ IVRIY(Hebrew)/ IVRIYM(Hebrews)/
IVRIRT(Hebrew language)/ YISHMA'E'LIYM(Ishmaelites)/

MITSRAYIM(Egypt)/ MITSRIY(Egyptian)/ KENA'AN(Canaan)/
SHOMERON(Samaria)/ YERUSHALAYIM(Jersulem)/
EPHRAYIM(Ephraim)/ ARAVAH(Arabia)/ KUSH(Ethiopia)/
CHITTIYM(Hittites)/ ASHSHUR(Assyrian)/
KASDIYM(Chaldean)/ ROMAIYM(Romans)/
PERATH(Euphrates)/ ARAM NAHARAYIM(Mesopotamia)/
RA'AMEC(Ramses)/ EYLAM(Elam)/ ASSWAGED(Subside)/
YACHIYD(Child)/ CHOKMAH(Wisdom)/ Cedom(Sodom)
MITSVAH(Commandment)/ NATSARIYM(Watchmen)/
TERAPHIYM(Idol)/ HALAKHA(Laws)/ Ciyn(sin)/
BESORAH(Message or Report)/ YASHAR'E'LIYM (Israelite)/
MISHPAT(Judgments)/ MASHIACHIY(Christian)/ B'SARI or
FLEISHIG   (Meat)/ MASHIACHIYM(Christs)/
ARAVIYM(Arabians)/ SOFER(Scribe) EDOMIYM(Edomites)/
CHAMETS(Leavened Bread) BA'AL ZEBUB(Satan) ARAM
NAHARAYIM(Mesopotamia)/ MATSTSAH(Unleavened Bread)
BHARATA(India)/ SERES(China)/ AVIYV(Abib 1st Month)/
ELOHIYM(god)/ EBED(Slave,Servant)/
MAKKEH(Beating,Strike)/ KLEPTO(Steal) MADAI(Medes,
Central Asia)/ Bible(Basic Instruction Before Leaving Earth)/
ASHKENAZ(Armenia)/TARSHIYSH(Mediterranean)/PUT(Persian
)/ KENA'AN (Canaanites)/ ARAM(Syria)

CEPHER 87 BOOKS

TORAH(Instruction)/ BERE'SHIYTH(Genesis) SHEMOTH(Exodus) VAYIQRA(Leviticus) BEMIDBAR(Numbers) DEVARIYM(Deuteronomy) TASLONIQIYM CEPHERIYM SHENIY(Second Books)/ YOVHELIYM(Jubilees) CHANOK(Enoch) YASHAR(Jashar) NEVIY'IYM(Prophets)/ YAHUSHA(Joshua) SHOFETIYM(Judges) SHEMU'EL RI'SHON(1 Samuel) SHEMU'EL SHENIY (2 Samuel) MELEKIYM RI'SHON (1Kings) MELEKIYM SHENIY (2 Kings) YESHA'YAHU (Isaiah) YIRMEYAHU (Jeremiah) CEPHER YIRMEYAHU (Epistle Of Jeremiah)/ YECHEZEQ'EL (Ezekiel) TOVIYAHU (Tobit) BARUK RI'SHON (1 Baruk) BARUK SHENIY (2 Baruk) TREI ASAR (The Twelve)/ HUSHA (Hosea) YO'EL (Joel) AMOC (Amos) OVADYAHU (Obadiah) YONAH (Jonah) MIYKAH (Micah) NACHUM (Nahum) CHABAQQUQ (Habakkuk) TSEPHANYAHU (Zephaniah) CHAGGAI (Haggai) ZAKARYAHU (Zechariah) MAL'AKIY (Malachi) KETUVIYM (Writings)/ TEHILLIYM (Psalms) MISHLEI (Proverbs) IYOV (Job) CHOKMAH SHALOMAH (Wisdom Of Solomon) SIRACH (Ecclesiasticus) MEGILLOTH (Rolls)/ SHIYR HASHIYRIRM (Song Of Solomon) RUTH (RUTH) QIYNAH (Lamentations) QOHELETH (Ecclesiastes) ECTER (Ester) HADACCAH (Additions To Esther) YAHUDITH (Judith) BEYT HA'MIKDASH HA'SHENIY (Second Temple)/ DIVREI HAYAMIYM RI'SHON (1 Chronicles) DIVREI HAYAMIYM SHENIY (2 Chronicles) TEPHILLAH MENASHSHEH (Prayer Of Azariah) SHUSHANAH (Susanna) BA'AL AND THE DRAGON (Bel And The Dragon)

EZRA V'NECHEMYAHU (Ezra) EZRA V'NECHEMYAHU (Nehemiah) EZRA SHELIYSHY (3 Ezra) EZRA REVIY'IY (4 Ezra) MAKKABIYM RI'SHON (1 Maccabees) MAKKABIYM SHENIY (2 Maccabees) MAKKABIYM SHELIYSHIY (3 Maccabees) MAKKABIYM REVIY'IY (4 Maccabees) BESOR'OTH (Synoptic Gospels)/ MATTITHYAHU (Matthew) MARQUES (Mark) LUQAS (Luke) MA'ASIYM (Acts)/ MA'ASIYM (Acts) CEPHERIYM TALMIDIYM (Disciples'Epistles)/ YA'AQOV (James) KEPHA RI'SHON (1 Peter) KEPHA SHENIY (2 Peter) YAHUDAH (Jude) CEPHERIYM PA'AL (Paul's Epistles)/ TIMOTHEUS RI'SHON (1 Timothy) TITUS (Titus) TASLONIQIYM RI'SHON (1 Thessalonians) TASLONIQIYM SHENIY (2 Thessalonians) ROMAIYM (Romans) GALATIYM (Galatians) TIMOTHEUS SHENIY (2 Timothy) QORINTIYM RI'SHON (1 Corinthians) QORINTIYM SHENIY (2 Corinthians) EPH'SHIYM (Ephesians) PHILIPPIYM (Philippians) QOLASIYM (Colossians) PHILEMON (Philemon) IVRIYM (Hebrews) CEPHERIYM YOCHANON (John's Gospel And Epistles)/ YOCHANON (John) YOCHANON RI'SHON (1 John) YOCHANON SHENIY (2 John) YOCHANON SHELIYSHIY (3 John) CHIZAYON (Revelation)